# Harrington on Cash Games: Volume I

## How to Play No-Limit Hold 'em Cash Games

*By*

DAN HARRINGTON
1995 World Champion

BILL ROBERTIE

**A product of
Two Plus Two Publishing LLC**

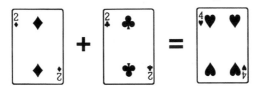

FIRST EDITION

FIRST PRINTING
March 2008

*Printing and Binding*
Creel Printers, Inc.
Las Vegas, Nevada

*Printed in the United States of America*

# Harrington on
# Cash Games: Volume I
## How to Play No-Limit Hold 'em Cash Games
# COPYRIGHT © 2008 Two Plus Two Publishing LLC

For information contact: **Two Plus Two Publishing LLC**
**32 Commerce Center Drive**
**Suite H-89**
**Henderson, NV 89014**

ISBN: 1-880685-42-6
ISBN13: 978-1-880685-42-6

*Yeller*: "Why you always bettin' out like that, anyways?"

*Doc*: "The bet was correct. He should not have called."

*Yeller:* "Better get yourself a new book Daddy."

From *The Cincinnati Kid* (1965)

# Table of Contents

# About Dan Harrington

Dan Harrington began playing poker professionally in 1982. On the circuit he is known as "Action Dan," an ironic reference to his solid but effective style. He has won several major no-limit hold 'em tournaments including the European Poker Championships (1995), the $2,500 No-Limit Hold 'em event at the 1995 World Series of Poker, and the Four Queens No-Limit Hold 'em Championship (1996).

Dan began his serious games-playing with chess, where he quickly became a master and one of the strongest players in the New England area. In 1972 he won the Massachusetts Chess Championship, ahead of most of the top players in the area. In 1976 he started playing backgammon, a game which he also quickly mastered. He was soon one of the top money players in the Boston area, and in 1981 he won the World Cup of Backgammon in Washington D.C., ahead of a field that included most of the world's top players.

He first played in the $10,000 No-Limit Hold 'em Championship Event of the World Series of Poker in 1987. He has played in the Championship a total of 15 times and has reached the final table in four of those tournaments, an amazing record. Besides winning the World Championship in 1995, he finished sixth in 1987, third in 2003, and fourth in 2004. In 2006 he finished second at the Doyle Brunson North American Championships at the Bellagio, while in 2007 he won the Legends of Poker Tournament at the Bicycle Club. He is widely recognized as one of the greatest and most respected no-limit hold 'em players, as well as a feared opponent in both no-limit and limit hold 'em side games. He lives in Santa Monica where he is a partner in Anchor Loans, a real estate business.

# About Bill Robertie

Bill Robertie has spent his life playing and writing about chess, backgammon, and now poker. He began playing chess as a boy, inspired by Bobby Fischer's feats on the international chess scene. While attending Harvard as an undergraduate, he became a chess master and helped the Harvard chess team win several intercollegiate titles. After graduation, he won a number of chess tournaments, including the United States Championship at speed chess in 1970. He also established a reputation at blindfold chess, giving exhibitions on as many as eight boards simultaneously.

In 1976 he switched from chess to backgammon, becoming one of the top players in the world. His major titles include the World Championship in Monte Carlo in 1983 and 1987, the Black & White Championship in Boston in 1979, the Las Vegas Tournaments in 1980 and 2001, the Bahamas Pro-Am in 1993, and the Istanbul World Open in 1994.

He has written several well-regarded backgammon books, the most noted of which are *Advanced Backgammon* (1991), a two-volume collection of 400 problems, and *Modern Backgammon* (2002), a new look at the underlying theory of the game. He has also written a set of three books for the beginning player: *Backgammon for Winners* (1994), *Backgammon for Serious Players* (1995), and *501 Essential Backgammon Problems* (1997).

From 1991 to 1998 he edited the magazine *Inside Backgammon* with Kent Goulding. He owns a publishing company, the Gammon Press (www.thegammonpress.com), and lives in Arlington, Massachusetts with his wife Patrice.

# Introduction

In *Harrington on Hold 'em; Volumes I, II,* and *III,* Bill Robertie and I examined no-limit hold 'em tournament play. In these two new books, we're going to look at the other side of no-limit hold 'em: the world of cash games.

Cash games differ from tournaments in just a couple of respects. Unlike tournaments, the blinds never increase, and antes are usually not allowed. In most cash games, you can buy in for a maximum of 100 big blinds; in some live games, you can buy in for much more. And unlike tournaments, you can rebuy when your chips get low. Other than that, the rules governing the two games are almost exactly the same.

These apparently small differences, however, are enough to make the two games very different. Players who play almost entirely cash games are unfamiliar with some of the nuances of tournament play. Many tournament specialists flounder around miserably when they try to play cash games.

Which game is more subtle, more intricate, more intriguing? That's easy. Despite the big prizes and glamour of tournament play, cash games are more difficult to master. In these two books, we'll see exactly why, and learn some of the strategies that will let you survive and even prosper in the cash game world, both online and live.

## Organization of the Books

The "Introduction" is a quick, general introduction to no-limit cash games. We'll give you a quick overview of some of the key-ideas that separate no-limit cash games from either no-limit tournaments or limit cash games.

Part One explains some basic ideas of no-limit play like pot odds, implied odds, and outs. If this is your first book on no-limit

1

play, you'll want to read this section carefully as these ideas are used constantly in the rest of the book. If you've already read the *Harrington on Hold 'em* books (or some other good introductory material), you can skip this section.

In Part Two, we discuss the key elements that make deep stack no-limit play so interesting. These include stack sizes and their effect on strategy, the deception principle, balance and hand selection, pot commitment, hand reading, multi-level thinking, and the importance of making good plays. When you've finished Part Two, you'll have a good general understanding of what you should think about when playing a cash game hand.

Part Three explains the difference between tight-aggressive play and loose-aggressive play, and shows how to play the tight-aggressive style preflop.

Part Four shows how to play on the flop when heads-up.

In Part Five, we show how to handle a multi-way flop with two or more opponents, and introduce "Harrington's Law."

Part Six shows how to play on the turn.

Part Seven discusses the intricacies of river play.

Part Eight deals with tells and observations.

In Part Nine, we introduce the basics of the loose-aggressive style, an effective (but more difficult) approach to the game than the tight-aggressive style.

Part Ten describes exactly what weak games are and gives advice on how to beat them.

Part Eleven gives some advice on managing your bankroll and other crucial topics including "Transitioning to Live Games."

Part Twelve is a conversation with one of the greatest no-limit cash game players of all time.

As with our other books, we'll discuss the general principles governing deep stack cash game play, and supplement this discussion with many examples taken from actual hands, some from live games and some from online games. Both Bill and I are in agreement that cash game poker, like tournament poker, can't be easily learned as merely an application of some abstract principles. Good play is more a sort of balancing act, where a collection of factors come together, get weighed against each other, and produce a play which represents a sort of weighted average of the different inputs. The best way to see this process in action is to first discuss the different principles involved, then watch as they are balanced against each other in actual play.

## No-Limit Cash Games versus No-Limit Tournaments

If you're like many readers of this book, you probably learned how to play no-limit hold 'em in the aftermath of the great poker boom that started with the World Poker Tour's debut on the Travel Channel in 2003. You started playing online sit-and-go's, then multi-table tournaments, and finally you tried a few live tournaments.

Recently you've started playing online cash games, but it's been slow going. The game seems quiet and even a little dull compared to tournament play. You've noticed players checking hands that, when shown down, seemed strong enough to bet. When you do get all your chips in the center, your opponent's hands seem much stronger than you expected. The game seems more or less the same on the surface, but success is elusive. You're wondering if you've been unlucky, or if there's something systematically wrong with your game.

Recently I sat down next to a friend of mine, a very competent online tournament player, as he tried his first session of no-limit cash game play. He made a full buy-in of 100 big blinds, about average for the table. After a half hour of uneventful back and forth play, he picked up an ace-king in early position. He made a standard raise and got three callers, including the two blinds. The flop came king-ten-nine, and he felt pretty good with his top pair, top kicker. To his surprise, the small blind bet and the big blind raised. My friend couldn't wait to push all-in, after which he got three callers! "How am I doing!" he whooped. "You might be third-best," I replied. When the cards were shown, he was actually fourth-best on the flop. His opponents had a set of tens, a set of nines, and a straight! (The straight held up.)

The transition from tournament to cash game play is difficult for many no-limit players. My friend made a very common error. His hand (top pair, top kicker), which is an excellent hand in most tournament situations, is a relatively weak hand in a deep-stack cash game when all the money goes in.

In tournaments, the players are only deep-stacked in the first and perhaps the second round of blinds. A typical multi-table tournament structure might start with stacks of $2,000 in tournament chips and blinds of $10 and $20. At that point your ratio of chips to big blind is 100, which is a legitimate deep-stack situation. By the time the blinds increase to $15 and $30, your ratio of chips to big blind is already down to 67, which is not really a deep stack, and the next blind increase will take you down below 50, which is not a deep stack at all.

Through some combination of study and trial and error, players learn to play very tight in these couple of early rounds, so they don't actually see many flops, then loosen their play a bit when the blinds grow and their stack shrinks. It's a reasonable approach for starting the tournament, but as a result they get very little practice in handling themselves in a deep-stack situation.

Cash games, on the other hand, are always deep-stacked, unless you choose to buy in for just a fraction of the maximum buy-in. In deep-stack play, as long as your opponent also has a lot of chips, *the goal is not to commit all your chips to the pot until you have a hand that's big enough for the situation.*

Exactly what does "big enough" mean? Like most poker advice, it depends. If you're up against someone playing a very short stack, say 20 to 30 big blinds, a high pair might be plenty. If you're up against a notoriously tight player and you each have 250 big blinds, and there's a pair on board, you might be nervous about pushing a straight all the way.

At each decision point in a deep-stack cash game, you'll be asking yourself a series of questions:

1.  How big is my remaining stack?

2.  How big is his remaining stack?

3.  How big is the pot?

4.  How strong is my hand relative to the action I've seen so far?

5.  Do I know anything about my opponent that suggests he's bluffing?

6.  If I bet, what will my response be if he pushes all-in?"

7.  Do I want to check the hand down?

And that's just a partial list.

Deep-stack cash games are difficult to play well. This book will help you.

# A Sample Hand

To illustrate some of the thought processes that take place in a no-limit cash game, let's take a look at a sample hand that's reasonably complex. It's from the third season of *High Stakes Poker,* a show that's broadcast on Monday nights on the Game Show network. (It's also highly recommended watching if you want to improve your cash game skills.) Each week eight top pros play a no-limit cash game with blinds of $300 and $600, and $100 antes. The ante structure is unusual; most cash games do not use antes. When antes are in place, the players have to play a little looser than normal because there's more money in the pot to be won in comparison to the blinds.

# 6 Introduction

The minimum buy-in for the game is $100,000, or 167 big blinds. The players can buy in for more. On a couple of occasions, players have brought $1,000,000 in cash to the table. (It makes an impressively large brick.)

For this session, the players were Phil Laak, Antonio Esfandiari, Daniel Negreanu, Mike Matusow, Chris Ferguson, Ilya Trencher, Dan Shak, and Dan Harmetz. The first five names will be very familiar to anyone who watches a lot of poker tournaments on television. The last three players are non-professional cash game specialists who have been giving a good account of themselves on the show.

For this hand, the positions, hands, and approximate stack sizes are as follows:

| | | | |
|---|---|---|---|
| 1. | Dan Harmnetz | $150,000 | A♦K♥ |
| 2. | Ilya Trencher | $100,000 | -- |
| 3. | Phil Laak | $200,000 | -- |
| 4. | Antonio Esfandiari | $200,000 | -- |
| 5. | Chris Ferguson | $150,000 | -- |
| 6. | Mike Matusow | $85,000 | Q♦9♥ |
| SB | Dan Shak | $120,000 | A♥3♠ |
| BB | Daniel Negreanu | $200,000 | 9♦7♠ |

The pot is $1,700 to start.

**Dan Harmetz.** Harmetz picks up ace-king offsuit under the gun. In most tournament situations, players would raise automatically with this hand. If the stacks were short enough, they would push all-in. But Harmetz just calls, a reasonable play. If he gets raised, he will call. Harmetz has been playing a tight, conservative game, and this call is consistent with what he's done so far.

Deep stack poker is mostly played after the flop. While there might be an occasional raise and reraise pre-flop, hands are not generally decided with a big pre-flop confrontation. Players usually like to see a little more of the hand before deciding how much of their stack they are willing to commit.

A more important question is whether it's mathematically incorrect to limp when you're the first in the pot, or whether you should instead always raise to put some pressure on the blinds. Some mathematicians in the poker community think that it's not correct to limp if you're first in the pot. The argument is pretty simple: If you limp and the hand is folded around to the big blind, and he has a weakish hand, he can't make an error by checking. If you raise, on the other hand, he has to call or fold, and either of those plays could be an error, depending on what he has and what you have. Taking away the chance to make an error from your opponent costs you some amount of money. (The actual amount can't be calculated, but it's both small and non-zero.) So you should always raise.

Many practical players acknowledge this point, but argue that there are solid reasons for limping which are more important than the theoretical pennies lost. Limping gives you an extra weapon in your quiver, and lets you see more flops cheaply than might otherwise happen. Limping also allows you to call with some very strong hands, giving your opponents different ways to go astray. On this issue, I side with the practical players.

One last argument. If you're at a table and you feel you're less experienced than the other players, you should definitely raise in this situation. You need to make the more experienced players pay a price to see a flop when you probably have the best hand pre-flop since, on average, you'll be outplayed after the flop.

Now, back to the hand.

**Ilya Trencher**. Folds.

**Phil Laak**. Folds.

**Antonio Esfandiari**. Folds.

**Chris Ferguson**. Folds.

**Mike Matusow**. Matusow calls with queen-nine offsuit. Players like to call on the button in deep-stack poker, especially in a multi-way pot, which this is now likely to be. Position increases in value with more players in the pot and the deeper the stacks. I'd only throw away a very weak hand in this situation, and queen-nine is certainly strong enough to play.

**Dan Shak**. In the small blind, Shak is getting enormous pot odds to call. The pot has now risen to $2,900, and it costs him just $300 to call, so he's getting almost 10-to-1. I'd play the vast majority of hands in this situation. Having an ace, his call is very easy.

**Daniel Negreanu**. Negreanu has the kind of hand he likes, nine-seven offsuit. These are good hands in deep stack poker if they can see a cheap flop. They're easy to release after the flop when they miss (which is most of the time) but when they hit, they can create concealed monsters, which are the kind of hands that can win your opponent's whole stack. Negreanu cheerfully checks to see a free flop.

The pot is now $3,200, with four players. The flop is

**Dan Shak**. Shak hit his ace on a board that rates to be pretty safe (for him) as long as there's no other ace out. (*In fact, however, two of his opponents just made trip nines!*) There are two clubs on board, so there's some possibility of a flush draw. In addition, his kicker, a trey, is very weak. *Should he bet?*

My answer is going to surprise a lot of readers: I wouldn't bet here.

In tournament poker, this same situation would often be a routine bet. But in tournament poker, your time horizon is very limited. You need to seize every opportunity as it presents itself or risk getting blinded away. Cash games don't have that same kind of pressure. They're much more of a game of patience. You don't need to swing at balls that just graze the strike zone; you can wait for the fat ones that you can blast out of the park.

Is this situation a fat one? Not at all. If anyone has a nine, Shak is pretty much dead. If someone has an ace, Shak is hoping to split the pot. No one who has an ace or a nine is going away anytime soon. If no one has an ace or a nine, will Shak's bet make him any money? Unlikely. The final point is that Shak is out of position. His best plan is to check, give the other players a chance to declare, and then reevaluate.

Should he be worried about the club flush? No. His hand and position aren't strong enough to be worried at this point. If he had a big hand, he could bet to charge the flush to play. But the flush is a long shot right now, and he has more pressing concerns.

He checks. Good play.

**Daniel Negreanu**. Negreanu has flopped trip nines, an excellent hand. His hand is certainly strong enough to bet. In fact, it's highly likely (he thinks) that he has the best hand. (*In fact, however, he doesn't. Matusow is sitting behind him with trip nines and a better kicker.*) He might get an ace to call, and he might get someone with two clubs to call.

Negreanu makes a more aggressive play, however. He checks with the idea of check-raising. His decision to slowplay is based on a couple of factors. Harmetz, who limped in first position, has yet to act. He may have an ace, and be willing to bet it. Behind him is Matusow, who has been very aggressive at the table. From last position, he might be willing to make a steal attempt if everyone checks in front of him. It's less likely, but possible, that one of them has two clubs and would be willing to bet if no one had opened the pot in front of them. In any of these cases, Negreanu can check-raise and perhaps gain an extra bet.

The check-raise isn't a risk-free move. If the hand is checked around and a third club comes on the turn, Negreanu won't be happy. But he judges it an acceptable risk, and he's probably right.

**Dan Harmetz**. Harmetz must bet. He has a pair of aces with top kicker, and unless someone has the last two aces or a nine, he's got the best hand. A lot of hands that he can beat might call: a weaker ace, a couple of clubs, or even a random low pair. If someone is holding two clubs, Harmetz wants to charge them to draw. So he bets, but it's an unusual amount. He bets $7,000, more than twice the pot.

Overbets (bets larger than the current pot) are uncommon, and more often than not indicate weakness. The bet is essentially saying "Go away and just give me the pot, I don't want to play this hand out." Note that it's not necessary to make an overbet in order to discourage drawing hands. A bet that's two-thirds of the pot, or a pot-sized bet, will deny drawing hands the proper expressed odds to draw. Sometimes a good player will move up to second-level thinking, and make an overbet with a good hand, saying "I'm strong, I'll make a bet usually associated with weakness in the hope that someone will try to push me off the hand."

Harmetz probably feels at this point that he has the best hand, and wants to encourage a call from someone who thinks he's bluffing. At this table, which has been marked by action, it's not entirely a bad idea. However, he doesn't yet have any idea where he stands, so I wouldn't go so far out on a limb. I'd make a normal bet of $2,200 to $2,400, and see what reaction I get.

The pot is now $10,200.

**Mike Matusow**. Matusow has trip nines with a pretty good kicker, a queen. He's very likely to have the best hand. But

Harmetz seems to have something, and he might be willing to come along for a raise. So Matusow raises to $15,000, an $8,000 raise. He's offering Harmetz very good odds to stick around. (If it's folded around to Harmetz, he'll be getting about 3-to-1 to call.) The pot is now $25,200.

**Dan Shak**. He originally checked to get some information from the table as to just how good his ace plus weak kicker might be. The results are in. It's not very good. He folds. Good move.

**Daniel Negreanu**. He's not thinking of folding his trip nines, although the action indicates it's possible he doesn't have the best hand. But now he has to seriously analyze the action.

If both bets are legitimate, someone has an ace and someone else probably has the last nine. Negreanu's kicker is a seven, which isn't great. If someone does have the last nine, then he's probably outkicked. But that's not as bad as it looks. Suppose Harmetz has ten-nine. Then his hand right now is three nines plus an ace plus a ten, versus Negreanu's three nines plus an ace plus a seven. Any card higher than a ten on the turn or the river would counterfeit the ten and leave a split pot. Of course, if Negreanu has the better kicker, the same logic applies in reverse!

There's also the slim chance that someone is betting a club flush draw or is on a total bluff. That would be good news, but Negreanu can't really act on it right now.

To further complicate the situation, Matusow is involved in the hand. Mike Matusow has great courage; he's completely capable of raising with nothing and following that bluff with another bullet on the turn and the rest of his stack on the river. (Phil Laak caught him doing exactly that in the second season of *High Stakes Poker*. Unfortunately for Mike, Phil was dealt a flush on the flop.) Negreanu has to be extremely reluctant to fold a big hand against Matusow.

So if neither opponent has a nine, Negreanu's in great shape, and if one does have a nine, there's some chance of a split pot and some chance that Negreanu just loses. In Negreanu's mind, a call looks justified here but a raise would be too loose. So he calls the $15,000. The pot is now $40,200.

**Dan Harmetz.** He overbet the pot, got raised, and then the raise got called. He's being offered 5-to-1 odds by the pot. (He has to put in $8,000 to call a $40,000 pot.) *Is it enough? Can he call?*

While the pot odds may look good, it's important in no-limit hold 'em to sometimes look beyond the odds and see if you're just beaten. So let's ask the basic question Harmetz should ask himself: At this point, what can my opponents have?

There are only three legitimate hands that can be in play here: an ace, a nine, or a club flush draw. Matusow could have any of these hands. He could also be on a total bluff; he's done that before. The real problem is Negreanu. Matusow's raise could be a bluff, but Negreanu's check followed by a call isn't. He's already seen a big bet and a raise, and he's calling anyway. So he's not kidding. He's got a real hand.

So what hand does he have? He can't have a club flush draw, for two solid reasons:

1. He's wasn't getting the odds he needed to call. He called getting just 25-to-15 odds, or 5-to-3. He was more than a 4-to-1 underdog to get the flush on the turn, and if the flush card comes, it put three clubs on board, which will kill the betting action, so there's no guarantee he'll get paid any more money.

2. He couldn't be sure that the betting was over since Harmetz was still alive in the hand. If Harmetz had a nine, he might reraise, and Negreanu would have to throw his flush draw away.

So Negreanu has an ace or a nine. But it's hard to call with an ace since two players have already said they have an ace or a nine, and if either of them has a nine, Negreanu is more than a 9-to-1 dog.

So Negreanu probably has a nine. But if he has a nine, Harmetz's ace-king is now more than a 9-to-1 dog. And if he doesn't have a nine, then Matusow may have one. So Harmetz needs to fold.

Here's a key principle of poker. You need to analyze hands by starting with the assumption that your opponent's plays are probably rational. That is, try to figure out what their bets, raises, and calls mean *if they're not bluffing*. Once you've done that, you can factor in the chance they are bluffing and see if that affects your play. Remember that no one bluffs routinely. In most cases, bets mean what they appear to mean. Analyze accordingly, especially as the pots get large.

Harmetz, however, calls the bet. The pot is now $48,200. The turn card is 5♣

**Daniel Negreanu**. Two new pieces of information have arrived for Negreanu:

1. Harmetz didn't raise when he could have. That decreases the chance that he holds a nine, and increases the chance that he held an ace, or even conceivably a flush draw.

2. The club on the turn gave a flush to anyone who was drawing.

Could either Harmetz or Matusow have had a flush draw? In each case, it's unlikely but possible. Harmetz overbet the pot initially, then called a raise with 5-to-1 pot odds. The overbet might have been a sort of scared semi-bluff, and the call (which concluded the betting) might have been a standard pot odds play with a flush draw. Matusow is capable of raising with a bluff, so he could have raised as a semi-bluff. Negreanu's best guess is still that he's facing an ace and the last nine, with Harmetz probably holding the ace because he didn't raise. But the club certainly didn't help his situation. At the very least, anyone with a single club in his hand is now drawing to a flush. Negreanu knows he's in trouble, so he checks.

**Dan Harmetz**. Harmetz's ace-king continues to shrink. It's almost impossible now that he has the best hand, so he checks.

**Mike Matusow**. Matusow still has trip nines with a good kicker. Did the club help either of his opponents?

Matusow should know that Negreanu didn't call with a club draw for the reasons listed when Harmetz called to end the flop betting: the pot odds weren't close to right, and Negreanu couldn't be sure of getting paid if a third club came. No pro would call with a flush draw there, and Negreanu is a consummate pro. So he hasn't got the flush.

Could Harmetz have the flush? Unlikely. The big overbet on the flop doesn't really fit with a flush draw. And the check here on the turn doesn't really fit either. If Harmetz just made his flush, he must know from the betting that he's up against two reasonably good hands. A bet now could justifiably expect to get paid off, but he just checked. So Harmetz shouldn't have the flush.

But if neither player has a flush now, either one could have a flush draw with just a single club. That's certainly possible (*although we in fact know there are no clubs in any of the hands*). So Matusow needs to bet. He might get a call based on the hand strength that's been shown, and he needs to charge anyone who has a single club and is drawing to beat him. With a $48,200 pot, a bet of about $30,000 is in order.

But Matusow just checks, and we go to the river. The pot stays at $48,200. The river is the Q♣.

**Daniel Negreanu.** Negreanu and his three nines are finished. He's losing to anyone who has a club, plus any better nine. He checks.

**Dan Harmetz.** Harmetz's ace has shrunk to nothing. He checks.

**Mike Matusow.** Matusow now knows he's going to win the pot. The arrival of the queen gave him nines full of queens, which could only be beaten by holdings of ace-nine (nines full of aces) or ace-ace (aces full of nines). But the two checks in front of him mean that neither of those hands are in play, and they also probably mean that neither of his opponents hit a flush.

Matusow will certainly bet, but what sort of bet can get paid? With no flushes out there and four clubs on board, will either of his opponents call any bet at all with trip nines? The answer is — probably not. But he needs to make some sort of bet, and his best chance is some sort of very small teaser bet, like $5,000. It's just possible that one of his opponents will find the pot odds irresistible and call. But Matusow actually bets $30,000.

**Daniel Negreanu.** Negreanu had already given up on the hand before Matusow's big bet. He folds.

**Dan Harmetz.** Also folds.

Matusow pulls down the $48,200 pot.

This was a great hand, with a lot of excellent decisions by the three main players. If you're somewhat new to no-limit hold 'em, this hand may have introduced some new ideas. In the upcoming chapters, we'll be talking about many of these ideas in depth, like pot odds, hand analysis, deception, and pot commitment. As you work your way through the book, you may want to review this hand from time to time. After awhile, decisions which may have seemed puzzling at first will start to become very clear.

# Part One

# Basic Ideas

# Basic Ideas

# Introduction

In this chapter, we're going to explain some basic ideas and terminology that you need to understand, both to finish reading this book, and to play poker. Much of the material here applies to all forms of poker, not just no-limit hold 'em cash games. If you've read a couple of poker books, and played no-limit hold 'em for a little while, you probably don't need to read this chapter. (Although a little review never hurts.) If you're just getting started in no-limit hold 'em, or if this is your first poker book, *then you need to read this chapter very carefully!* In fact, you should read it twice. Although most players take ideas like expected value and pot odds for granted, they (and others) are crucial building blocks in the process of becoming a good player.

Warning: this chapter contains a little mathematics, but it's nothing that you didn't learn in middle school. And we'll go very slowly. Poker's not about being a math whiz. It's about understanding basic concepts, and developing a keen eye for situations and the logic that underlies them.

Let's proceed.

# The Four
# Principles of Poker

Poker books are full of rules and principles for playing good poker. (This book is no exception.) Some rules, however, are more important than others. There are four rules which I think are the most fundamental, and I call them "The Four Principles of Poker." These principles don't apply just to no-limit hold 'em. They are the foundation of all forms of poker. Good players understand them intuitively, and they form the cornerstone of a sound, all-around game. We'll use them over and over again as we analyze hands in this book, but for now, let's state them in their pure form.

**Principle No. 1: The Strength Principle.**

> In general, you want to bet your strong hands, check your middling hands, and fold or bluff with your weakest hands.

Each part of this principle is fairly easy to understand, but let's quickly review the reasoning.

1.  Obviously you want to bet your strong hands to build a bigger pot when you're very likely to win.

2.  You want to check hands of middling strength because it's harder to make money when you bet such a hand. Better hands are likely to call or raise, while weak hands are likely to fold.

3.  Folding weak hands is obvious. Choosing your weakest hands for bluffing might not be so obvious, but the basic idea is that

19

if you bluff with a weak hand and the bluff works, you've gained value from a hand that had none. If you pick a hand with some value (like a medium pair) for bluffing, but then get raised off the hand, you've lost value with a hand that had some to begin with. (Bill Chen and Jerrod Ankenman, in their book, *The Mathematics of Poker,* were able to prove this principle for a variation of poker with simple rules.)

**Principle No. 2: The Aggression Principle.**

> In general, aggression (betting and raising) is better than passivity (checking and calling).

Aggressive actions give you two ways to win: your opponent can fold to your bet, or he can call your bet and you can win at the showdown. Passive action only gives you one way to win, at the showdown. Two ways to win are better than one way to win. We refer to the value you gain when your opponent folds as your *folding equity* — sometimes abbreviated as FE, and exploiting folding equity is a key part of no-limit hold 'em.

**Principle No. 3: The Betting Principle.**

> In general, a successful bet must be able to do one of three things: force a better hand to fold, force a weaker hand to call, or cause a drawing hand to draw at unfavorable odds.

A bet can make money in only three different ways. If you can chase a better hand out of the pot, you've won a hand you should have lost. If you get a weaker hand to call, you've gotten more money into a pot you rate to win. If a hand is drawing to beat you, and you can make that hand pay, you've also made money.

If you don't think a bet can accomplish any of these things, you probably shouldn't be betting.

**Principle 4: The Deception Principle.**

> Never do anything all of the time.

In order to be successful at poker, you need to keep your opponents guessing about what you have and what your bets mean. In order to keep them guessing, you have to make sure that all of your actions can have multiple interpretations.

With the Four Principles firmly in mind, let's move on to some of the other basic concepts.

# Expectation
# and Expected Value

In life, situations have outcomes, and outcomes have values. Expected value is what you think (or calculate) a situation is worth on average before it eventually resolves itself.

As a practical example, let's imagine you're in the business of house flipping. You look around and you find a run-down house in a pretty good neighborhood. The house is listed at $300,000. You and your contractor put your heads together and decide that if you put $80,000 worth of improvements into the house, it can fetch a price of $500,000 in this market. A real estate agent will charge 6 percent of the selling price to sell the house.

1. What's the expected value of this business situation to you? And,

2. Should you actually buy the house?

The answer to No. 1 is pretty easy. It will cost you a total of $380,000 to buy the house and get it into shape, after which you can sell the house for $500,000 less the commission of $30,000, or $470,000. Your profit, or expected value on this transaction, is $90,000.

$$\$90{,}000 = \$500{,}000 - (\$300{,}000 + \$80{,}000 + 30{,}000)$$

Seems pretty good for a couple of month's work.

No. 2 is a little harder. In fact, we don't know enough yet to answer it. Before we can decide whether or not to take this opportunity, we need to know what other deals are available. A good house flipper would look at several properties, perform a similar analysis on each one, then pick the property with the largest expected value (profit).

A good poker player thinks like this at crucial points in a hand. He decides what his choices are, makes a quick calculation (or perhaps just an educated guess) at the expected value from each choice, then picks the play with the higher value. Here's a quick example.

# Example

You're playing a small stakes no-limit hold 'em game at your local casino. Your hole cards are

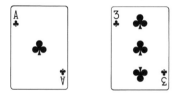

The turn card has just appeared, and the board is

giving you a draw to the nut club flush. The pot right now contains $50. You're up against a single opponent, a tight, conservative player. Right now you have just $20 left in front of you. Your opponent has much more. He bets $20, so you will have to put in the rest of your chips to call. From what you've seen of his play, you believe he would make this bet only with a pretty good hand, at least two pair or trips (three of a kind). Your choices are to call or fold. *What should you do?*

This is a fairly simple hold 'em problem because your action here, whatever it is, ends the betting. After your play, you'll either win or lose based on how the last card falls. If it's a club, you'll win. If it's not a club, you'll lose. To make a decision, we'll calculate the expected value (also known as EV) of each play, and we'll pick the play that has the higher EV.

We'll start with folding because that's pretty easy to calculate. If you fold you can't lose anything and you can't win anything. Your EV is therefore 0.

"What about the money I already put in the pot before this!" you scream in anguish. Fuggedaboutit. That money is gone. Ancient history. The money in the pot belongs to the pot. It doesn't matter who put it there. Each betting decision is a fresh decision, and the money in the pot is nobody's money anymore until the hand is decided.

Now let's see what happens when you call. This is a bit more involved. There are 13 clubs in the deck, and right now you know the location of four of them, two in your hand and two on the board. There are a total of 52 cards in the deck, and you've seen six of them. That means there are 46 cards still unseen, 9 of which are clubs and 37 of which belong to one of the other three suits. So the chance of drawing a club on the river (and winning) is 19.6 percent.

$$0.196 = \frac{9}{46}$$

and the chance of drawing a non-club (and losing) is 80.4 percent.

$$0.804 = \frac{37}{46}$$

Before we go further, let's quickly round these numbers off to 20 and 80 percent respectively. In poker, we're rarely trying to get mathematical exactitude in our calculations. Instead, we're happy with good approximations that let us do computations quickly and easily. In almost all cases, a good approximation will lead us to the same answer as an exact calculation, with much less time and effort.

So we win 20 percent of the time, and when we win, we pick up $70. (The $50 pot plus our opponent's $20 bet.) On average, that's a win of $14.

$$\$14 = (.20)(\$70)$$

When we lose, we lose our $20 call. On average, that's a loss of $16.

$$-\$16 = (.80)(\$20)$$

Now we can calculate the expected value of calling. Since these are the only two possible outcomes after calling, our expected value is just the sum of the expected values of each event or -$2.

$$-\$2 = -\$16(\text{when we lose}) + \$14(\text{when we win})$$

Our expected value, or EV, when calling is -$2. That is, we expect to lose, on average, about $2 every time we call in this exact situation.

Notice that the expected value of calling is nothing like the actual result. In actuality, we're either going to win $70 or lose $20. But if we were to set up this same situation hundreds or even thousands of times, each time shuffling the deck and dealing a fresh river card, the long-run result would approach the expected value, namely a loss of $2 per hand.

Now we have all the information we need to answer our original question: call or fold? Calling loses $2 per hand, but folding has an expected value of zero, so folding is better. It doesn't win any money, but it loses less than the alternative.

Every play in poker has an expected value. In simple cases, like this one, a good player can calculate the answer in his head. In more complex cases, you make educated guesses. But you're always trying to pick the play that has the highest expected value *given what you know about the situation.*

# Pot Odds

A player confronted with the situation in the previous example wouldn't actually have gone through the EV calculation we just described. Instead, he would have used a shortcut, by calculating the *pot odds* he was being offered and comparing them to the *odds of making his hand*. Let's see how this works.

Pot odds are a simple and extremely useful concept. Just compare the money in the pot to the amount of money required to call the bet. In the previous example, there was $70 in the pot, and you had to put in $20 to call, so the pot odds were 70-to-20, or 3.5-to-1.

Once you know the pot odds, you can decide if you want to call the bet by comparing the pot odds to your actual chance of winning. If the pot odds are better (i.e. higher) than your winning chances, then you'll make money by calling. If the pot odds are worse (i.e. lower) than your winning chances, then you're not being paid enough to take the risk, and you should fold.

In the last example, you had nine winning flush cards and 37 other losing cards. So the odds against your winning were 37-to-9, or just over 4-to-1 against. The pot odds you're being offered (3.5-to-1) are lower than the odds against your winning, so you should fold.

Here's another example.

# Example

You hold

and the board is

The pot right now is $150. You have $50 left in your stack, and you face two opponents, one of whom has $200 left, while the other has $100. The player with $200 moves all-in. The second player calls. *What should you do?*

The first point to note is that since you have only $50 left, the situation is the same as if the first player had bet $50 and the second player had called. The pot is now $250 and it costs you $50 to call. The extra money that was bet, above what you had, will go into a side pot that won't affect you.

So the main pot is offering you 250-to-50, or 5-to-1 pot odds. Are your winning chances better than that? Let's see.

With four clubs on board, the first player's bet practically announces that he has a club in his hand, and very probably a high club. (If he doesn't have a club, and he's facing two opponents, he won't bet because there's too good a chance that he's beaten, and will be called.) The second player's call implies that he has a club also. Who has the higher club? You don't know and it's not your problem. Right now you're probably facing two flushes, and all you have is a set of aces.

But all is not lost. No matter how many flushes you're facing, you can still win by making four of a kind or a full house, and a number of cards can come on the river that will do exactly that. You could draw any of the three remaining fours, any of the three remaining eights, any of the three remaining jacks, and the lone remaining ace. That's a total of ten cards to give you a winning hand, out of the 46 cards in the deck you haven't seen yet.

So the deck has 10 winning cards and 36 losing cards, making you 36-to-10 against drawing a winning hand. That's 3.6-to-1 against, which is much less than the 5-to-1 odds you're being offered by the pot. So you should call. You're an underdog to win, but you're being paid enough, when you win, to want to play.

If you have a real eye for detail, you may have noticed you're actually doing better than this calculation would indicate. None of the cards you want to complete your hand are clubs, because the clubs of all those ranks are already out on the board. You believe that your opponent's hands contain at least two clubs, which are cards you don't want. So there are only 34 useless cards unaccounted for, and still 10 good ones. Your actual odds against hitting are 34-to-10 against, or 3.4-to-1. If you noticed this fact, pat yourself on the head. You've got the kind of attention to detail that will make you a really good poker player.

# Expressed Odds
# and Implied Odds

Now let's take the idea of pot odds a little bit farther. Poker odds actually come in two flavors, *expressed odds* and *implied odds*. Expressed odds are the kind of odds we've considered so far. Your call ends the betting, so there is no more action. You either win or you lose, and you know exactly what you can win; it's the amount in the pot right now.

Implied odds are a little more complicated. Suppose your opponent makes a bet, but the bet doesn't put you all-in. If you call, there may be more action in the hand. If you hit your hand, you may be able to win more money later, but if you miss your hand, you won't have to put any more money in the pot. Implied odds are the odds offered by the pot, *taking into account the money you may win at a later time.*

Unlike expressed odds, which you can calculate directly as we just showed, implied odds require some educated guesswork. You'll need to estimate the answers to questions like these:

- If you hit your hand, will your opponent call a future bet?

- How big a bet will he call?

- If there's a large probability that he'll call a small bet, and a small probability that he'll call a big bet, how big a bet should you make?

## Example

No-limit hold 'em cash game. Right now you hold

and the board is

You have $500 left in your stack, and your opponent has the same amount. The pot is $180, and your opponent bets $100. You believe that he paired his ace on the flop. *Should you call or fold?*

We know from working through our previous example that of the 46 cards unseen in the deck, nine will make our flush and 37 will not, so we're a 37-to-9 underdog to hit a winning hand, or about 4-to-1. The pot now contains $280 after our opponent's bet, and it costs us $100 to call. The expressed odds given by the pot are just 280-to-100, or 2.8-to-1. By themselves, that's not good enough to call the bet, since we're 4-to-1 underdogs to make our hand.

However, if we call the $100, there will be another round of betting. On the river, the pot will be $380 ($180 plus his $100 plus our $100), and we will each have $400 remaining in our stacks. Some or all of that $400 might get bet on the river. That's to our advantage because we aren't going to put any money in unless we hit our hand. If a non-spade comes on the river, either he'll bet and we'll fold, or he won't bet and we'll show our hand down. In either case we presume we'll lose the pot, but we won't lose any more money.

But if a spade comes on the river, there are a few possibilities:

1. He might bet into us, in which case we can raise, and he might or might not call our raise.

2. He might check, and we could bet a small amount, like $100. He'd now be getting 4.8-to-1 pot odds to call this bet, which are pretty good odds, so he'll probably call.

3. He might check, and we could bet a medium-sized amount, like $200. Now he's only getting 2.9-to-1 pot odds to call, so he's not as likely to call. But he might.

4. He might check, and we could go all-in for our last $400. Now he's only getting about 2-to-1 odds to call, so he's even less likely to play. But there's some chance he'll still call.

The truth is, we don't know how much our flush will be worth to us. Partly, that's because I haven't given you any information about this particular opponent, except to say we think he has at least a pair of aces. Is he a loose, belligerent player who doesn't like to be pushed around? Then he'll probably call a bet, and he might even call a large bet. Is he timid and weak? Then he might go away without a peep. And what if he is a good card reader? Then our flush may lose much of its value.

Without knowing anything about our opponent, it seems reasonable to think that we can collect something on the river. Let's estimate our profit on the river, if we hit, as somewhere between $100 and $150.

Now let's go back to our call on the turn and see how this new estimate affects our decision. At that point, the pot contained $280 and it cost us $100 to call. We were getting 2.8-to-1 expressed odds, not enough if we were 4-to-1 underdogs to make a winning hand.

But now we think we're going to win some extra money on the river, somewhere between $100 and $150, and we're not going to lose any more money.

1.  If we win an extra $100, then our *implied odds* are really 380-to-100, or 3.8-to-1. Still a little short.

2.  But if we win an extra $150, our implied odds are 430-to-100, or 4.3-to-1. Comfortably adequate.

Looks like a close decision. We can't make a big mistake here. What to do? In these close cases, I like to play. Call a bet on the turn, and then bet $200 on the river if a spade comes. I can't be making a big mistake, and I might get paid off.

In all close decisions, you should try to make the play that creates the appearance of giving action. A table image of an action player, one who likes excitement and who will bet, raise, and call with a variety of hands, is more profitable than the table image of a rock who needs something close to the nuts to put his money in the pot.

# Calculating Outs

After the flop, you will often find yourself in a position where you need to improve your hand to win. A card that will improve your hand to a winning hand is called an "out." Estimating the number of outs you have after the flop or the turn is an important skill. If you can calculate your outs, you know how big an underdog you are right now, and what pot odds you need to call a bet.

Counting outs involves some calculation and some guesswork. A card that appears to be an out at first may not be. If you are drawing to a straight while your opponent is drawing to a flush, some of the cards that give you a straight will give him a flush at the same time. On the other hand, if your opponent is betting like he's strong but he's actually bluffing, you may not need any outs at all.

For a quick example of counting outs, consider this hand. In middle position before the flop, you hold

You raise, and an opponent in late position calls.

The flop comes

34

You check, and your opponent bets. Right now you have nothing. How many outs do you have to a winning hand?

The first point to notice is that your opponent could have a variety of hands. Your decision to check on the flop showed weakness, so his bet might be an attempt to pick up the pot with nothing. It might also mean he hit the flop and has a real hand. Let's list some hands he might have, and see how many outs we have against each of them.

- **He has a big hand:** He might have hit two pair or a set. That's not a likely result, but we must consider it. In that case you need a straight or a flush to win. You have what is called a *double belly-buster straight draw*; that is, you need either a king for a high inside straight, or a nine for a low inside straight. There are four kings and four nines, so that's a total of eight outs. You also have a *backdoor flush draw*. You need a spade on the turn and another one on the river to complete that draw. The chance of a spade on the turn is 10/47. The chance of following that with a spade on the river is then 9/46. A quick way of looking at this is ten outs on the turn, but only about one-fifth of those make a flush on the river. That's a total of about two more outs. That gives us a total of eight straight outs and two extra flush outs, or about 10 outs in all.

  But we're not quite done yet because he can improve his hand to beat us even if we hit one of our outs. If he currently has a set, for instance, any card that pairs the board on the turn or river will give him a full house or better. If he has a set, that's about a 30 percent chance of improving. If he has two pair, it's about a 20 percent chance of improvement. Taking this into account, we need to reduce our outs from 10 down to 7.5 or 8 in this variation.

- **He has a pair of aces:** This happens when he called with ace-x in his hand and paired his ace on the flop. We still need to improve to win, so this is like the previous case, except it's much harder for him to beat our straight or flush when we hit it. We'll give ourselves the full 10 outs in this case.

• **He has a pair of jacks:** He may have started with a hand like king-jack or jack-ten, hit middle pair on the flop, and decided that your check indicated you didn't have an ace. In addition to the 10 outs you had before, the queens now represent three additional outs, for a total of 13.

• **He has a lower pair:** He may have something like a pair of nines or a pair of sevens, and simply decided this was a good opportunity to take down a winnable pot. If this is the case, the three tens in the deck have become new outs for you, making a total of 16.

Notice, however, that we're now moving into a grey area. In this last case, the tens are technically outs for you, given his actual hand. But if you hit a ten, you'll have no idea if you just made the best hand or not. The same is true to a lesser extent with the queens. The straight cards are unambiguous outs; everything else is a little fuzzy.

This last example is much more like a real-world hand than the simple examples we gave earlier. There it was enough to say "Oh, I'm drawing to a flush, I have nine outs," or "I have an open-ended straight draw, I have eight outs." In real hands, you have to give some thought to just what your opponent's bets or checks might represent, and adjust your outs accordingly. In this last hand, I'd estimate that given my straight, flush, and high card possibilities, 10 outs is a good average number. Then I'd decide if I wanted to play the hand or not.

For some assistance, here's a table of outs covering the most common situations you'll encounter:

| Number of Outs | Drawing Hand |
|:---:|:---|
| 4 | Two pair needing a full house; an inside straight draw |
| 6 | Two overcards needing to make a pair |
| 8 | Open-ended straight draw |
| 9 | Flush draw |
| 11 | Flush draw plus a pair needing to improve to trips |
| 12 | Flush draw plus an inside straight draw |
| 15 | Flush draw plus open-ended straight draw |

As a handy rule of thumb, 14 outs makes you about even money against a made hand.

# The Rule of Four
# and The Rule of Two

If you know how many outs you have and want a quick and dirty estimate as to your percentage winning chances in the hand, use the Rule of Four and the Rule of Two.

> **The Rule of Four:** If two cards are still to come and you will be able to see both cards, multiply your number of outs by four to get your winning chances in the hand.

For example, if you have six outs with two cards to come, your winning chances are around 24 percent.

> **The Rule of Two:** If only one card is still to come, multiply your outs by two to get your winning chances.

For example, if you have nine outs and only the river card remains to be seen, your winning chances are around 18 percent.

When there are exactly two cards to come, you can get an even more exact percentage by using Solomon's Rule:

> **Solomon's Rule:** With two cards to come, multiply the number of outs by four, then subtract the number of outs in excess of eight to get your winning percentage.

With 14 outs, for instance, your winning chances are approximately 50 percent.

$$50 = (14)(4) - (14 - 8)$$

# Bet Types

A bet at the poker table can fall into several distinct types. Each type of bet has its own rationale and goals. Let's quickly look at the four main types of bets: value bets, probe bets, bluffs, and semi-bluffs, and explain why they are made.

## The Value Bet

A value bet is exactly what its name implies. You believe that you probably have the best hand at the table right now, and you'd like to get more money into the pot while that's the case. You don't need certainty to make a value bet. Except in the very rare cases where you hold the mortal nuts (best possible hand) your belief that your hand is best is just an educated guess. In poker, however, you have to act on your educated guesses, so you bet. A normal value bet is usually in the range of half the pot up to the whole pot.

A value bet can accomplish a number of good things, including:

- **Getting more money into the pot when you are a favorite:** One of the prime goals in poker is to build big pots when you are a favorite, and keep the pots small when you are an underdog. A value bet accomplishes the first goal.

- **Chasing away better hands:** If you're wrong, and you don't have the best hand right now, a bet might still get a marginally better hand to fold, winning a pot that you were otherwise a favorite to lose.

- **Denying proper odds to drawing hands:** If an opponent has a draw to a hand that beats you, and you bet an amount that denies them the proper drawing odds they need, they either have to fold or put money into the pot when their expectation is negative.

● **Taking control of the hand:** Your bet establishes you as the leader in the hand. On a later street, your opponents may be reluctant to bet hands which are, in fact, better than yours, thus giving you a free card.

# The Probe Bet

Probe bets are smaller than value bets (one-third to one-half the pot, typically) and have a different function. They occur when you don't really think you have the best hand, but you want to bet anyway for a number of possible reasons. Like a hunter in front of a thicket, you're "probing" at the pot to see just what you can flush out.

A probe bet might accomplish any of the following:

● **Winning the pot:** Unexpected, but a great result.

● **Establishing control:** By taking the lead and establishing yourself as the man in the pot, you may get a free card or two on later streets.

● **Heading off larger bets:** Players with marginal hands are more inclined to bet than they are to raise. By betting first, you might induce someone who would have made a bigger bet to just call, enabling you to see a later street (or the showdown) more cheaply.

● **Flushing out weak opposition:** In a multi-way pot, a probe bet might convince a couple of opponents to throw their hands away rather than call with hands that might have beaten you with a lucky draw.

# The Bluff

A bluff is just what it implies — a bet made with a very weak hand in an attempt to represent a big hand in order to win a pot that otherwise can't be won.

In addition to winning the hand right on the spot, bluffs have a couple of other important functions.

1.  **Setting up future (bluff) bets:** This is also known as "firing multiple bullets." If you bluff on the flop, and get called, you don't have to give up on the hand. You can bluff again on the turn ("firing a second bullet") and if that gets called, yet again on the river ("firing three barrels"). It's very hard to call three progressively larger bets with a hand that's not the pure nuts. Your chances of winning the pot are pretty high if you can fire three barrels. When it doesn't work, however, you might lose your whole stack.

2.  **Establishing credibility:** In poker, if you never bluff, you can't win. Once your opponents figure out that your bets mean what they're supposed to mean, they essentially know what you have, and from then on you'll win small pots and lose big ones — a recipe for failure. In order to make your opponents call you when you have a big hand, they must believe that you're capable of making big bluffs. So once in a while, you must do it.

# The Semi-Bluff

The semi-bluff, a term first coined by David Sklansky, is a very particular kind of bet, not exactly a value bet and not exactly a bluff, but a little of both. It's a bet made by a drawing hand, against a presumably made hand. The bet has two ways to win: the made hand may fold, or the drawing hand may hit its draw and win, possibly winning a big pot.

As an example, suppose you have

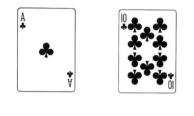

and the flop is

You have a club flush draw plus an overcard (the ace, which is higher than any card on the board), and you bet. If your opponent folds, you win the pot, not a bad result. If your opponent has a pair, he might call your bet. Now you can take the lead if any club comes, or any ace, a total of 12 outs. If you don't hit your hand on the turn, your show of strength on the flop may discourage your opponent from betting, so you could hit your hand again on the river. With 12 outs, you're about 44 percent to make your hand if you get to see two cards.

A little math will show how powerful a move the semi-bluff can be. Let's look at our previous example again. Suppose you believe there is a 30 percent chance that your opponent will fold when you bet. If you call, you've calculated that there is a 44 percent chance that you'll hit your hand and actually win at the showdown. If those estimates are right, then you'll win 30 percent of the time immediately and another 30.8 percent

$$.308 = (.70)(.44)$$

at the showdown, for a total of 60.8 percent. Your semi-bluff has made you an actual favorite. (Although you would show a loss if the bet was a high multiple of the pot.)

Before you decide to start semi-bluffing at every opportunity, note that a couple of things can go wrong with this rosy scenario. Here's a short list:

1. Your estimate of 30 percent folding chances might be too high given the hand your opponent may hold.

2. When you make your semi-bluff, your opponent might raise rather than just call, after which your estimates go out the window.

3. If you miss your draw on the turn, your opponent might make a big bet with just one card to come, a bet you can't call.

4. You might make your hand only to discover that your opponent made an even bigger one.

In short, semi-bluffs are a tool in your arsenal, but not a mechanical winning strategy. Use them carefully.

# The Check

After our previous section on the merits of various kinds of bets, it might seem that checking (instead of betting) isn't worth much. Quite the opposite. Apart from the obvious case of not wanting to put money in the pot with a hopeless hand, checking is an important strategic option and has a number of merits. Let's list them now.

**Merit No. 1: Preserving a medium-strength hand.** If you have no hand, the only way to win the pot might be to bluff. But if you have a hand of modest strength (for example, bottom pair on the flop) you may have a hand which we call "good enough to check." It's not a hand you especially want to bet, but it's not so weak that you have to bluff. Instead, it's a hand that might win on its own if the hand is checked down. So you check, risking the minimum to try and see an eventual showdown.

**Merit No. 2: Shortening the hand.** Suppose the flop comes and you find yourself with a hand like top pair. Right now that hand, on average, rates to be the best hand at the table. However, if the hand goes all the way to the river, with bets and calls on each street, and your top pair never improves, your hand does not rate to be best at the end. This creates a paradox. You may have what appears to be a strong hand, but with the pot growing geometrically on each street, it's not a hand that you want to bet on every street. Checking is one solution. You might choose to check the flop and bet the turn, or bet the flop and check the turn. Either way you succeed in *shortening the hand*. By reducing the number of streets where betting occurs, you can keep the final pot more in line with the projected strength of your hand.

**Merit No. 3: Trapping.** Checking a good hand shows weakness, and misleads your opponents as to the true strength of your hand. The quick way to exploit this deception is with a check-raise, but you might also check and call a bet, saving the chit of deception to cash in on a later street.

# Controlling Pot Odds

When you make a bet, you are in essence controlling the odds your opponent sees to call that bet. The ability to control odds is one of the great features of no-limit hold 'em, one that adds much of the skill to the game. In limit poker, the size of the bets are preset, and as the pot grows large, the bets become almost insignificant. If you're drawing to a flush in limit poker, and you're a 4-to-1 underdog or so, but the pot is so big that your opponent's bet still offers you 10-to-1 pot odds, you have an easy, even mindless, call. Much of limit poker looks exactly like this, as made hands make maximum bets and draws simply keep calling with better and better pot odds, until finally the hand resolves itself.

But in no-limit poker, drawing hands are much more problematic. If your opponent puts you on a drawing hand, he can shut you down with a pot-sized bet, which reduces your drawing odds to 2-to-1 or so, and requires you to either believe you have such massive implied odds that you can keep going, or get out.

On the other hand, making small bets, offering good pot odds, may just be an inducement for your opponent to correctly stick around and draw out on you. Take a look at the following typical example.

## Example

An online no-limit hold 'em cash game with $2 and $4 blinds. Preflop, everyone folds to you in the cutoff seat. You have

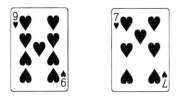

and you make a mini-raise to $8. The button folds but the small blind calls for $6. The big blind folds. The pot is now $20, and you have position on your single opponent.

The flop is

Your opponent checks. That's a very scary flop with three cards higher than your nine-seven, and some straight possibilities floating around. Right now, you have only an inside straight draw (a jack gives you a straight). Having no idea where you stand, and with just four outs, you check.

The turn is the 6♠. That's helpful because you pick up yet another inside straight draw, this time on the low end where an eight will give you a straight. Now you're up to eight probable outs.

Your opponent now bets $4. That's a very strange bet, offering you 6-to-1 pot odds. Right now you've seen six cards, so 46 remain in the deck. Of those, as far as you know, eight fill your straight and are winners, while the other 38 probably lose. The odds of filling your hand are 38-to-8, or a little less than 5-to-1. You actually have the expressed odds you need to call! Any implied odds are just a bonus. (Your opponent could have something like ace-jack, in which case you're drawing dead. But such a big hand isn't consistent with his betting so far.)

You call, making the pot $28. The river is the 8♣ filling your straight. He checks, and you bet $16. That's a good amount; you're pretty sure you have the winning hand, but you don't want to bet so much that you won't get paid. He calls, and shows the

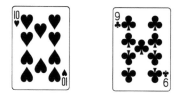

You win a nice pot.

Notice what your opponent did. On the flop he was scared with just bottom pair. But you checked, and on the turn an apparently innocuous card came. At this point he felt he could try to take the pot, but he was scared, so he made a tiny bet. The bet was so small that you were justified in staying with a weak drawing hand — eight outs with just one card to come equals 16 percent chances using the Rule of Two. As a result you drew out, beat him, and won the pot plus another $16 on the river. Had he been willing to make a decent-sized bet, say $12 to $14, you would have gone away on the turn and he could have claimed the pot.

Bets shouldn't be proportional to the strength of your hand. They need to be proportional to what you're representing in the situation.

# Part Two

# The Elements of No-Limit Hold 'em Cash Games

# The Elements of No-Limit Hold 'em Cash Games

# Introduction

No-limit hold 'em cash games revolve around the proper application of a few key concepts. The concepts themselves aren't particularly difficult to understand in the abstract. After you read this section, you'll probably walk away thinking, "I understood all that. Cash games aren't really so tough." Disabuse yourself of any such notion quickly. Cash games are very hard to play well, which is why there are only a handful of top cash game players.

While the concepts themselves may seem simple, even elementary, they interrelate in a myriad of different ways. That's why we urge you to not just skim through these sections quickly, but to read them slowly and carefully. Pay particular attention to the sample hands and hand examples in every chapter. Each hand example will illustrate multiple concepts and show how they interrelate in a real hand. As a group, the hand examples are every bit as important to understanding the game as the text itself.

# Stack Sizes

Let's start by discussing the effects of different stack sizes, a concept which interrelates with the other ideas in this chapter. In our series of books on tournament play (*Harrington on Hold 'em; Volumes I, II* and *III*), we introduced the concept of M which was the ratio between your stack size and the total of the blinds and the antes. M was a quick way to determine how many rounds of the table you could last before you were blinded off assuming you played no hands in the interim. Once you knew your M, you knew how aggressively you had to play to have a chance of staying alive. With a small M — 5 or less, you simply looked for a good situation and pushed all-in. With larger Ms, you could afford to play a style closer to normal poker.

In the early rounds of tournaments, your M could be much larger. In a typical sit-and-go, your starting M might be 50; in a major tournament, it might be anywhere from 100 to 200. As the tournament progressed, however, your M dropped rapidly, and even by the second level your M was likely to be under 100.

In no-limit cash games there are no antes and the blinds never change, so we can drop the 'M' notation and just describe a stack in terms of the number of big blinds it contains. When you enter an online no-limit cash game, your maximum buy-in is generally 100 big blinds, and the minimum is generally 20 big blinds. (As the game goes on, stacks may get bigger than 100 and smaller than 20.) When you enter a live game, the buy-in policy will vary from casino to casino. The minimum buy-in will generally remain very small, but the maximum could be 200 big blinds, 500 big blinds, or, in some cases, anything you want.

When you sit down in a game, you'll see a wide variety of stack sizes at the table. Different stack sizes imply different strategies. Here's how I like to characterize the different possible stack sizes in a game:

- **30 big blinds or less:** These are the short stacks at the table. In cash games, unlike tournaments, you're never forced to play with a short stack, so you can assume players whose stack is short actually want it that way. Players who want short stacks generally have one of two reasons: they want to reduce their risk, or they're playing a carefully thought out short stack strategy.

  Playing a short stack to reduce your overall risk is a reasonable choice, especially for a novice player. I used this approach myself when I began playing no-limit cash games. If something goes wrong and you lose your whole stack, just buy back in and start over again.

  There is also a well-defined short stack strategy outlined by Ed Miller in the book *Getting Started in Hold 'em*, which in turn was based upon some of David Sklansky's ideas in *Tournament Poker for Advanced Players*. We'll say more about this approach in a later section, but it basically involves selecting premium hands and trying to get all-in whether preflop or on the flop.

- **40 to 60 big blinds:** These are medium stacks. They don't have any independent significance unless you're playing a somewhat mechanical strategy based upon trying to get all-in on the flop with a mixture of very strong hands and semi-bluffs. Like the short stack strategy, we'll have more to say about this at a later time.

- **100 to 200 big blinds:** At this level we're starting to get into true deep stack play. Play begins to focus less on pushing premium starting hands and more on maneuvering to win an opponent's entire stack.

- **More than 200 big blinds:** True deep stack play. Hand values change. Winning an opponent's entire stack becomes, up to a point, the central focus of the game.

# Stack Sizes
# and Hand Selection

In small stack play, hand selection is dominated by premium hands, pairs, and big cards. Since your stack isn't big enough to cover a long series of escalating bets, your basic strategy is to wait for a good hand, bet it preflop, then continue to push it on the flop unless the board is especially unfavorable.

After a couple of bets, most of your stack will be in the pot. Suppose you started with a stack of 20 big blinds, bet 3 big blinds preflop, and another 8 on the flop. You now have only 9 big blinds left in your stack and the pot might already have 20 big blinds in it. If your opponent puts you all-in at this point, you'll be getting 3-to-1 or 4-to-1 pot odds. If you have top pair, you probably won't be able to fold.

If you're likely to get all-in early in the hand, you need to focus on cards that have a good chance of being the best hand quickly. Hence you play pairs, especially the big pairs, and high card combinations. You can't play the trickier hands like small pairs and suited connectors because those hands need time to develop, and with a short stack you don't have time.

With deep stacks everything changes. Hand values *normalize*, which means that the gap between "strong" hands (premium pairs and ace-king, for example) and "weak" hands (small or medium suited or unsuited connectors) gets smaller and smaller as the stacks get larger and larger. A good player in a big stack game doesn't want to wait solely for premium hands. He can play more hands, and some of the hands will be the so-called weak hands that he would have routinely dumped in the muck had he been short-stacked.

This last point is crucial and can't be overemphasized. In no-limit cash games with deep stacks, you will of course play your premium hands. You're not going to throw away a pair of queens or ace-king before the flop except in extremely unusual situations. But you'll mix in with your good hands an astute selection of other hands: ten-nine offsuit, seven-five suited, four-trey offsuit, and so forth. Not only are these hands not as weak as they appear, they are in fact the hands which are most likely to win your opponent's whole stack!

Many beginners who transition to no-limit hold 'em cash games from tournament or limit play come with a simplistic and very erroneous view of how the game should be played. "Deep stacks? No problem! I'll just wait patiently for a big hand, then get all my chips in and clean up. Easy money." Sounds simple, but this approach breaks down quickly. Let's look at a couple of sample hands and see what's likely to happen.

# Sample Hand No. 1

You're in a $5-$10 live game. You bought in for $1,000 and your stack is now $950. You've played very tight so far, waiting for a good hand. In second position you finally pick up

The under the gun player folds and you raise to $30. You get one caller, on the button. His stack appears to be about $1,800. The blinds fold and you go to the flop with a pot of $75.

The flop is

You've flopped top pair and top kicker. You like your chances. You act first and decide to bet $60 into a $75 pot. It's a good solid bet. Your opponent folds. You rake in the pot. Your ace-king suited made a total profit of $45 on the hand, the cost, as it happens, of the blinds for three complete rounds of the table.

# Sample Hand No. 2

Same game, a couple of rounds later. Your stack has drifted back to $965. In second position you pick up

Another promising start. The first player folds and you raise to $30. This time you get two callers, Player F in the cutoff seat and Player G on the button. The blinds fold and the pot is $105.

The flop is

Very similar to the last hand you played. Once again you like your chances with top pair and bet $75. Player F calls $75 and Player G folds. Action! You like it. The pot is now $255.

The turn is the Q♣. This looks like a good card to you. You were a little worried about a spade draw and now that has missed. Also, if someone was playing ace-queen or ace-jack, they might be inclined to call another bet. But now there are two potential flush draws on board, and you can't let them draw for free. You make a nice solid bet of $200. Your stack has $660 left.

Player F raises you another $400 to $600. The pot is now $1,055 and it costs you $400 to call.

This wasn't what you expected. His raise will cost you almost two-thirds of your remaining stack. You realize he could have a set of queens, nines, or eights. He could even have a straight if he called originally with jack-ten. You don't feel like losing your whole stack on a pair of kings. You fold.

As the dealer collects the pot you ask "What did you have?"

"Lessons are extra," he replies, and mucks his cards. You lost $305 on the hand.

What went wrong? Actually, less than you might think. On the end, he probably had you beaten, and many beginners would have lost their whole stack with top pair, top kicker. You didn't, so that's good news.

Mainly, what went wrong was that you were out of position and transparent. You had top pair, top kicker, and you played exactly like you had top pair, top kicker. In a deep stack game, opaque is good and transparent is very bad. You were new to the game, playing very tight, and after a few rounds your opponents surmised that on the few occasions when you were in a hand, you probably had high cards. When the king came on the flop and you bet, your opponents had a simple problem. You probably have something like top pair, top kicker, so if they can beat that hand, or if they have a draw to beat that hand, they can stick around, otherwise not. Most likely Player F had you beaten on the flop with a middling set, and called expecting you to bet again on the turn. It's also possible he had the straight draw and expected to collect large implied odds if he hit. If the queen did complete his straight, you fooled him by not paying off.

The key lesson from these two hands, however, is what you won and lost. In the first hand, you hit the flop, everyone else missed, and you made $45. In the second hand you hit the flop but someone else did too, and you lost $305. That's not a completely unusual result for hands like premium pairs and ace-king. When they win pots, the pots tend to be small. When they lose, however, the pots tend to be big.

Why are the winning pots small? Because experienced players won't put a lot of money in a pot unless they can beat a hand like top pair, good kicker. If you have a hand like J♥J♣, and your opponent bets before the flop, and the flop comes something like A♦7♣4♥, and your opponent bets again, how much money will you lose with your pair of jacks? The answer is — not very much. The ace is simply too obvious and too threatening, so you'll get out.

Why are the losing pots big? Because when you flop top pair, good kicker, or an overpair, you have a problem. How long should you stick with the hand if you don't improve? You can't fold whenever someone calls you on the flop and bets on the turn because that pattern is easy to read. But if you stick around when you're actually beaten, the geometrically escalating nature of the bets means you can lose a lot of money very quickly. In Sample Hand No. 2, our hero lost one-third of his stack after folding on the turn. But if his opponent did have a set, as advertised, he would have lost his entire stack by the river.

Does this mean premium hands aren't good? Not at all. They're profitable hands because they win lots and lots of pots. The only problem is that those pots are typically smaller than the pots they lose, so on balance those premium hands are not as profitable as they would be in a short-stack game or a limit game.

So the naïve beginner's strategy of waiting patiently for a premium hand and then cleaning up doesn't really work well in a game of competent players. (It works just fine in a small-stakes weak game.) What's a better approach? To see, let's ask ourselves a more fundamental question. What has to happen for us to win our opponent's whole stack?

# Big Hand versus Big Hand

When big stacks collide, winning your opponent's whole stack requires two things to happen:

1. You must have a big hand.

2. Your opponent must have a hand big enough to warrant getting all his chips in the pot, but smaller than yours.

Most players with any experience will not put their whole stack at risk after the flop with just a pair, or even two pair, as their holding. Back in Sample Hand No. 2, that appeared earlier in this chapter, even our inexperienced hero had the sense to get out when he held a pair of kings but it became clear that he would have to get his whole stack in the pot. It was simply too easy and too likely for his opponent to hold a set. When big stacks go all-in against each other, the hands are usually full houses versus straights, or flush versus flush, straight versus set, or set versus set. Each player in the pot needs some reason to believe that his hand is likely to be best, and that means each needs a big hand.

# Normalizing Hand Values

Earlier we said that in deep stack poker, hand values normalize; that is, the gap between "strong" preflop hands and "weak" preflop hands shrinks as the stacks get larger. To see why this should be the case, let's consider these two hands as they go against each other in a pot:

1.   Hand 1: A♥K♦

2.   Hand 2: 8♣7♣

Let's imagine that two players play a variation of hold 'em against each other. In this mechanical variation, each player has 10 big blinds in their stack. One player gets dealt the ace-king offsuit in every hand, while the second player is dealt the eight-seven suited. After each deal, the players both shove their 10 big blinds in the pot, and the board is dealt, after which we see who wins. Which hand would you rather have? Clearly, you'd rather be the player with the A♥K♦. You'd be about a 58-to-42 favorite against the player with the 8♣7♣, hand after hand after hand.

Now let's play a second mechanical variation. It's a little more complicated. One player is dealt ace-king offsuit each time, as before, while the second player is dealt eight-seven suited. Now the five cards of the board are dealt. If either player makes a set or bigger, he raises his hand. If neither player raises their hand, or if only one player raises their hand, the deal is annulled and the players try again. If both players raise their hand, they shove all their chips in the pot and see who wins. Who would you rather be in this variation?

Under these rules, almost all hands go right in the muck. But when the players actually contest a pot, the edge goes to the eight-seven suited. Whenever both players make the very same hand (a set, a straight, or a full house) the ace-king has the advantage. But the eight-seven suited will make more straights (because he can make a straight on either end of his holding) and more flushes, obviously. Since the chance of making exactly the same level of hand at the same time are slim, the eight-seven will win a slight majority of the hands that are actually contested.

With these mechanical examples, we can see why hands like eight-seven and five-four aren't at as big a disadvantage vis-à-vis the premium hands as the stacks get deep. They can risk a small amount to see a flop, then choose to get involved or not depending on whether they have a big hand or have a draw to a big hand. Mostly the flop misses them and they can let the hand go for a small price. When they do make a hand or a draw, however, they can take aim at their opponent's whole stack, a monstrous payoff for a small investment.

## Implied Odds Justification

Another way of seeing the relationship between hand selection and stack sizes is to consider what happens with expressed odds and implied odds as we vary stack sizes. When you enter a pot, you are entering because you like the combination of expressed odds and implied odds relative to your hand and the money you're putting in the pot. As stacks grow larger, the relationship between expressed odds and implied odds changes, and with that change comes a change in the hand mix you wish to play.

When the stacks are short, the expressed odds are more important than the implied odds because the implied odds are obviously bounded by the size of the opposing stack. Therefore with short stacks you need to play hands that are immediate favorites against the hand you're likely to be facing; hence pairs (especially premium pairs) and high cards predominate.

As stacks grow, the implied odds associated with any hand you elect to play grow along with the stacks. Therefore a simple relationship emerges:

> **Big stacks** *imply* **big implied odds** *which* *imply* **play more hands.**

So the simplistic "play tight and wait for premium pairs" strategy employed by beginners turns out to be almost the opposite of the proper strategy for a reasonably tough game. A more optimal approach to hand selection is to play all the normal "good" hands, but mix in an appropriate number of promising hands (suited connectors, unsuited connectors, small pairs, and others) in cheap situations where you wish to speculate.

# No-Limit Hold 'em and Venture Capitalists

A good no-limit hold 'em cash game player is playing much the same game as a venture capitalist in the stock market. A venture capitalist buys small to medium sized stakes in start-up companies. He's not trying to be Warren Buffet; he doesn't invest because he expects most of these companies to turn into solidly profitable concerns. In fact, he realizes that most of the companies in which he invests will either be just marginally successful or go bankrupt altogether. But he tolerates that result because he's looking for the rare gem that will develop into Microsoft or Home Depot. In pokerspeak, he's playing a game with huge stacks and monstrous implied odds, and he's happy to splash around with very speculative hands, waiting for the board to give him the occasional quads or royal flush.

# Hand Distribution as a Defensive Weapon

Adding some speculative hands to your distribution serves a defensive function as well. By playing a mix of hands, *you're actually reducing your opponent's implied odds on his speculative hands*. Let's see how this works.

Suppose you're known for playing only premium pairs and high cards. What's more, you don't let your hand go easily when you hit it. You open for a raise in early position. A bunch of players fold, and now your knowledgeable and shrewd opponent on the button looks down at a pair of deuces. Against another player, he might contemplate laying his hand down. Against you, he has a mandatory call. Why? Because his implied odds are so good. If you have some sort of hand when he hits his set, he'll be able to get you to call at least an extra bet and perhaps two, all that he needs to justify his original call.

But suppose you play a mix of hands. Now your early raise might still be mostly high cards and pairs, but might also be a speculative low pair, suited connector, or even something worse. Now what happens when your shrewd opponent picks up a pair of deuces on the button? He can't be so certain any longer of getting paid when he hits his set! If you started with one of your speculative hands and missed the flop, you won't mind letting your hand go when the button makes a move, and consequently he won't get paid. As a result, his implied odds are poorer, and he must play fewer of his speculative hands against you.

# Hand Selection in Tournament Play and Cash Play

In *Harrington on Hold 'Em*, our series on tournament play, we described both a tight-aggressive style and a loose-aggressive style, and contrasted their various strengths and weaknesses. The tight-aggressive style we described there is tighter than the style we're recommending in this book on cash games. That very tight style is effective for tournament play because much of the action in tournaments occurs with stacks between 20 and 50 big blinds. With stacks of that size, pairs and high cards predominate, as we've already discussed.

The tight-aggressive style that we'll outline in this book for cash play is actually somewhat looser than the tight tournament style. The switch to a looser style is forced by the fundamental relationship between stacks and implied odds:

**Big stacks** *implies*
**better implied odds** *implies* **play more hands**.

As in tournaments, cash games have both loose and tight styles as well. We'll describe the characteristics of a loose cash game approach later in the book, but we'll just quickly mention here that the difference is one of degree. Both tight and loose players play with a mix of premium value hands and what we're calling speculative hands, but the loose players play more speculative hands, more often.

# Stack Sizes
# and Bet Count Tables

No-limit hold 'em cash games are usually played with stack sizes that seem very large compared to the blinds. If you come from the tournament world, having a stack of 100 or 200 big blinds seems like a huge amount of money in front of you.

But these amounts are somewhat deceptive. What actually matters when betting a hand is not the number of big blinds that we have in front of us, but the number of bets we have in front of us. When we convert our stack sizes into actual bets and raises, a surprising picture emerges.

Let's do a quick calculation and see what we mean. Suppose you have a stack of 100 big blinds. You pick up a pair of aces in early position. You decide (perhaps unwisely) to push this hand to its limits. Your intention is to make a standard raise of three big blinds preflop, and then to bet the pot each round until your opponent gives up. How many bets can you make before you run out of chips?

Your first bet is your preflop raise to three big blinds. Let's say you get one caller and the blinds fold. The pot is now 7.5 big blinds.

Your second bet is a pot-sized bet on the flop. We'll keep the mathematics simple and round off this bet to 8 big blinds. Your opponent calls again. The pot is now 23.5 big blinds and you've bet 11 so far, so your stack is down to 89 big blinds.

The third bet is the pot-sized bet on the turn, 24 big blinds. Your opponent calls again. Now the pot is 71.5 big blinds and your stack is down to 65 big blinds.

Your stack actually isn't big enough to make a fourth pot-sized bet on the river. You're short by 7 big blinds.

So your massive stack of 100 big blinds wasn't big enough for four bets if you assume that all except the preflop bet were pot-sized bets. You could have made your stack last longer if you had bet less each round, or if your starting stack were bigger.

Below is a table which I call the "Bet Count Table." It shows how big a stack is required to make a certain number of bets given that you start with a preflop bet of 3 big blinds, and then bet the same percentage of the pot each time after that. It's an important table which illustrates a crucial truth about no-limit hold 'em.

## The Bet Count Table

| Stack (in the Blinds) Required For | | | | |
|---|---|---|---|---|
| **Bet Size** | **3 Bets** | **4 Bets** | **5 Bets** | **6 Bets** |
| One-half pot | 15 | 31 | 63 | 127 |
| Two-thirds pot | 20 | 48 | 113 | 265 |
| Three-quarters pot | 24 | 62 | 156 | 391 |
| Pot | 35 | 107 | 323 | 971 |

(Note, by the way, that a bet followed by a raise in the same proportion counts in this table as two bets. So if there was a preflop raise, and on the flop the first player bet three-quarters of the pot, and his opponent then called and raised three-quarters of the new pot, his raise is the third bet of the hand.)

What should be obvious from the table is that even relatively large stacks don't let you make many bets in the hand. If you're starting with 100 big blinds and making bets that are larger than half the pot, you can only make four such bets before you start bumping up against your stack limit. With 150 big blinds, you can make the fifth bet if you're betting two-thirds or three-quarters of the pot. If you're making pot-sized bets or raises, even 150 big blinds can't get you close to making the fifth bet.

The lesson to take away from this table is that the number of bets you can make in a no-limit hold 'em hand is severely constrained, even though the stack sizes seem huge, because the bets are growing geometrically. The first bet is cheap, as is the second. The third bet, however, is a sort of transition bet, and bets beyond this one contain the threat of involving most of your stack. Keep this table in mind as we move to the next chapter on pot size and pot commitment.

# Stack Size, Pot Size, and Pot Commitment

As you make bets during the hand, you need to consider not only the strength of your hand and the likely strength of your opponent's hand, but also the relationship between the growing pot, the strength of your hand, and the stack sizes of you and your opponent. You don't want to create a pot that's too large, given the strength of your hand. You also don't want to create a pot that's too large compared to your remaining stack if you're unwilling to get your whole stack involved. Let's take a look at these two ideas more closely.

## Idea No. 1: Balancing the Strength of Your Hand and the Size of the Pot

No-limit players have a succinct rule to describe the relationship between hands and pots: *small hand, small pot; big hand, big pot.* It's a simple way of stating that if you have a hand that's suited to playing a small pot, try to arrange your bets to keep the pot small. If you have a hand that's suited to playing a big pot, do your best to make the pot a large one.

What are big pot and small pot hands? I'll make some sweeping generalizations here because we need to start somewhere. After the flop, a small pot hand is a hand that's an overpair to the board, or top pair, top kicker, or worse. These hands are often best on the flop but have a limited upside. Barring unusually good turn and river cards, they'll at best improve to something like three of a kind or a good two pair.

A big pot hand, however, is a set or better, or a hand with a strong draw to a straight or a flush. Flopping a set is not only a powerful hand in itself, but also a pretty good draw to a full house. What about two pair on the flop? That's an intermediate hand. It's very likely to be best on the flop, but can easily be overtaken on the turn and the river.

These are quick categorizations, useful as general rules. In real life, let common sense prevail. If you have a pair of tens against two opponents with some action before the flop, and the flop comes queen-jack-ten, all of one suit, you have a set, but you don't want to play a big pot with this hand. You've got a small hand for the situation and you'd be happy to end the hand right there.

When you have a "small" hand, your goal is to keep the pot small and see if your hand is best or not. You can keep the pot small in a variety of ways, including making smaller bets (betting half the pot instead of three-quarters of the pot, for instance) and checking a street instead of betting it. Under some circumstances, you may be happy to check the hand entirely, right down to the showdown.

When you have a big hand or the nuts, your goal is to build the pot by making larger bets, by raising instead of calling, and by betting on each street. Your goal is to get the pot large enough so that a final all-in bet on the river isn't such a big overbet that your opponent goes away, but instead offers him attractive enough odds to call.

Both of these approaches, of course, are constrained by the need to be deceptive and to confuse your opponent about just what you're doing. Still, the general outline of your play is clear. With a small hand, try to keep the pot small, and with a big hand, build it up.

Many beginners typically get into trouble with small pot hands by playing them too aggressively. The next sample hand is a typical example.

# Sample Hand No. 1

You're in a $2-$4 online game. You joined the table a few hands ago and your stack is now $394. You pick up

in middle position. In front of you, everyone folds. You think you have a good hand for your position and raise to $12. The button and the big blind both call. Each player has a stack that appears to be about $600. The pot is now $38.

The flop comes

The big blind checks. You have top pair with a good kicker. You think you probably have the best hand, and in addition there are some possible draws out against you. Someone with two clubs has a flush draw, and someone with jack-ten has an open-ended straight draw. You decide to bet the pot, both as a value bet and to charge the draws. You bet $35. The button folds but the big blind calls. The pot is now $108.

The turn is the T♠. You're glad it wasn't a club, but now there are more possible straight draws against you. You decide you still probably have the best hand, but you're still worried about letting the draws have a free card. The big blind checks again. You're convinced now that he's on a draw. You want to bet, and you decide that about 70 percent of the pot is probably a good amount. You bet $70. The big blind calls again. The pot is now $248. You've bet $117 so far, and your stack is down to $277.

The river is the A♦. The big blind bets the pot, $250. *What do you do?*

Unless you had some extraordinary knowledge that your opponent was bluffing, you should fold. You have second pair, and at this point you can only beat a bluff. There are a number of hands that could very plausibly account for your opponent's sequence of actions: A♣9♣, king-jack offsuit, or a pair of nines or fours. Your bets more or less announced that you have a queen with a good kicker, and with all the money you've put in the pot, your opponent probably expects you to call. His bet indicates he's not terribly worried about that, so fold.

What went wrong?

There was nothing wrong with your preflop bet with a good hand, and the flop was pretty good for you, so it was reasonable to bet there. The size of the bet on the flop, however, was a little large. If you're in the habit of making half-pot continuation bets, then a half-pot bet here (about $20) would have been a good idea. It would have been enough to charge the draws, and it would have chased away anyone who missed the flop entirely. A half-pot bet would also fit the strength of your hand, which is a hand that wants to keep the pot small.

The real problem, however, was the big bet on the turn. Your position gives you an advantage, and you can exploit that advantage by checking behind your opponent. With a top pair type hand, and an opponent who has already called you twice, the ideal result now would be to check the hand down and see if you win. By making another big bet, you're in the process of creating a monster pot, one which your hand doesn't justify.

"But what about all the draws?" you reply. "Surely it's a blunder to give him a free card?" Yes and no. Among other things, poker is a game of balancing conflicting objectives. You do need to deny a free card to drawing hands; you also need to make sure that the pot doesn't get out of control for the strength of hand you actually have. When those two goals conflict, you'll have to give precedence to one or the other.

Which takes precedence? Just ask yourself which error is most likely to hurt you. If you overbet the hand, you're guaranteed to be building a pot that's too big for your relatively modest hand. If you fail to charge a potential draw, two things must happen before you actually get hurt:

1.  He must actually have the drawing hand you're worried about instead of some other hand, and

2.  He must actually hit the draw.

Given his possible hand distribution and the betting action, the chance that he actually has a draw is probably no more than 30 percent. The probability that he hits a draw, given that he has one, is about another 30 percent. So we're comparing an event that's less than 10 percent to happen — he has a draw, and he hits it, to an event that's 100 percent to happen — building a big pot with a small hand. Conclusion? Stop worrying about the draw and be glad to check the turn.

How do you keep the pot small with a small pot hand? Mostly by limiting the number of bets you're willing to make or call. A typical strategy might be to bet the flop and, if called, to check the turn. Another way is to check the flop, see what happens, and if no one takes any action, bet the turn. By playing the hand slower, you can in effect remove a betting round and keep the pot under control.

# Sample Hand No. 2

You're watching a $5-$10 live game in a casino. You happen to know the hole cards of two players in the hand. (Don't ask.)

The small blind has A♥Q♠, and a stack of about $1,000. Player D, in fourth position, has K♣K♦, and a stack of about $1,000 as well. Let's watch as the hand develops and see what we think of the play.

The first three players fold. Player D raises to $30 with his pair of kings, an obvious play. Everyone folds around to the small blind.

With ace-queen offsuit, the small blind has a perfectly reasonable call, even out of position. He calls $25. The big blind folds. The pot is now $70.

The flop comes A♣T♠6♦. That's a great flop for the small blind who now has top pair with a good kicker. He could still be trailing if Player D happened to raise with ace-king, ace-ten, or a pair of aces or tens. But there are many more hands Player D could have where the small blind has taken the lead, so for now he should assume he has the best of it until Player D gives him some evidence to the contrary.

Since Player D led before the flop, it's reasonable to assume that's he'll make a continuation bet on this flop. Even if he raised with something like a pair of queens or jacks originally, he'll probably bet the flop to represent a pair of aces and see if that's enough to win the hand. The small blind checks to allow Player D to bet first, which is a good play.

With his pair of kings, Player D obviously didn't like seeing the ace arrive on the flop. He has to decide whether to bet or not. Let's look at the reasons for and against betting.

Most players in D's position would bet here, and if asked why, they would give one or more of the following reasons:

1. "I need to be aggressive."

2. "I want to find out where I stand."

3. "I make continuation bets all the time when I miss the flop, so I need to make them when I have a hand as well."

4. "I want to get more money in the pot if I'm ahead."

All of these reasons are flawed in this situation. Let's see why.

The small blind either has an ace or he doesn't. The fact that he checked doesn't provide much evidence one way or the other. If he doesn't have an ace he checked because he thinks he's beaten, and if he does have an ace he checked to trap you because you were the preflop aggressor. Either way you don't know (right now) what he has.

If he has an ace, he won't fold to your bet. He might fear that you have a better ace than him, but he can't fold to the first bet in any case. So your "aggression" can't push him out of the pot with a better hand.

If he doesn't have an ace, but instead has some lower pair, he'll fold to your bet and you'll win the pot. But you gain very little by claiming the pot now because it's a pot you were very likely to win later. Suppose he had a pair of nines. In that case he had only two outs to improve to the better hand, a 5 percent shot on the next card. The vast majority of the time, you're still beating him on the turn and he'll still fold when you bet.

"Wait," you say. "What if he has an ace with a mediocre kicker, like A8. Now if I bet I'm representing an ace with a good kicker, and I might be able to chase him off the hand, winning a pot that I'd lose if the hand went to a showdown. What about that?"

That's true. You might be able to chase him off ace-eight or ace-seven, if in fact that's what he has. But what if he has ace-king, ace-queen, or ace-jack? You're probably not going to chase him off those hands. So now the question becomes, how much money are you willing to risk to find out just which kind of ace he has? Suppose you do bet. Since the pot is now $70, perhaps you bet $50. No matter what ace he has, he's not going to fold. How can he? He called with some ace and then he hit his ace on the flop. If he has a low kicker, he might feel a pang of regret and start wondering if you have an ace with a better kicker, but he'll certainly call the first bet; otherwise he'll feel like a complete idiot. Now the pot is $170 and we'll suppose a blank comes on the turn. Will you bet again? Suppose you now bet $120. The lower his ace, the more likely that this bet chases him away. But if he sticks around, will you fire another shell on the river? Remember, you're possibly beaten at this point, firing money in the pot in the hopes that he has an ace that he can lay down, and willing to risk an awful lot of money to find out the answer.

What you have right now with your pair of kings is what's called a *way ahead/way behind* situation. Since the board has almost no draws, you're either ahead or behind in the hand, and whichever it is, the relative standing isn't likely to change. If you're behind to something like ace-queen offsuit, you're about a 10-to-1 underdog. If you're ahead to something like a pair of eights, you're about a 9-to-1 favorite.

If you're in a way ahead/way behind situation and you believe you could equally well be either ahead or behind, you don't have much reason to get more money in the pot. Bets will be called by hands that beat you and folded by most hands that are clearly weaker, so betting doesn't rate to gain much and can just be a lost bet if your opponent is in a position to know he's winning.

(Note, by the way, that it's only the relative absence of draws that makes this way ahead/way behind analysis relevant. If the board is draw-heavy, you aren't, by definition, in a way ahead/way behind situation.)

In many way ahead/way behind situations, both players are trapped in the middle and the hand gets checked down, which is not a bad result for either player. It's a variation on our first principle of poker: bet your strong hands, check your middling hands, and fold or bluff your weak hands. In this case the appearance of the ace has changed the pair of kings from a premium hand to a middling hand. With a middling hand, the kings' goal is to either check the hand down, or try to get to the showdown as cheaply as possible. The small blind's check enables

Player D to check and eliminate a betting round. Under the circumstances, with a single pair that may not be best, that's a very good thing.

So Player D should check. But Player D actually takes the lead and bets $50. The pot now contains $120.

The small blind should now raise as a value bet. It's the logical consequence of his original check since he had no reason to believe that he didn't have the best hand at that point. He's beating most aces, and all smaller pairs. He's only losing to ace-king, two pair, or one of the three possible sets. That's a very small number of hands, and there's no reason to believe that Player D has any of those hands yet. So a raise is in order. Since a call would bring the pot to $170, a good raise would be another $120 more. However, the small blind only calls. The pot is now $170.

The turn card is the J♣. The small blind checks. This is consistent with his previous call since his position hasn't improved and has, in fact, deteriorated just a bit. Conceivably Player D made his bet with a pair of jacks, in which case he now has a set, or ace-jack, in which case he has two pair.

Although the check was consistent, a bet wasn't unreasonable since the small blind has no reason as yet to believe that Player D flopped a hand bigger than top pair, good kicker. The small blind is being conservative, however, in keeping with the small hand, small pot philosophy.

Player D also checks. This check is clear since the small blind's call on the flop probably indicates he has an ace. Since he didn't raise, Player D can conclude he probably doesn't have ace-king or ace-queen, and won't be afraid he's facing one of those hands.

The sequence of betting the flop and checking the turn, or vice-versa, is characteristic of no-limit hands where both sides have nothing better than a pair. By eliminating one of the two middle betting rounds, the players effectively put a cap on the pot. Since a pair is generally not a hand that wants to see a big pot, this is a good result for both players. By the river, a single pair has become a small hand, and, as we know, a small hand wants a small pot.

The river is the 8♦. The small blind bets $120. It's a good river value bet. Nothing in the hand so far indicates that he stands worse at this point. If Player D has somehow made two pair or a set, he'll probably raise, and the small blind will have to deal with that when it happens. But making good river value bets is a crucial and very profitable part of no-limit cash games, and based on what the small blind now knows, this is an excellent bet.

Note as well that by checking the turn and making a bet on the river, the small blind has played in such a way that his bet is more likely to be called. Player D would have had a harder time calling a turn bet because it contained the threat of yet another bet on the river. The river bet, on the other hand, threatens no future bets, so Player D can accurately quantify his risk. This is a key maneuver to remember when you're pretty sure that you have your opponent beaten and you think his hand might be good enough to call just one more bet.

The pot is now $290 and Player D needs $120 to call, so his pot odds are about 2.5-to-1. He's probably beaten, and he knows it. The small blind called a bet with an ace showing and bet again on the river. It's hard to credit him with a hand weaker than an ace. But it just might be an elaborate move, and the pot odds are reasonable, so Player D calls. The small blind shows his A♥Q♠ and takes the pot.

**Summary**: Although the players made a couple of questionable plays, the pot ended about where it should have given what the players knew and the strength of their hands. With small hands, they didn't let the pot get outsized by betting and raising, even if that meant erring too far on the conservative side.

The "big hand, big pot, small hand, small pot" mantra is easy to understand in theory. In practice, some players get into trouble by not recognizing that a hand which might be "big" in the abstract is actually small given the particular circumstances. Typical examples occur when the board has four to a straight or four to a flush, and you have either the low end of the straight or a middling flush card. Straights and flushes are normally big hands, but in these situations where the bulk of the hand is on the board, they're actually small hands. Treat them as small hands and look to win with a showdown, rather than bidding up the pot.

# Idea No. 2: Courting or Avoiding Pot Commitment

Pot commitment is a key idea in no-limit hold 'em. If the pot has grown very large, an all-in bet from your opponent may offer you very attractive odds to call, given the strength of your hand. When this situation occurs, you're said to be *pot-committed*. When you're pot-committed, moreover, nothing can really stop the rest of your money from going in. If he doesn't push all-in, you often should; the odds of your winning will still be good enough regardless of where the all-in bet originated.

Toward the end of tournament play, pot-commitment decisions occur constantly and are often trivial. If your M is 8 and you pick up a pair of queens, the strength of your hand and your critical situation in the tournament makes you automatically pot-committed. The only practical questions concern the best way to get your stack in the pot. Do you push all-in to start, or do you make a small raise or even a limp, hoping your opponent will put you in? Whichever method is right for the particular situation, your goal is the same.

In cash game play, pot commitment decisions are much rarer, because all-in moves are fairly rare. When they occur, however, they are very important because they decide the fate of your entire stack. Handling pot commitment decisions well in the course of cash game play requires keeping two questions in your mind as you play each hand:

1. How much of my stack do I want to get involved given the hand I have and the hand I think my opponent has?

2. If my opponent pushes all-in (either now or in response to a bet I'm contemplating) will I be compelled to call or can I lay my hand down?

Let's take a look at a pot-commitment example.

# Sample Hand

You're at a $5-$10 live table. Your stack is $805. In first position you pick up

and raise to $25. Player E in fifth position calls $25, as does Player G on the button. The blinds fold. The pot is now $90.

The flop is

You have top pair, top kicker and decide to bet $80, almost a pot-sized bet. Player E folds but Player G calls $80. The pot is now $250.

The turn card is the T♠. You're now a little concerned about possible straights and flushes, so you decide to bet the pot to chase the draws away. You bet $250. Player G calls again. The pot is now $750.

The river card is the 2♣. You count your stack and realize you have just $450 left. You're worried you may be beaten, even though the deuce didn't help any of the draws. You still want to see a showdown, however, because your top pair may be good. You decide to make a blocking bet (a bet designed to preempt a larger bet) of $150 in the hope that your opponent will be reluctant to raise and will just call, and you can see a flop cheaply. You bet the $150. Your opponent raises to $450, putting you all-in.

You count the pot. It now contains $1,350, and you have to put in your last $300 to call. Your pot odds are 1,350-to-300, or 4.5-to-1. You decide those odds are too good to fold your top pair, so you call. Player G turns over

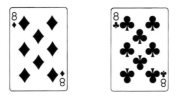

and wins with his set of eights. *What went wrong?*

You basically made two errors. You built a huge pot with a relatively small hand (top pair), and because the pot was so big, you got pot-committed on the end and lost the rest of your stack.

You could have improved your play at a number of stages. The bet on the flop was fine with two opponents, but it didn't need to be a pot-sized bet; something smaller, say $50, would do just as well. Remember from our bet-count tables just how radically the choice of bet sizes affects the growth of the pot. Your hand is still only one pair, so growing a big pot isn't your goal. Ideally, you're hoping that this flop bet will take down the pot right now.

Once your flop bet was called, and the turn didn't improve your hand, you have to consider very seriously whether there's any point to betting the turn. Betting here will create a very large pot for your hand, and takes you a long way to being pot-committed on the river.

Let's work through the reasoning process you should have used on the turn. The first question to answer is "What hands might reasonably have called on the flop, and how much do I want to bet at these hands on the turn?" We can break down Player G's calling hands into a few key groups.

1. **The hands that were already beating you:** He was beating you if his hole cards were AA, 88, 77, A8, A7, or 87. He could have called (perhaps unwisely) with any of those hands preflop. In this case, you certainly don't want to bet. You have no outs against the sets and only three outs against two pair.

2. **Hands that beat you on the turn:** If he had ace-ten or tens, he just became the favorite. Both hands fit his betting perfectly, and again you don't want to bet since you have very few or no outs.

3. **Value hands that were losing on the flop and are still losing:** Any lower pair or any lower ace that didn't make two pair could have reasonably called on the flop, unwilling to give up the hand just yet. These hands are all still losing and only have two or three outs to beat you. You don't need to bet at these hands because they're such big underdogs to catch up. You'd like to bet, however, because you're ahead.

4. **Drawing hands:** He could have called on the flop with an open-ended straight draw. In that case, his hand was either ten-nine, nine-six, or six-five. It's extremely unlikely that he called an early-position raise and a call preflop with a nine-six, so the ten-nine and the six-five are the candidates here. Both hands still have a straight draw, while the ten-nine has

a pair of tens as well. Both hands can be prevented from drawing with a half-pot bet or more.

As you look at this list, you can see that we're back in a way ahead/way behind situation with the exception of the straight draws. When you're behind, you're way behind and you can't chase your opponent off a hand, and when you're ahead you're way ahead, and your opponent will mostly fold to a bet. A bet serves a purpose if he's on a draw, but there are very few such drawing hands.

So the conclusion is that a turn bet is unlikely to serve any positive purpose. In addition, the pot gets too big for your hand, and pot commitment raises its ugly head. So you should have checked the turn rather than bet.

There were more mistakes on the river, but they didn't matter much. A small blocking bet wasn't going to stop the hands that were beating you from making a value raise, which in this case had to be an all-in move. Should you have called? Were you in fact pot-committed? From your actions, the minimum hand anyone could expect you to have was a very good ace. Player G knew you had great calling odds. So how likely can it be that he can't beat a good ace? Not very. But 4.5-to-1 are great odds on the end, and most players would take them.

# Summarizing Hand Strength, Pot Size, and Pot Commitment

The two big ideas of this section, small hand, small pot, big hand, big pot, and pot-commitment, are closely related. Let's consider what sort of hand we might have and see how these ideas interact. (In the following section, remember that the term "hand" refers to the entire situation you're facing. A pair of queens is a "big hand" preflop until your opponent suddenly moves all-in, after which it shrinks a bit.)

**Hand Type No. 1: We have a big hand.** Here our job is to create a big pot and try to get our opponent pot-committed by the river. Usually we won't slowplay big hands; instead we'll bet and raise. In no-limit hold 'em, the implied odds created by the big stacks cause betting and raising to dominate slowplaying. Slowplaying tends to pick up an extra bet when the opponent has a marginal hand. Playing directly accelerates the process of getting him pot-committed because of the geometrical increase in bet sizes. Getting your opponent pot-committed with a good, but still weaker, hand is a key step to winning his whole stack instead of just a slice of it. When betting, try to bet amounts that are callable, but which grow the pot rapidly enough that an all-in river bet still offers good odds.

Note that when we talk about a big hand, we're not just referring to the nuts. A big hand is just a hand that rates to be best when called in the situation. From time to time, a very good hand, correctly played, will cost you your whole stack; that's just part of big-stack poker. Don't push modest hands foolishly, but don't be afraid to push all-in with a hand that your judgment tells you is likely best.

What is a big hand? Here's a rough and quick guide based solely on card strength, but keep in mind that any knowledge you have about your opponent, or a good guess as to what he thinks about you, may allow you to modify this outline substantially.

- **Preflop:** Aces and kings are big hands in any situation. Don't fold kings because you think your opponent has aces; you'll be wrong much more often than you'll be right. In particular situations, queens, jacks, and tens may be big hands as well.

- **On the flop:** on uncoordinated flops, sets are big hands, and usually top two pair as well. On coordinated flops, sets remain big hands. Big bets on drawish flops generally represent semi-bluffs rather than made hands. Straights, flushes, and full houses are of course huge. Made full houses are an exception to the "Don't slowplay" rule. They're not only strong, but they use up most of the cards that could make a hand against you. Slowplay them and give someone a chance to catch up, then try to make all the money on the river.

- **On the turn and river:** Straights, flushes and full houses are of course big, but so much information is now available in terms of both cards and betting sequences that good analysis should be able to narrow down the possibilities.

**Hand Type No. 2: We have a drawing hand.** Drawing hands offer choices. They can be pushed on the flop as semi-bluffs because of their potential to make very big hands. If you have a big draw — 12 to 15 true outs, then an all-in move with a sufficiently big pot to win is usually a profitable play because of the fold equity combined with the chance of actually making your hand. Without the fold equity, the hand isn't as strong, so you usually don't want to call an all-in bet with a weaker draw. Draws can also be played modestly, of course, as long as you have the proper expressed and implied odds to call.

**Hand Type No. 3: We have a medium-strength hand.** What constitutes "medium strength" of course is highly situation-dependent. But in general, these are the problem hands in big stack no-limit hold 'em. You need to be somewhat aggressive because the better medium-strength hands are often the best hands outstanding after the flop. But you don't want to become pot-committed with these hands either. As the pot gets large, these hands will not usually be best. Use the bet count table as a guide here. Typically, in the absence of any demonstrated strength from your opponent, these hands will be worth a bet on the flop or the turn, but not both. In the most general sense, a medium-strength hand like top pair, good kicker is happy with a betting sequence that includes a bet on the flop, a check on the turn, and a modest bet on the river. Exceptions abound, of course.

**Hand Type No. 4: We have a weak hand.** Big pots and pot commitment shouldn't be a problem with a weak hand. You'll either fold these hands or use them occasionally as bluffs on the flop. If your bluff gets called or raised, you should be done with the hand unless you have some specific knowledge of your opponent that says continued bluffing should be profitable.

In summary, if we have a small hand, we want to keep the pot small and avoid pot-commitment issues. If we have a big hand, we're trying to grow the pot and get our opponent pot-committed. Exactly how we accomplish these objectives is a tactical problem; it depends on our cards, what we know about our opponent, our own image, and how the hand has developed. Study the problem examples throughout the rest of the book for specific examples of how to handle the tactics of big-stack games.

# Hand Reading

Hand reading is simply the process of reconstructing your opponent's likely hand (or hands) given the clues you have in front of you. To perform the reconstruction, you ask yourself a number of questions, each intended to eliminate some possible hands from the set of hands he might hold.

1.  What is his style? What hands have I seen him play in the past?

2.  What hands might he hold given his pre-flop action?

3.  What hands account for his actions after the flop?

4.  How does his position affect the hands he might play?

5.  What does he know about me? What hands might he elect to fold given what he knows of the hands I am likely to play?

6.  How does the presence of players yet to act affect what he might have done?

7.  Is he ahead or behind in the session? How might this affect his hand choices?

The more good questions you can ask, and the more answers you can give, even if only approximate, the better chance you have of whittling down his possible hands to a small, manageable number. In some extraordinary cases, players have been able to put their opponent on his exact hand, and play accordingly.

Hand reading works because most players play most hands in a relatively logical way most of the time. By bringing logic to bear on their decisions, you can keep eliminating hands that don't fit the observed data.

Having said that, good hand reading is an art form. You can get better with practice, and it's certainly a skill well worth practicing, but in most cases you'll need to be satisfied with reducing a large number of possibilities to a relatively small number. And sometimes your opponents will just choose to play a hand in a completely counter-intuitive way, and fool you completely. That's poker.

# Sample Hand

Let's take a look at a good example of hand reading in practice. Here's a hand between Mike Sexton and Phil Gordon from an episode of the *Poker After Dark* television series on NBC.

Each week of *Poker After Dark* is actually a mini-tournament with six players, broken into five episodes plus a summary episode. Because the blinds begin very small and increase slowly, and because most hands are actually shown, situations in the first couple of days play almost exactly like cash games. The level of play is also quite high which makes for a great educational experience in deep stack poker.

In this hand the blinds are $150 and $300. Both Sexton and Gordon have stacks of about $20,000, or not quite 70 big blinds. These are not super-deep stacks, but they're still deep enough to allow for some maneuvering. Sexton is on the button, while Gordon is in the big blind.

We should also mention the styles of the two players. Mike Sexton plays a tight-aggressive game; when he acts, he generally has solid values for his position. Phil Gordon also plays a tight-aggressive game, but he's a little more likely than Sexton to make a bluff pre-flop with a weak holding. So far in this session he's stolen a couple of pots with bluffs, but since none of his raises were called, and since he hasn't played an unusual number of hands, presumably the rest of the table is not yet suspicious.

Howard Lederer, in first position, folds. Chad Brown, in second position, folds. Gabe Kaplan, in the cutoff seat, folds. Mike Sexton, on the button, picks up

He raises to $800, a perfectly reasonable raise for this hand. With only two players to act behind him, he's a very big favorite to have the best hand. Michael Konik, in the small blind, folds. Phil Gordon, in the big blind, picks up

With this hand, he's obviously not going to fold. Although Sexton plays solid hands, it's premature to think he has a pair higher than the jacks. Since the table has been playing tight, Sexton could have noticed this and decided to raise with any pair. He could also have two high cards, all of which are now slight underdogs to the jacks. Given his position on the button, he could have even raised with a hand like ten-nine. Given his style, however, he's probably not raising with absolutely nothing. In addition, his raise was a bit on the smallish side, and Gordon is being offered 2.5-to-1 pot odds to stick around. (He needs to put in $500 to call a pot of $1,250.) That would seem to indicate that

Sexton doesn't mind a call so much, probably indicating that he has a reasonable hand.

Should Gordon raise? There's certainly nothing wrong with that play. With a hand as strong as jacks, most players would elect to raise, in part to take the pot down now rather than try to play the jacks out of position after the flop. If overcards come on the flop, it will be difficult for Gordon to play the hand well.

But Gordon elects to call rather than raise. The call has two advantages:

1.  Calling keeps the pot small, and Gordon doesn't yet have a hand so big that he necessarily wants to play a big pot with it.

2.  Calling makes his hand hard to read. Sexton will have great difficulty putting him on a pair of jacks later on, so a flop like ace-jack-small could put him in position to win a really big pot, perhaps Sexton's whole stack.

Gordon's call is completely reasonable. The pot is now $1,750.

The flop comes

Gordon acts first. This is about as bad a flop as he could hope to see with his jacks. If Sexton was playing two high cards or even a single high card, his hand now beats Gordon's, and there's little chance that he's going away anytime soon. Gordon wisely checks.

Sexton's reaction to this flop is almost the same as Gordon's. Gordon could easily have called his raise with an ace, or conceivably a hand like king-jack. (King-queen is unlikely because Sexton holds two of the queens, and king-ten is a weak and troublesome hand for a tight player to make a call out of position.) Of course, Gordon might have called with a smaller pair, in which case Sexton is well ahead. But that's still no reason for Sexton to bet. Weaker hands than his will fold, and stronger hands will call, so a bet can't make him any money. A much better approach is to wait, and let his positional advantage gather some more information on the turn.

The pot remains at $1,750. The turn is the 6♣, putting three clubs on board.

From Gordon's point of view, very little has changed. The third club has created a few more hands that beat him, like T♣9♣ or 9♣8♣. However, with the A♣ and K♣ already on board, most of the suited combinations that would have raised pre-flop have been ruled out. Gordon still has no reason to bet as Sexton's initial check could easily indicate a trap with a pair of aces, or a pair of kings that he simply isn't going to fold. Gordon checks.

Sexton now has a little more information. He's seen Gordon check twice, and he's seen a third club arrive. The arrival of the third club is not a matter of great concern. With the A♣ and the K♣ out of the picture, what two clubs could Gordon have held to call the raise pre-flop? Something like Q♣J♣ or J♣T♣ are possible, but few good players would want to call a raise with two low suited connectors since those hands really only play well in multi-way pots. It is possible that Gordon holds a single club, in which case he's drawing at a flush. But is denying him a free card a good reason to bet?

Sexton correctly realizes that it's not. At this point he has two good reasons for checking rather than betting:

1. If Gordon has him beaten with an ace or a king, he'll call a bet at this point, and Sexton would simply be getting more money in the pot with the worse hand.

2. If Gordon is losing because he called with a medium pair, he may not call a bet now, although he might call on the river.

Why would he call on the river, but not on the turn? In either case, Gordon would believe he was probably losing, but good pot odds might tempt him to want to pick off a bluff. If Sexton's bet comes on the turn, Gordon's pot odds are an illusion because he could still have to face a much bigger bet on the river. But if Sexton's bet comes on the river, Gordon's call would end the hand, and he could make a call based on pot odds alone.

So Sexton checks again. Excellent play.

The river card is the 6♦. This card doesn't change the situation for either player. There are very few hands that would have raised or called pre-flop with a six, except for a pair of sixes, and that hand went from a winning set of sixes to winning quad sixes, no change at all.

Because Gordon has to act first, he remains at a disadvantage. If Gordon bets, Sexton will at least call with almost all the hands that beat him. He'll raise with a flush, although that's an unlikely holding. He might choose to raise with ace-king or ace-queen, although a call is more likely.

If Sexton has a worse hand, say a pair of eights, nines, or tens, he'll probably call to try and pick off a bluff, and Gordon will make some money. But Gordon has to balance that profit against all the losses when Sexton calls with a better hand or raises, a raise that will force Gordon to fold. So Gordon correctly realizes that his hand now has value only as a bluff-catcher, and checks.

Sexton now has enough information to put the hand together.

1.  Gordon called preflop, an action which could indicate a wide range of hands, particularly since Sexton raised from the button. But since Gordon is a fundamentally conservative player in a deep-stack situation, and since he would be out of position for the rest of the hand, he didn't call with nothing.

2. A flush draw was very unlikely all along because he couldn't have held either of the top two clubs, and calling a raise with two low suited connectors is a poor move heads-up. If he had hit the flush, he would have had to bet on the river or pass up any real chance of extracting value with the hand. So Gordon doesn't have a flush.

3. Could he have an ace? If Gordon had a good ace, like ace-king or ace-queen, and probably even ace-jack, he was likely to raise preflop. That didn't happen, so let's for now put him on a medium or low ace. He didn't bet on the flop, which is still reasonable. He would have had top pair with a weakish kicker, certainly not a hand that was eager to see a big pot. On the turn he checks again. An ace wouldn't have been that afraid of a flush, but might have wanted to bet to charge a hand with a single club from drawing. So the turn check makes the ace holding more unlikely. But the river check with the ace after two checks from Sexton is very unlikely. So he probably doesn't have an ace.

4. Could he have a king? Yes, but there aren't a lot of possible kings. He doesn't have ace-king or a pair of kings because he would have bet at any number of points in the hand. King-queen is unlikely because there aren't many queens left in the deck. King-jack is possible, and would more or less account for the preflop call and all the subsequent checks. King-ten is less likely just because it's a weaker preflop call, but it also matches all the subsequent checks. Hands worse than king-ten are dubious calls from a tight player.

5. Could he have a lower pair? Certainly. All the pairs from jacks down through deuces are reasonable preflop calls (although a tight player might fold the deuces, treys, and fours out of position), and all would be checking post-flop for the same reasons Sexton has been checking. He doesn't have

a pair of fours or sixes, because those hands have to bet on the river (if not before) to get paid off.

6. Will a lower pair call a bet on the end? Yes, if the pot odds are reasonably good. Gordon would have to assume that Sexton could be betting with a small pair as well, given his checks on the flop and turn. The higher Gordon's pair, the more likely it is the best low pair, and the more likely he will call. Of course, Sexton has the best pair lower than a king, so he wins all these showdowns.

So Gordon's most likely hands are lower pairs, with some possibility of a king-jack or king-ten. All of these hands rate to call a moderate-sized value bet that offers good pot odds. So Sexton bets $700 into a pot of $1,750. Gordon realizes he's probably beaten, but the 2.5-to-1 odds are tempting. There's always a chance he's facing a bluff, or he might be facing a lower pair that's still betting for value. So Gordon calls, and Sexton wins the hand, a well-played hand by both players.

# Defending Against Hand Reading

When you play a hand, your opponents will want to use some of the techniques in this chapter to analyze your play and try to read your hand. You, in turn, want to make this process as difficult as possible for them. For most players in live games, this means cutting down on any physical tells — wearing dark glasses, remaining quiet, not jiggling their knees or tapping their fingers and the like.

But as we saw in the Sexton/Gordon hand, Mike Sexton didn't need any physical clues at all to figure out what his opponent had. Since Gordon's plays were all logical given his holding, Sexton just had to look at the hand through his opponent's eyes and conclude what hands would have made these actions. After four streets of information, Sexton was able to reduce Gordon's possible holdings to just a couple of possibilities.

# Diversifying Betting Sequences

One way to fight against being "read" in this fashion is to make sure you *diversify your betting sequences*. Simply put, you need to make sure that any betting action by you is capable of multiple interpretations by an observant opponent.

Let's consider a concrete example. You're in fourth position at the table. There are three folds to you, and you pick up

You make a raise to three times the big blind, and the player one off the button calls. The button folds, as do the small and big blind. The flop comes

*What do you do?*

Keep that thought in mind, and now let's consider the same situation with a different flop. This time the flop comes

*Now what do you do?*

Most beginners and intermediates in no-limit cash games follow an obvious strategy. In the first case, they bet since they have top pair and top kicker, and they want to make some money on their hand. In the second case, they sometimes make a continuation bet, to pick up the pot without a fight, and they sometimes check.

Notice that someone who plays like this is easily exploitable. If they bet, they may or may not have a pair or better. But if they check, you know they missed the flop, and you can probably pick up the pot with a strong bet.

That's too much information to give an observant opponent. It won't matter much if you're at an online table full of strangers, or if you just sit down in a live game for an hour or so. But if you're in a regular game or playing a long session, you have to do better. Let's see how you can.

One simple method would be to bet half your hands, whether you hit the flop or not. In this situation (where you lead off pre-flop with a strong non-paired hand, and get called), you will make a pair or better on the flop about 30 percent of the time, and miss the other 70 percent. If you bet half the time no matter what happens, then your opponents won't be able to dedeuce anything from your post-flop action. If we look at a sample of 100 such hands, you'll bet 50 of them, which will consist of 15 occasions where you made a hand and 35 where you didn't. The same percentages will apply when you check; 15 times you'll actually have a hand, and 35 times you won't.

Of course, there will also be hands where you started with a strong pair, so that after the flop you have at least a pair, and perhaps two pair or a set. These hands you will also sometimes bet and sometimes check, making your post-flop distributions stronger in both cases.

The exact percentage of time you choose to bet and check in each group isn't terribly important. (It's highly dependent on the prevailing style of the game you're in.) No one could ever observe you closely enough to figure out what these numbers are in every case, and in fact no good player has rigid percentages to go by. The important idea is that *each betting sequence has to contain samples of each hand type.* If you check after the flop, your observant opponents need to know that your action may indicate a weak hand, a medium hand, or the nuts. The only way that can occur is if you rigorously make sure that you sometimes take every possible action with every hand type. (Exception: Don't fold the nuts to vary your play! There are other obvious exceptions as well.)

This strategy has multiple good effects. First, your opponents have great difficulty reading you. They've seen plenty of examples where your actions were the opposite of what they expected, and now they're not confident of their ability to put you on a hand.

Second, your opponents lose interest in playing marginal pots with you. If they get burned too many times, they just don't want to play anymore.

Eventually, they start to play passive, tentative poker, or its evil twin, crazy-aggressive poker. Either of those styles is money in your pocket.

# Sample Hand

You're in a live game in Las Vegas. Blinds are $5 and $10. This hand, you're in fifth position. You've played in this game before and you're familiar with most of the players at the table. Right now your stack is $1,100, and you're up about $100 on the session. Your reputation is that of a tight player.

Player C in third position is a conservative, tight, but very tough player, and very successful in this game. Of all the players at the table, you'd rather not play a pot against him if you can avoid it. He wins too many of them. He usually shows down strong hands, but every so often he seems to play some unusual cards.

Players A and B fold. Player C opens for a standard raise of $30. Player D folds. You look down and see

No matter how tough Player C may be, you're not folding this hand. On the other hand, Player C wasn't raising with junk, so he must have a hand too.

You could raise or call with your hand. You decide to play it conservatively and call, which might leave your hand well-disguised if you hit it. You call $30.

The players behind you all fold, so it's a two-way pot. You have ace-king suited and position. The pot is $75.

The flop comes

You're pretty happy with that flop. You have top pair and top kicker. It's very unlikely that a tight player was raising in early position with any hand containing a deuce. There are no draws on board to worry about. You even have a backdoor flush draw as a bonus.

Player C bets $50, two-thirds of the pot. The pot is now $125. You almost certainly have the best hand. If Player C has the last two aces in the deck, he's going to win some money from you. Otherwise, you're in good shape. You decide to raise. If Player C has a weaker ace, he won't fold, and he may think you're trying to represent the hand he has.

How much should your raise be? If you just called, the pot would be $175. A good raise on that pot would be in the neighborhood of $100 to $150. If Player C has a hand like ace-jack, he has very few outs. You'd like to keep Player C in the pot if you can, so you decide to go for the low end of that range. You put in $150, a $100 raise which makes the pot $275.

Player C calls $100, making the pot $375. You decide he wouldn't call your raise with nothing, so you can eliminate a lot of his possible hands here. He doesn't have king-queen, or any other collection of two high cards without an ace. With his preflop raise and his bet and call on the flop, you decide he has one of the following hands:

1.  A pair of aces. Unlikely, since you can account for two aces, but still a remote possibility.

2.  A high pair below aces, perhaps as low as sevens. Raising with a lower pair is unlikely but possible. Could he have raised with a pair of deuces? As Gus Hansen is prone to say, that would be 'sick, sick, sick.' But that's much less likely than the chance he has aces, because he would certainly have raised with aces, but almost certainly not deuces.

3. Ace-x, where 'x' is as low as an eight or a nine. You don't see this particular tight player leading off early with hands like ace-six or worse. Even ace-nine or ace-eight seems like a bit of a stretch (for a raise from a tight player in early position).

You're in good shape against everything but aces. The turn comes the J♥. That's not a good card for you. Two hands which were definitely in Player C's range, jacks and ace-jack, are now beating you. In addition, you know that Player C is putting you on just about the same range of hands that you're estimating for him, so that card could cool his action if it didn't help him.

Player C checks.

You consider what betting means in terms of pot commitment. You've bet $180 so far, so your remaining stack is $920. You can see that Player C has a few hundred dollars more than you. If you bet $250 and get called, the pot will balloon to $875 and your stack will shrink to $670. Now if your opponent pushes all-in on the river, you'll be getting 1,545-to-670 odds to call, about 2.3-to-1. That's not a compulsory call with top pair; you can theoretically walk away from the hand, although given how the hand has developed, you may feel you have to call.

Still, you only have top pair, and in no-limit cash games, top pair isn't usually a hand where you want to get your whole stack involved. Although you still think you're a favorite to have the best hand, you decide that the absolute strength of your hand doesn't yet justify plunging into a possible all-in situation. You check behind. The pot remains at $375.

The river card is the K♦. It's an odd card. It looks good, but it actually doesn't change your status relative to Player C by very much. You're now beating ace-jack once more, but a pair of kings has joined a pair of jacks as hands that beat you. No-limit hold 'em is a tough game in part because a card can arrive that appears to help your hand, but when you actually analyze the hand range your opponent could be playing, the card has little effect. Player C bets $100, making the pot $475. That's a very small bet. It's probably a blocking bet; that is, Player C wants to see the showdown without investing a lot of money, and figures if you don't have the nuts, you may just shrug your shoulders and call this bet, rather than stick in a raise.

Since a blocking bet shows weakness, the proper response to a suspected blocking bet is usually a healthy raise. But before you raise, you need to go back through the list of possible hands and see just where you think you stand. Let's review what we think Player C might have to make sure that a raise is really a good investment.

1. **High pairs:** We thought Player C could have raised in early position with a high pair, perhaps sevens or better. Right now we're losing to aces, kings, and jacks, but beating queens and tens through sevens. If our high pair range was right, we're beating five of the eight possible pairs. If he could have raised with any pair, we pick up four more pairs we beat (sixes through treys) and only one pair that beats us (deuces).

2. **Ace-x hands:** We thought Player C might have raised with anything from ace-king down to about ace-eight. We're tied with ace-king, and now that a king appeared, we're beating all the others. In fact, the only ace-x hand that can beat us is the highly unlikely ace-deuce.

We had decided that, although Player C could conceivably have opened with two high cards that didn't contain an ace (like king-queen or king-jack), he wouldn't have bet and then called a raise on the flop with that hand. Too bad, since we're now beating all these hands.

Summarizing, we're beating all the ace-x hands (except ace-king, where we split) and most, but not all, of the pairs. We decide that his apparent blocking bet is just that, and a raise here on the end is justified by the odds.

How big should our raise be? The pot is $475 and our stack has $920. If we call $100, the pot becomes $575 and our stack is $820. A raise of half the pot is about $300, meaning our stack afterwards would be only $520. We're getting pot-committed, but we decide the situation is favorable enough, and we make the raise, putting in a total of $400.

The pot is now $875 and it's a $300 raise to Player C.

Player C puts us all-in. The pot becomes $1,695, and we have to put in our remaining $520 to call. We're getting better than 3.2-to-1 on our money.

Those odds sound pretty good, and we sure don't want to get bluffed out of a hand this big. We call. Player C turns over A♠2♥ and scoops the pot with deuces full. We are unhappy.

# Recap: What Went Wrong?

Our analysis of this hand was actually fairly superficial. Did you catch that? Let's go back to a couple of crucial spots in the hand and see where a careful player would have done better.

Our preflop play was alright. We chose to just call with ace-king suited rather than raise. As it happens, the raise would have won the pot. Player C would have realized that his ace-deuce was possibly dominated by a better ace, and thrown his hand away. But calling a certain percentage with ace-king for deception is a good play. Nothing wrong there.

Our play was reasonable on the flop, but contained the seeds of future trouble. His initial bet didn't really tell us much. It could have been a value bet, or it could have been a continuation bet bluff. Our raise with ace-king was perfectly proper. But his call of our raise needed to set off alarm bells. We're supposed to be a tight player, and he's supposed to be a tight player. We just saw a bet, a raise, and a call. That's a lot of action from two tight players. We needed to be more careful in thinking about just what hands he might have had.

The flop contained an ace and two deuces, and both players indicated they were willing to get involved in the pot. Since there were no draws available, both players had to recognize what was being said by the betting: each player had been helped by the flop. For the flop to help, you need an ace or a deuce in your hand. A priori, the ace is a more likely card. But once the betting gets serious, you have to give some consideration to the possibility that a deuce is out there.

Our real error came after the flop when we tried to interpret the results: we completely discounted the chance that Player C held a deuce (because he was a "tight" player) and we continued to think that there was some chance he held a pair between kings and sevens. Suppose, for instance, he had a pair of jacks. His raise preflop is perfectly sensible. We call. An ace comes on the flop. He bets. Also a sensible move. He needs to find out if the jacks are still any good. We raise. Does he call with his jacks, out of position? It's reasonable that we would have called his preflop bet with an ace, and our raise says that we not only called with an ace, we called with a pretty good ace. If we're telling the truth, he has only two outs (the last two jacks). If we're not telling the truth, how much should he invest in the hand before giving up? Most players would lay down the jacks after the raise. So we have to start to discount the chance that he has a pair, and put him on either an ace or a deuce. Right now the ace is more likely, but as more money gets involved, the chance that he actually has a deuce starts to rise. Actually only the strong aces are likely because the weak aces don't have any hands they can beat. If we have a strong ace (indicated by our raise) or a deuce, the weak aces are losing to everything.

So on the flop, our appraisal of his hand range was both too narrow and too wide. Too narrow because we had completely discounted that he had a deuce, whereas there was now some chance that was the case, and too wide because we were including hands like medium pairs and weak aces which we could beat, but which he couldn't still be playing.

Our turn play was fine. The jack hurt us because it turned ace-jack, one of his reasonable hands, into a winner. When he checked, we were right to check behind because our situation wasn't that strong, and we shouldn't have had any desire to build a big pot here.

On the river, however, we went completely off the rails. The king looked helpful, but was pretty much irrelevant; it simply moved the ace-jack hand back into the win column for us. Aside from that, we were in mostly the same situation as on the flop: losing to a deuce or a pair of aces, tying ace-king, and beating ace-queen and ace-jack.

When he made his small bet, which we read as a blocking bet, but which was actually a "suck bet," (a small bet with a great hand intended to offer the opponent irresistible odds), we should have just called. Our position wasn't good enough to get a lot of money committed to the hand. Remember, this was the third time, since the flop, that our opponent had voluntarily committed more money. He bet the flop, he called a raise, and now he's betting more money.

Instead, we fell into the trap of listing many hands that we could beat, instead of asking "Could he have played the hand this way with those cards, and would any of those holdings call our raise on the end?"

Consider a hand like ace-ten, for instance. Let's work through how the hand looks to our opponent if he has ace-ten.

1.  Could he have bet that hand preflop? Yes, especially if it was suited.

2.  Would he have bet on the flop? Yes, certainly.

3.  Would he call our raise on the flop? Maybe, but probably not. He's now out of position, losing to any deuce plus ace-king,

ace-queen, and ace-jack. He's beating the small aces. He showed strength perfectly consistent with his preflop raise, and we raised him anyway. That doesn't sound like we have ace-weak kicker, or a small pair. It sounds like his hand is right at the bottom of our possible range, and that's a real good time to fold.

4. Would he check the turn? Sure. He thinks he's beaten.

5. Would he make a small bet on the river? Maybe. We didn't bet the turn, so possibly our hand isn't as strong as the flop betting made it seem. But we could just as easily be lying in wait on the river. A small blocking bet is a possible play to see a cheap showdown which he just might win.

6. Would he call our raise on the river? No. He's beaten, he knows it, and we know it. He should fold.

The very same reasoning applies to almost all the hands we can beat, except for ace-jack. Ace-jack could have played the hand just the way it happened, and might call our river bet and pay us off. But that's the only hand we can beat that will pay us off. Every other hand that can put us all-in on the river can beat us.

So we should have just called his small bet on the river, and seen his hand. We were getting 5-to-1 odds on that bet, which is fine for seeing a hand even if we think we're mostly beaten.

Reopening the betting with a raise was a big mistake, and calling on the end was another big mistake despite the better than 3-to-1 pot odds. At that point, as the hand played out, we could only beat a bluff. If this was a bluff, it was artfully crafted from the flop, and sometimes you just have to admit this is a bluff you won't catch rather than pay off your whole stack to a better hand.

# Deception

Apart from the tactical errors, however, the real lesson of the hand was the immense potential profit from Player C's deceptive play. He raised in early position with ace-deuce suited. This isn't a standard play or even a good play in some abstract sense. It's easy to explain to any beginner why this play isn't "right." "In early position, ace and a weak kicker is treacherous ... if an ace flops you won't know where you stand ... your deuce will often be counterfeited..." We know all the arguments. Player C was undoubtedly well aware of them. So why did he do it?

We just saw why he did it. He hit his hand strong, and because the play was so unexpected, his opponent discounted the holding and lost 110 big blinds, his whole stack. That's a big, big payoff, and it's also an essential lesson for big stack poker. The potential payoff for deceptive plays is your opponent's whole stack when things go right.

The crucial question is not "Should you play ace-deuce in early position?" But rather, "Just how often can you play ace-deuce (or any other weak but well-hidden hand) before the cost of playing weak cards offsets the surprise value of the cards?" That's a hard question to answer, and different types of players answer the question in different ways.

The tight-aggressive player would answer the question this way. "I'll mostly throw this hand away, but occasionally, perhaps 5 to 10 percent of the time and when it is suited, I'll play it. I'll play it more often at a tight table of straightforward players because there's more of a chance that hands will lay down to me. A lot of players at a tight table would fold better aces than mine once I raise, and if I get action I'll know I'm in bad shape. At a really loose-aggressive table, I might never play the hand, because I can't stand a raise with it."

The loose-aggressive player would answer the question a little differently. "I'll play this hand 15 to 20 percent of the time (and again when it is suited) in early position. With no one in the pot ahead of me, I don't mind setting the pace. I get called more often than a tight player would, and mostly the caller won't have an ace. If an ace flops, I'll find out quickly if the caller had an ace or not."

A similar line of reasoning holds for other deceptive hands. You play them occasionally to mix up your game, make yourself both unreadable and unclassifiable, and reap the rewards when you flop a huge hand and your opponent flops a big hand which he believes must be best because "There's no way you would have raised from that position with that junk hand."

# Hand Analysis: Weighing the Evidence

Analyzing hands usually presents you with several pieces of information, one after the other: their preflop bet, a check on the flop, followed by a call, a bet on the turn, and so forth. Should all these pieces of information be given equal weight?

I think not. Here's the principle I like to follow:

> When performing hand analysis, weigh the evidence in proportion to the associated bet size.

Give more weight to a bet of 30 big blinds on the turn than to a bet of 3 big blinds preflop. Give more weight to a bet than a check. In practice, this means that bets later in the hand carry more weight than bets earlier in the hand.

Intuitively, this principle makes a lot of sense. Players, especially loose-aggressive players, will often fool around preflop with marginal hands just to see a flop. Those bets shouldn't carry a lot of weight. Later in the hand, players have seen more evidence and the pot is getting larger relative to their stacks.

Clearly, bets made under those circumstances should carry more weight.

How much more weight should be given to larger bets? Here I would use a heavy measure of common sense. A bet of 30 big blinds on the turn should be given more weight than a bet of 3 big blinds preflop, but it shouldn't be given 10 times more weight. All bets have some intrinsic meaning. Just be aware that larger bets made later in the hand with more available information should count for more than early bets.

# The Metagame

Much of what we discuss in this book is the detailed play of individual hands. Topics like what cards to play, whether to bet or check this sort of hand on the turn, and what deductions to draw from the other actions at the table, are all part of the tactics of the game. But beyond all this is another aspect of poker, which we call the *metagame*.

The metagame is that aspect of poker which goes beyond the tactics of the individual hands themselves. Here we're in the realm of table image and table presence. It's the sum of everything that you know about the other players, and everything they know about you. In order to craft the metagame image you want, you will sometimes have to play hands in strange and non-optimal ways. As others see your plays and react to them, your metagame image takes shape.

Note that the metagame is something different from just playing deceptively. When we play deceptively, we are trying to increase our chances of winning money in the current hand by making plays that don't reflect the true situation.

For example, we call a raise with eight-six offsuit and flop a straight. If a couple of players check to us, we may elect to check as well, rather than fire out a bet. We judge that there's no extra money to be won right now by betting, but a check, feigning weakness, might collect an extra bet (or even two) on the turn or river by allowing our opponents to hit a little more of a hand. By playing deceptively, we are trying to increase our equity in the current hand with shrewd play.

When we make plays designed to influence the metagame, we're doing something quite different. In metagame play, we are *sacrificing* equity in the current hand to *increase* our equity in other hands at some point in the future. In effect, we become investors, transferring a small amount of value from our current hand to an unknown but real set of future hands, hopefully growing the equity in the process.

Suppose, for instance, we play regularly in a medium-stake game with a group of tight players, competent, but unimaginative players. Over time, the players come to know each other quite well. Tonight we sit down and, in early position, we raise with four-deuce offsuit — since we're concentrating on the metagame, it's now okay not to be suited. We eventually make two low pair and, at the showdown, lose to a player with two higher pair. Rather than comment on the decisions that went into this particular hand, let's instead step back from the table and ask ourselves this question: In terms of equity, what exactly has happened?

The highest-equity play for a weak hand like four-deuce offsuit in early position is to fold. Folding has an expectation of zero, and raising will be negative, no matter how well we play afterwards. So by raising, we've cost ourselves some money, on average, no matter whether we win or lose the actual hand.

But look what happens on future hands. Suppose later in the evening we pick up a pair of aces in first position. We raise. Before, opponents would have assumed we had a big hand when we raised early. But now they know we could be playing four-deuce. So they are more inclined to call. So the value of our aces, whatever it was before, has increased by some amount. In fact, the ripple effect of the four-deuce play will be felt over many hands, and the value of all our real hands has increased.

Chess players will be familiar with this concept because in chess it happens frequently. Players make material sacrifices (often of a pawn, sometimes of a piece) in order to reap a reward of other assets later in the game (development, center control, attacking chances). But the central idea is the same: You sacrifice something concrete now for something larger and real but more intangible later.

The goal of metagame plays is to create an image of a player who is dangerous and inscrutable. When you make a move, players don't know what you're doing. They've seen you make plays before with big hands and with nothing. They can't be sure what your bets, raises, and calls mean. That makes you a player they don't want to play against, and that image is a money-making asset.

## Playing the Metagame

Metagame plays are easy to describe but require discipline and courage to execute. Let's look at a master in action, from the second season of *High Stakes Poker*.

For this hand, the positions, hands, and approximate stack sizes are as follows:

| | | | |
|---|---|---|---|
| 1 | Antonio Esfandiari | $160,000 | -- |
| 2 | Gus Hansen | $400,000 | -- |
| 3 | Daniel Negreanu | $300,000 | J♥T♥ |
| 4 | Corey Zeidman | $100,000 | -- |
| 5 | Barry Greenstein | $100,000 | -- |
| 6 | Anton Filippi | $120,000 | A♣6♣ |
| SB | Doyle Brunson | $500,000 | K♠K♥ |
| BB | Eli Elizera | $80,000 | 7♥4♣ |

Blinds are $300 and $600, with $100 antes. There's a live straddle this hand of $1,200. (The player in first position, in this case Esfandiari, has made another blind bet of $1,200. If the action gets limped back to him, he'll have the option to raise.) The pot is $2,900 to start.

**Gus Hansen.** Folds.

**Daniel Negreanu**. Daniel has

He's been very active at the table, both aggressively raising with marginal hands, and aggressively calling raises with any reasonable holding. His game plan has been to establish himself as the table captain. He's justifiably proud of his ability to play after the flop and escape from awkward spots by shrewdly putting his opponents on hands. He makes an initial raise to $4,000, a normal raise considering the straddle. He's varied his raise sizes throughout the session, so it won't be easy for the other players to know what this raise means.

**Corey Zeidman**. Folds.

**Barry Greenstein**. Folds.

**Anton Filippi**. Filippi started as one of the relative unknowns at the table. He's played a conservative game without lapsing into excessive tightness or passivity. When he's had a good hand for the situation, he hasn't been afraid to push it.

Right now he knows that Negreanu has been playing a lot of hands, including a lot of medium connectors like jack-ten, ten-eight, and seven-six, suited or unsuited. His

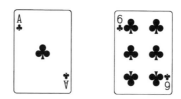

is probably a favorite over Negreanu's starting hand. Add to that his position on the button, and he's got an easy call. He calls $4,000. The pot is now $10,900.

**Doyle Brunson.** Brunson picks up

in the small blind. He almost certainly has the best hand at the table, and since the pot is already large enough to be worth claiming at this point, a raise to something like $12,000 to $15,000 is the obvious play.

But Doyle doesn't raise. Instead he just puts in $3,700, calling the bet.

Every good player limps occasionally (very occasionally) with kings. It's a dangerous play, much more dangerous than limping with aces. If you limp in early position, and two or three players just call, and an ace comes on the flop, it's almost impossible to call a bet. Unless you can simply throw your hand away with no regrets in that situation, you can't really make that play.

You might limp with kings as part of randomizing your play, but mostly it's done in early position at a table with known aggressive opponents. You're hoping for a couple of calls, followed by a big bet from someone pouncing on the limpers. Then you pounce on him, and you've made some money to immediately justify the risk you took.

Doyle's idea looks like something quite different. After Doyle, only two players remain to act in the hand. It's highly likely that if Doyle just calls, the other players will either call or fold, and we'll go to the flop with three, four, or five players in the hand. In addition, Doyle will be first to act after the flop. Putting it mildly, that's not a favorable situation for the kings. In fact, it will be nearly impossible for anyone to put Doyle on a pair of kings for the rest of the hand.

And that is the point. Doyle's going to play this hand like he had a small pair or one of Negreanu's favorite ten-eight suited type hands. Negreanu's taken the lead, so it's likely he'll be pushing the action all the way. Against a player who prides himself on his ability to read his opponents, Doyle's going to present him with a situation he can't possibly read, and see what happens.

If it doesn't work, Doyle will have wasted a pair of kings and a chance to pull down a modest pot. If it works, he might win a big pot. But whether it works this hand or not, Doyle will have effectively made another point in the metagame: "Forget it, kid. You can't read me."

**Eli Elizera.** Elizera calls $3,400 with seven-four offsuit. I'd fold this hand. It's not a great candidate for improvement, Elizera's position is relatively poor, and the hand has already gotten somewhat expensive. In no-limit hold 'em, the idea with these mediocre hands is to see a good number of flops *when the price is cheap and the circumstances are good.* Here the price isn't so cheap and the circumstances aren't so good. Let it go.

**Antonio Esfandiari.** Folds.

The pot is $18,000 pre-flop, a big pot even for this game. The flop comes

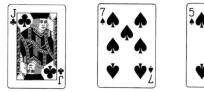

**Doyle Brunson**. That's a pretty good flop for Doyle's hand given that it didn't have a king. No ace appeared which means that Doyle's pair of kings still rates to be best.

The normal play here would be to bet somewhere between $12,000 and $15,000. The board has two spades, and the cards are just connected enough so the kings would like to make it expensive for any drawing hand to continue.

Checking here, with the idea of check-raising, is also a standard and reasonable plan. Negreanu is third to act, he's very aggressive, and he already took the lead before the flop. It's likely that he'll bet on the flop after two checks, in which case the kings can come over the top.

Doyle checks, but he has a third plan in mind.

**Eli Elizera**. Eli hit middle pair with a very weak kicker. It's not a strong hand and he has no way of knowing where he stands against three opponents. He wisely checks.

**Daniel Negreanu**. Negreanu has hit top pair with a medium kicker. Given his starting hand, that's a pretty good result. Two of his three opponents have checked, another good result. The board has some drawing potential, so he needs to bet.

What's the right amount? A standard bet would be something between half and three-quarters of the pot, which here would be about $9,000 to $14,000. Negreanu picks $8,000. It's a low bet, but still enough to deny great odds to a straight or flush draw if they aren't certain they can collect some more money when they hit. Since he's pretty sure there are no high pairs out against him, he may be hoping to encourage a middle pair to stick around.

**Anton Filippi**. His ace-six of clubs has missed the flop completely, so he has no reason to stay in the hand. He folds.

**Doyle Brunson**. Doyle could check-raise, but that's not his plan for this hand. Although it's dangerous, he's going to ride this to the end, encouraging Negreanu to keep value betting against his apparent draw. He calls $8,000.

**Eli Elizera.** His middle pair and feeble kicker doesn't look so good against a bet and a call. He wisely folds.

> The pot is now $34,000. Only Brunson and Negreanu remain. The turn is the 9♣.

**Doyle Brunson.** The board is now a little more threatening, with various straight possibilities all over the place. Brunson could bet, but he continues with his plan of representing something — a flush draw, a middle pair, perhaps a straight draw plus a low pair. In any event, a hand that might have been good enough to call last round, but can now be pushed out of the pot. He checks.

**Daniel Negreanu.** The check-call on the flop told him Brunson had something. The nine might have helped him or not. It's possible the nine made Brunson's hand, but it's more likely that Brunson is now drawing at a winning hand.

> Negreanu bets $30,000. It's almost a pot-sized bet, and if Brunson is on a draw, this should make him go away. If Brunson made his hand, Negreanu will find out when he makes a big reraise. The pot is now $64,000.

**Doyle Brunson.** Brunson just calls $30,000. His strategy may be working, or Negreanu could by now have made a better hand. At any rate, it's now too late and too risky to bet. The pot is now $94,000.

The river is the A♥.

**Doyle Brunson.** That's a dangerous card. It's possible Negreanu was playing with an ace and a pair in his hand, or even bluffing with just a lone ace. In either case, he now has top pair. He could also have made a hand on the turn. Whatever the case, it's now far too dangerous for the kings to make any kind of value bet even if that were Brunson's intention on the last street. He checks.

**Daniel Negreanu.** After Brunson's check, Negreanu said "I just don't think I win. You've probably got two pair," and turned over his cards. From Negreanu's point of view, what else could Brunson reasonably have? His call preflop and his check-call on the flop might have indicated some sort of drawing hand, but the call of the pot-sized bet on the turn, with just one card to come, wasn't a good call for a draw. Would he have called a pot-sized bet on the turn with a hand like ace-seven? Hard to believe. Would he have called pre-flop with seven-five, checked on the flop and then not raised after Negreanu bet? Negreanu's problem is that no plausible hand really fits all the actions here, but Doyle must have something since he's called all the way to a showdown. So Negreanu checks, and Brunson shows the hidden pair of kings.

The hand went about as well as it could for Brunson. He both won a big pot and got to show the hand down, in effect sending a clear message to Negreanu. "I can have anything at any time." It's very hard to play pots with confidence against someone when you know they can't be read.

# When Not
# to Make Metagame Plays

Metagame maneuvers are primarily useful in the early part of a hand, before the flop and on the flop. As you get to the river, the pot is growing in size. As the pot gets larger, the cost of a "mistake" (a non-optimal play for the situation in front of you) grows. You start to face a situation where the future equity gain can't make up for the present loss.

Still, there will be opportunities. Don't always bet the nuts on the river when first to act. Once in a while, check the nuts, and let someone try to steal the pot from you.

# Metagame Evolution

Metagame play can cause the action to steadily evolve over a period of hours, or even over multiple sessions. Let's say a player at an aggressive table wants to establish pre-flop limping as an option because he feels (correctly or not) that he can outplay his opponents after the flop. Play might then develop as follows:

1.  The player begins to limp with his medium-strength hands and some pairs.

2.  His opponents, being aggressive, raise his limps with a variety of hands.

3.  To make his strategy work, our hero calls these raises.

4.  As the opponents discover that he's limping with medium-strength hands, they raise even more.

5.  Our hero now has to start limping with some of his very strong hands to protect the integrity of his limps. At the same time, he begins raising with some of his old limping hands.

6.  The opponents discover that his limps may mean a very strong hand, and cut back on the frequency of their raises, while increasing the strength of their raising hands.

7.  A rough equilibrium is eventually reached with our hero limping with a balanced selection of hands, and being raised by an equally balanced selection. Meanwhile, other players begin to limp as well.

# Avoiding Big Mistakes

All games with a significant skill component share a common characteristic. It's not enough to play brilliantly; if you are a winner over time, you win because your opponent makes more mistakes than you do.

Consider a chess grandmaster playing at the highest level — a Garry Kasparov or a Bobby Fischer. Matched against weaker players, their game looks flawless. They play well; their opponent makes one slight mistake, then another. The opponent's game begins to deteriorate. All choices start to look awkward, then downright bad. Finally a blunder, and the game is over.

When two top players are matched against each other, the game is more interesting. The players make many fine moves, but with a few minor, very subtle errors. Each tries to exploit the other's small mistakes. Tension is maintained for a long time as good moves alternate with small, almost imperceptible errors. Finally, perhaps under the pressure of the clock, one player makes an error that's too serious to overcome, and his opponent moves in for the kill. A masterpiece, cheer the critics.

In two-person games like chess, we tend to think of top players as winning because their grand conceptions just overwhelm the opponent. That can be true on occasion, but it's really a metaphor that obscures the main point. Games are about not making errors. If the sum of all your errors is less than the sum of all your opponent's errors, you win. Otherwise he wins.

When we move to a multi-player game like no-limit hold 'em, the picture gets more complicated. To define an error in no-limit hold 'em, we go back to Sklansky's Fundamental Theorem of Poker. An error is a play you wouldn't make if you knew what your opponent had. If your opponent holds the nuts on the river and bets at you, it's an "error," in this particular sense, to call. It doesn't matter if you were getting wonderful pot odds to justify the call given the range of hands he might have held. If you knew what he held you would have folded, so it's an error to call.

Here's a useful way of thinking about a game of poker. You and each of the other players start with an abstract bankroll of equity, entirely separate from your chips. Off in another room, a computer is assigned the job of keeping track of all these little bankrolls. Meanwhile, you and the other players at the table are making errors all the time. The computer busily tabulates all these mathematical errors and puts them in a big bubbling vat, the equity pool. As each hand ends, the computer scoops out the vat, counts the total, and credits it to the winner of the hand.

Now the winner might have actually made some terrible blunders and been the biggest contributor to the pool. Doesn't matter. The computer isn't trying for fairness; his job is just to tabulate the errors and keep the accounts in balance.

At first, the money at the table and the balances in the computer's counting room don't seem to bear much relation to each other. But as the players play hundreds, then thousands, then tens of thousands of hands, each player's cash stack starts to look very similar to his theoretical account. The players who, over time, have made the smallest contributions to the equity pool now have the largest stacks, and vice versa. Eventually the players who made the most contributions see their stacks wiped out, and they either have to quit playing or contribute more money.

Over time your results will reflect your ability to minimize errors. You don't have to make a lot of brilliant plays to be a success at no-limit hold 'em. What's important is not to make a lot of really bad plays. Sounds easy? Well, it's not that easy, but it's not an impossible task either. Let's think for a minute about where the really big errors in no-limit hold 'em are likely to come from.

If you started out playing limit hold 'em, and are now trying no-limit, you need to be aware that it's possible to make much bigger mistakes at no-limit than at limit. To see why, imagine that after the flop you have the second-best hand in a limit game, with no chance of drawing out to beat your opponent, but you mistakenly decide to call your opponent's bets down to the end. Note that these are real "errors" in the sense we're talking about. If you knew your opponent's hand, you would certainly fold. But instead you keep calling, and the cost of your series of calls is about 10 big blinds.

Now let's look at the same situation in a no-limit game. You have 200 big blinds in your stack, and so does your opponent. Preflop, he bets three big blinds and you call. After the flop he has the nuts, but you mistakenly decide to call him all the way down. On the flop he bets roughly the pot, eight big blinds, and you call. On the turn he bets roughly the pot again, this time 24 big blinds, and you again call. On the river he bets the pot again, now 72 big blinds, and you call for the final time. This time your post-flop errors have cost you, not 10 big blinds, but 104 big blinds!

A similar situation arises in tournament no-limit hold 'em. For much of the event, most players are short-stacked. When you're short-stacked, you can make errors, but they aren't likely to be serious errors because your chance of winning with a short stack is small. When a player with a stack of ten big blinds or so pushes all-in with a seven-five offsuit and gets called, he might be embarrassed and he might actually have made a mathematical error, but the size of the error doesn't really amount to much.

So how do we avoid making big mistakes at deep stack no-limit hold 'em?

# Hand Susceptibility

Let's try to understand just what kind of hands are susceptible to big mistakes. Look at the kinds of hands you might have on the flop and see whether you can make a major error with them:

- **Very strong made hands:** The decision with these hands is whether to bet out or try and trap with either a check-raise or a check-call followed by a bet on the turn. It's hard to make a serious mistake here because in a sense you already know your opponent's hand — it's worse than yours. The only unknown is whether or not it's strong enough to call a bet. But the size of any error you might make is very limited.

- **Very weak hands:** It's also hard to make a mistake here because you don't plan to get involved with these hands. You might decide to bluff at a pot, a play which might work or might not, but again your potential error is pretty much limited to the size of a bet — a few big blinds at most.

- **Drawing hands:** Again, not too much can go wrong here. Since you know your opponent's hand (it's probably better than yours right now), you just need to know the odds that you can improve to a winning hand. Then pot odds can tell you if calling a bet is justified or not. If you calculate the expressed odds right, you could still make a mistake estimating the implied odds, but in terms of big blinds thrown away, that's not going to be a major error.

- **Medium strength made hands:** We'll count as medium strength anything from overpairs down to underpairs. Next to the hands where you miss the flop entirely, these are the most common hands on the flop, and these are the hands where big errors can be made. Compared to the other possible hands, you really don't know where you stand. You might be even or a slight favorite against a draw, and otherwise you're either way ahead or way behind, but you don't know which.

The medium hands on the flop are the bread and butter of no-limit play. It's essential to play them well because this is where the big mistakes can be (and are) made. We'll have plenty to say about them in the course of this book, with lots of examples. Pay attention, because playing these hands correctly after the flop will largely determine whether you're a winner or a loser.

# Dealing with Short Stacks

For most of "Part Two: The Elements of No-Limit Hold 'em Cash Games" we've talked about the problems of deep stacks confronting other deep stacks. However, not all stacks in a deep-stack game will be deep. Some players at the table may have very short stacks, either because they just lost a big hand, or because they have deliberately chosen to play with a short stack.

When a deep stack meets a short stack heads-up, the deep stack's extra chips do him no good. The confrontation is essentially a battle of two short stacks, and strategies appropriate to short-stack poker apply. Premium pairs and high-card combinations predominate, and drawing hands (low pairs, suited connectors) don't have the implied odds needed to play.

When several deep stacks are in a hand along with a short stack, an interesting dynamic emerges. Essentially, the deep stacks play against each other; from their point of view, the short stack in the hand is irrelevant. Curiously, this presents the short stack with an opportunity. He can play his own game, and from his point of view, the deep stacks will be playing poorly. Their decisions, which have to take implied odds into consideration, will be errors in his small-stack world.

Ed Miller, in his excellent book *Getting Started in Hold 'em*, presents a self-contained short-stack strategy, based upon playing only premium pairs and high cards, with some adjustments for position. The main idea is to play a small number of hands and to get your money in quickly, either preflop or on the flop. Although not a huge money-maker, the strategy is easy to learn and enables beginners to sit in higher-stakes games and gain experience without being at a disadvantage. When I started playing no-limit cash games in the 1980s, I used a similar strategy to good effect while I was learning how to play.

If you're in a game and there are short stacks at the table, you need to ascertain if they're playing a well-defined short stack strategy or if they're simply playing a normal game with just a little money. The giveaway of a real short-stack strategy is super-tight play combined with an eagerness to get all-in quickly. What can you do if you're against a savvy short-stack player? If you're heads-up, you can narrow their hand range to a few possibilities, and you can be pretty sure they're never bluffing when they put their money in. That knowledge should let you make close to optimal decisions. In a multi-way pot, you can't really do much because what happens vis-à-vis the other big stacks is much more important.

# Part Three

# Tight-Aggressive Preflop Play

# Tight-Aggressive Preflop Play

# Introduction

In the course of the next several chapters we'll explain in detail how to play on the four different streets of a no-limit cash game: preflop, after the flop, after the turn, and after the river. We'll show how to play these streets from the perspective of a fundamentally tight-aggressive player. Before we do that, however, we'll need to explain a little about the difference between the two major styles of play: tight-aggressive and loose-aggressive.

First, let's note that these are not the only possible styles. There's also tight-passive players (known as "rocks"), who play few hands and like to call rather than raise; loose-passive players, who slop into a lot of hands but only call because on some level they think poker is about seeing hands, but betting is rude; and probably a few other bizarre predilections too unworthy to note. Successful players, however, play some variation of an aggressive style, betting to put pressure on opponents and lay claim to pots in accordance with the Second Principle of Poker.

When a tight player enters a pot, he basically wants one of two situations to occur:

1.  Either he has a hand which rates to be best at the moment, given what he knows about his hand, his position, and his opponents, or

2.  He doesn't think his hand is best, but he believes that the expressed and implied odds he's receiving from the pot make playing worthwhile.

An example of the first situation is a player who raises preflop under the gun with a pair of jacks. There are only three hands in the deck better than jacks, and right now there's less than a 15 percent chance that one of the eight or nine players behind him has one of those three hands. So the odds are very good that he has the best hand, and he raises.

An example of the second situation is a player who calls on the button with seven-six suited after three limpers have already come into the pot. Right now he has only a seven-high, and it's highly unlikely that the limpers all have worse hands than this. But he assumes the total of his expressed odds and implied odds are good enough, so he plays.

In addition to these value-type plays, a good tight-aggressive player knows he has to mix in some different kinds of hands from different positions, so from time to time he'll raise in early position with a six-five suited, or call an early raise with jack-ten offsuit. He has to make enough of these non-standard plays to make his hand mix essentially unreadable, and to convince the other players at the table that a bet from him on any kind of flop can present a viable threat.

A loose-aggressive player will play all the same sorts of value hands as a tight-aggressive player, but he'll bring even more non-standard hands into his mix. The difference between a good loose player and a good tight player is one of degree. Both understand the need for variety in hand selection, but the loose player is willing to push the edge of the envelope a bit more.

For the next few chapters we're going to focus on the play of a hand from the tight-aggressive point of view. In "Part Nine: Playing the Loose-Aggressive Style," we'll look more closely at the looser style of play and the issues it raises.

# Hand
# Evaluation and Stack Sizes

In no-limit hold 'em, *the hands you want to play depend on the stack sizes at the table.* This will seem like a puzzling statement at first, particularly to those with a tournament background. Let's see what we mean.

Imagine one day you walked into a casino with a very unusual poker room. In this poker room, every table spread a game with exactly the same blind structure, $5-$10. However, each table had a fixed buy-in, and each table differed from every other table. Over here at table A, everyone buys in for $200. In the far corner at table B, the buy-in was $500. In the right-hand corner at table C, the buy-in was $1,000. And in the center of the room at Table D, you had to buy in for $3,000.

For awhile you walk around the room and observe the play at each table. The players, you are told by the manager, are all very competent. "These boys really know their poker." And indeed, they do give off a sense of being very good players. No tourists or rubes here. So now a question: What kind of hands do you expect to see being played at each table?

As you observe Table A, with buy-ins of 20 big blinds, there are no surprises. Many hands end when first player on the flop with a raise takes down the pot. When hands go to showdown, often with an all-in and a call either preflop or on the flop, it's clear the players started with good cards. You see aces against queens, ace-king against jacks, kings against ace-queen. Yes indeed, these boys are playing good solid cards.

As you move on to Table B, with the 50 big blind buy-in, the play seems a little more ragged. Aces get cracked by a pair of sixes that flopped a set. Kings lose to a queen-jack suited that pushed all in with draws to both a straight and a flush. These boys seem a lot looser than the lads at Table A.

At Table C, the players seem wilder still. Players start showing down hands like medium connectors and ace-small suited. It seems harder and harder to predict what the players have from their preflop betting.

By the time you get to Table D with the 300 big blind buy-in, you're not sure what to expect. The first hand starts with a raise and a call preflop, then a flop of ace-four-deuce. Just as you think that perhaps someone paired their ace, the players go nuts and start betting, raising, and reraising. Pretty soon they're both all-in with a monster $6,000 pot. The first player flips over two aces for top set. Very reasonable, you think, but what could the other guy possibly have? He cracks a wry smile and turns over five-three offsuit for a wheel. The wheel holds up on the turn and the river, and he pulls down a monster pot.

As you walk away, you think that the high-stakes players in this room must be a bunch of lunatics. But they're not. In fact, you saw high-quality play at every table. The players were simply adjusting their starting hands to reflect the relative stack sizes.

Table A, with its stacks of 20 big blinds, was high-card city. The players waited for their big pairs or two high cards and got their money in the pot as fast as possible. Tiny pairs and connectors weren't playable, because you couldn't get the odds you needed to make these hands work.

Table B, with the 50 big blind stacks, showed an evolution. Now the stacks were large enough so that hands like small pairs and good drawing hands were getting the implied odds they needed to play. By the time we reached Table C, with its 100 big blind stacks, weaker drawing hands like unsuited connectors and ace-x suited were being added to the mix.

Finally, at Table D with its gigantic stacks, any hand in good position that could form a disguised monster against a strong, but second-best hand was now a candidate to be played.

In no-limit hold 'em, the playability of a hand is directly related to the size of the stacks at the table. In tournament play, this effect is masked because the deep-stack part of a typical tournament is relatively short. In a sit-and-go, it might consist of one round of betting and just a few hands. In multi-table tournaments, you might get two or even three betting rounds. After that, the blinds have risen to the point where play resembles that at Table A in our example.

(In tournament play, a further situation arises which confuses this issue in the minds of many players. As the blinds continue to rise relative to the stacks in tournaments, players can't wait any longer for high cards or premium pairs. Instead, they start raising or moving all-in with hands like small pairs and the suited connectors. This isn't, however, because of implied odds or the deception value of these hands, but simply because of the fold equity from being first in the pot.)

In cash game play, however, it's the stack sizes which determine which hands you can play and how valuable those hands are. To see why this is so, let's go back to the scene at Table D and consider the two hands that were involved in that big all-in: a pair of aces and five-three offsuit. What happens to these hands as we start at a table with small stacks and progressively move to tables with larger and larger stacks?

At a small-stack table, it's no contest. The aces are massively stronger than the five-three. Heads-up, preflop, the aces are a 5-to-1 favorite to win. At a table with 20 big blinds each, the money will all get committed either preflop or on the flop, which strongly favors the aces.

But look what happens when we move to a table with 300 big blinds each. Let's say the aces raise to 3 big blinds preflop, and the five-three decides to call. The pot becomes 7.5 big blinds (assuming no other players are involved in the pot). The five-three have risked 1 percent of their stack as a 5-to-1 underdog.

Now comes the flop. Most flops will miss the five-three entirely. The aces will bet, and the five-three will fold. Net loss: 1 percent of their stack.

But suppose we get a flop like king-six-four. That looks like a pretty safe flop for the aces, who bet, say, 5 big blinds. The five-three, with a well-disguised open-ended straight draw, calls 5 big blinds. The pot becomes 17.5 big blinds. The five-three got 5 more big blinds involved in the pot, but this time, with the straight draw, as just a 2-to-1 underdog with two cards to come.

Notice something else as well. The player with the five-three knows almost exactly what's going on in the hand. Their opponent seems to have something like a high pair. They have a straight draw. But the aces are flying blind. They know they have an overpair, but they're clueless as to what they're facing. Their best guess at this point is that they're facing something like a pair of kings, or perhaps some medium pair like eights or nines.

On the turn, a deuce arrives. This still looks all right for the aces. After all, the guy didn't call a preflop raise with a five-three, did he? So the aces bet again, this time 15 big blinds. And the straight just calls, laying a trap. The pot becomes 47.5 big blinds. Each player still has 277 big blinds in their stack.

On the river an ace arrives, giving the aces top set. The aces now have the second nuts (we're assuming there is no flush draw on board.) With what clearly appears to be the best hand, the aces take their last chance to make some money and bets 30 big blinds, hoping for a call from a smaller set. Mr. Five-three now raises to 120 big blinds. The pot is 197.5 big blinds, and Mr. Aces has 247 big blinds left in his stack.

Now what? Mr. Aces has every hand beaten except precisely a five-three. He could be getting raised by a small set, thinking it's up against an ace-king that has improved to two pair. Or he could be against a set of kings that has slowplayed throughout. This is a pretty good situation for Mr. Aces, and despite some nagging doubt, he finally decides that fortune favors the bold, so he pushes all-in. Mr. Five-three calls and doubles up with his most unlikely straight.

Now let's carefully take a look at just what happened in this hand, paying careful attention to precisely what portion of the stacks were involved in each case.

1.  Mr. Five-three called a raiser in early position with a five-three offsuit. To a tight player accustomed to playing small-stack poker or even limit poker, that looks crazy. Right now he's a 5-to-1 underdog against a pair of aces. *But he only got 3 big blinds, or 1 percent of his stack involved as a 5-to-1 underdog.*

2.  On the flop, Mr. Five-three called another bet for 5 big blinds, this time with a well-disguised open-ended straight draw. *This time he got 2 percent of his stack involved as a 2-to-1 underdog.*

3.  On the turn he hit his straight, which was the nuts at that point. *He got 5 percent of his stack involved as a 100 percent favorite.*

4.  On the river, Mr. Aces had the severe misfortune of hitting his hand, and all the rest of the money went in. *Mr. Five-three got the last 92 percent of his stack involved as a 100 percent favorite.*

In short, 1 percent of Mr. Five-three's stack went in as a big underdog, 2 percent went in as a small underdog, and 97 percent went in as an unbeatable favorite.

So what's the lesson here? Is five-three a hitherto underestimated hand? The answer is: yes and no. But before we explain further, let's state the general principle that's in operation, Harrington's First Law:

> The gap in strength between strong hands and weak hands is inversely proportional to the stack sizes.

In other words, when stacks are short, a pair of aces is just as big a favorite over a five-three offsuit as a pure calculation of heads-up winning chances would indicate. The reason is very simple: with four betting rounds and short stacks, most or all of the money is going in on the early betting rounds, when the aces are still a big favorite.

But when stacks are very big, the advantage of the aces shrinks dramatically. The reason? Only a small percentage of the stacks are going in on the early rounds, when the aces are strong. If the five-three doesn't hit the flop, no more money goes in. If the five-three hits the hand, huge amounts of money go in on the later streets, when the aces are at a big disadvantage.

So now we get to the paradox of no-limit hold 'em. The premium pairs are strong hands, but only in the sense that they win a high percentage of pots. The pots they win, however, tend to be small. The weird connecting cards, small pairs, and ace-x suited hands lose most pots, but they have the potential of winning the very big pots.

Another way to explain the paradox is in terms of the deception principle. The more deceptive your hand, the more likely you are to get paid in a big pot. Premium pairs and ace-king are the least deceptive hands possible. If you raise in early position and keep betting on the flop, do you think your opponents are asking themselves "If he is secretly playing a seven-four suited, can I beat him?" No! They're saying "If he's got a big pair, can I beat him, or am I drawing to beat him?"

The weird connectors, however, are the most deceptive hands possible. If you play a nine-seven and the flop is ten-eight-six, no one will jump to the assumption that they're facing a made straight; it's just too unlikely. They might well believe they're facing a straight *draw*, and bet accordingly. But if the turn and the river don't seem to fill that draw, you'll get a lot of action on your hand.

To summarize: In small-stack poker, you need to stick closely to big pairs and premium cards. As the stacks get larger, you can broaden your range of playable hands to include the small pairs, suited connectors, and ace-x suited hands. As the stacks get really large, you can play (under the proper circumstances) any cards that can make a concealed monster that your opponent can't see.

One last caveat. Note the phrase "under the proper circumstances." Big-stack poker isn't a license to play half the hands, or to call a raise and a reraise with garbage. Your use of unusual hands has to be selective, or people will quickly see what you're doing and counter effectively. Playing these hands selectively, in position, and at a reasonable price is the proper recipe.

# Limping, Raising, and the Deception Principle

When everyone has folded to you preflop, and you've decided you're not going to fold, you have a choice: You can limp (call the big blind) or you can raise. If you decide to raise, you have another choice: you can vary your raises in any number of ways, or you can try to raise the same amount every time, or you can raise the same amount depending on your position at the table. Let's examine these choices in light of our Deception Principle.

If you make certain assumptions about the players at the table and what they're likely to do in response to a limp or a raise, it's possible to prove, mathematically, that raising is better than open-limping — limping as the first player to enter the pot. I first became aware of this several years ago when a group of computer scientists were working on developing a neural network program to play poker while learning from its own mistakes. The first idea the program "learned" was that, when first in the pot, raising was better than limping because of the fold equity when everyone else gave up their hand.

In his book, *The Mathematics of Poker*, Bill Chen makes a different argument that yields the same conclusion. Only by raising can you put the big blind in a position where it's possible for him to make a mistake. If you raise, he might call you, or reraise you, or fold. Any of these choices could be a mistake, based on the cards you each hold. But if you limp, the big blind has a free shot to see the flop. You've taken away his ability to make a mistake by folding. His ability to make an error is worth some (however small) amount of money to you, therefore you're giving some amount of equity away by limping.

While I recognize the validity of these arguments logically, I believe there are strong practical reasons for making open-limping a tool in your repertoire. Here's a quick summary of the arguments for open-limping:

1.  **Open-limping lets you see more flops cheaply:** One of your goals is to see a lot of flops at a low price. A limp is cheaper than a raise, and at many tables a limp will begin a cascade of limpers, building a large pot for a minimum investment.

2.  **Open-limping allows you to disguise some big hands:** When you open-limp, it won't just be with suited connectors or small pairs. On occasion, to mix up your play, you'll open-limp with some big hands as well. Your opponents will have a harder time figuring out just what your plays mean.

3.  **Open-limping favors good post-flop play:** If you believe (as most good players do) that you play well after the flop, then open-limping lets you get there more often. If you believe you're weak in post-flop play, then always raising preflop is a good way to cut down on the number of flops you see.

4.  **Open-limping encourages players to get involved:** Whenever you get involved in a hand, both your and your opponent's stacks are potentially at risk. If you're the better player, this favors you, and if you're a much better player, it can favor you a lot. Remember that the (theoretical) error involved in limping instead of raising would be measured in small fractions of a big blind, but the gain from winning an opponent's whole stack when he gets involved, but misplays his hand, could be hundreds of big blinds.

These arguments aren't conclusive and they certainly aren't mathematically based. But good poker isn't all mathematics. As a practical matter, I've found that combining raising with open-limping presents my opponents with more problems than simply always raising when first in the pot. However, there are some very strong players who disagree.

If you find yourself in a game where you believe you're overmatched (but want to play anyway) then you should definitely drop open-limping in favor of always raising when first in the pot. In this case, shortening the hands definitely favors the overmatched player.

One last point to note: At an aggressive table with lots of raising going on and very little limping, you can't limp. In this case you have to raise if you decide to play and you're first in the pot. You can't allow yourself to get in a position where you're limping and being raised by aggressive players behind you; whether you throw your hands away or call out of position, the long-run cost will be too great.

What about sizing your raise when first in? Here there are three main theories:

1.    Always raise the same amount when first in. (Typically three times the big blind.)

2.    Vary your amount by position, but always raise the same amount from the same position. (Typically smaller raises in early position, larger raises in late position.)

3.    Vary your raises as you wish.

The first two strategies have the advantage of guaranteeing that your raises aren't giving away information about your hand. The last strategy lets you play with your opponent a little more. As with open-limping, the more you feel you may be overmatched, the more rigid you need to make your playing style. The more confident you feel in your abilities, the more you can size your raises as seems appropriate. Remember, your opponents will try to figure out what your raises mean. If your raises in fact have particular meanings (big raises with big hands, small raises with small hands, for example), they will eventually get it. If your raise changes are essentially random, they won't ever get it.

# Adopting Complementary Strategies

The idea of complementary strategies is crucial to successful no-limit hold 'em. Simply put, the idea is this:

> Every action, or sequence of actions you take in a hand, must be capable of multiple interpretations.

Put even more simply, the idea looks like this: Don't let your opponents know what you have.

Suppose you raise to three big blinds from under the gun. Technically, the only hands that are strong enough to make this raise are premium pairs, ace-king, and maybe ace-queen. But if you only make that raise from that position with those hands, you're giving your opponents too much information. It may take awhile, but eventually they'll figure out what that raise means, and take advantage.

On the other hand, you can't raise with a lot of weak hands under the gun, partly because they're weak and they'll cost you money in the long run, and partly because your opponents will eventually figure that out as well. We have a conundrum here. So what's the solution?

Let's assume that you're playing a style in which you're willing to either limp or raise if you're first in the pot. Let's also assume that there are hands you're always willing to play in first position, hands you will play occasionally, but not always, and hands you will never play. For example, you might classify potential hands as follows:

- **Premium pairs:** Always play.

- **Ace-king, ace-queen, ace-jack suited:** Always play.

- **Medium pairs:** Always play.

- **Small pairs:** Sometimes play.

- **Ace-small (lower than queen) suited:** Sometimes play.

- **Suited connectors (jack-ten or higher):** Always play.

- **Suited connectors (below jack-ten):** Sometimes play.

- **Ace-jack offsuit, king-queen ofsuit:** Sometimes play.

- **All else:** Never play.

Now for each group of potential hands, decide just how often you need to take each of the possible actions. Let's start with the premium pairs. Since you're always going to play a premium pair, the probability of folding is zero. You mostly want to raise with these hands, but you need to limp once in a while so that your opponents know they can't simply attack your limps with impunity. Suppose you decide that you'll raise 80 percent of the time, and limp the other 20 percent. That's a fine balance.

Now you move on to ace-king and ace-queen. Here you might decide to raise 70 percent of the time with ace-king (limping the other 30 percent) and just 50 percent of the time with ace-queen (limping the other 50 percent). Again, these are reasonable numbers.

You continue this way through the list of possible under-the-gun hands. When you get to the hands that you sometimes play, you have to include a folding percentage as well as raising and limping percentages. For example, let's look at the suited connectors below jack-ten. You decide that you don't want to always plays these hands because then you'll have too many weak hands in your early position mix. So you decide you'll fold them 40 percent of the time, limp 40 percent, and raise 20 percent. When you're done, you have a strategy for playing the under the gun position that's very difficult, if not impossible, for an alert observer to exploit.

The same procedure works for selecting hands in other positions. You should have a strategy for early position hands, middle position hands, late position hands, and even the small blind if it's folded around to the blind.

If you're playing online, you could actually create a chart for the various situations and keep it by your computer. For live games, however, I don't recommend trying to commit some large and complex chart to memory. Instead, try to use some common sense rules when the situation arises.

For example, suppose I'm playing a live game and it's folded to me in the cutoff seat. I have a pair of fours. With three players left to act it's probably the best hand, so I'm not folding. Since I'm in late position, I should almost always (but not quite always) be raising. So I'll estimate that I should be raising 90 percent of the time and limping 10 percent. That kind of quick estimation is good enough for any real-world purpose.

Once you've got some numbers, how do you actually decide what to do? Readers of *Harrington on Hold 'em; Volume I* know the answer to this question. Use the second hand of your watch as a random number generator. If you decide you want to raise 75 percent of the time and limp 25 percent, just glance down at your watch before deciding on your play. If the second hand is between 0 and 45 seconds, raise. If it's sitting between 45 seconds and 60 seconds, limp.

This method produces an unbiased random number which is both powerful and necessary. Attempting to rely on your own hazy judgment of what you've done with a given hand in the past is notoriously unreliable. Say you pick up a pair of aces in first position. You know you've decided that you should raise 80 percent of the time and limp 20 percent with this holding. But what do you do right now? You know that raising is inherently the stronger and safer play, but limping is necessary to balance your strategy. But you want to win this hand! So you raise. It doesn't take many such decisions before your strategy is totally out of whack.

The overall effect of this randomizing process is to make your raises and limps very difficult to interpret. Your raises from any position can imply anything from a pair of aces to a low suited connector. Your limps are equally opaque. This approach ensures that you'll get more action on your good hands (because it becomes clear that you're not just a locksmith) and more respect on your weaker hands (because no one can be sure they're weak). That combination puts you in an excellent position for playing the rest of the hand.

# Factoring in
# Your Post-Flop Skills

In formulating the makeup of your preflop hand selection strategy, you should take your post-flop skills into account. If your post-flop skills are below average, you need to win a larger percentage of your hands preflop. That means fewer limps, more raises and reraises with strong hands, and larger raises.

Good post-flop skills mean just the opposite. You can limp more, make fewer and smaller raises, and play a wider mix of hands.

This idea can't be underestimated and you need to be accurate in your evaluation. It's my experience that most poker players, even those who play fairly well, believe they are more expert than they really are. What this means is that if you're not sure how well you play post-flop relative to your opponents in a particular game, tend to error on the conservative side: specifically as stated above, go with fewer limps, more raises and reraises with strong hands, and larger raises.

# Playing Individual Hands

Now we'll move on and look at some of the issues for each particular type of hand. In general, each hand type has its own set of characteristics and goals. Be aware also that your goals with a hand can change markedly depending on what the other players at the table have done so far. If you pick up a pair of nines in middle position, for instance, and no one has entered the pot, you're happy to put in an initial raise. If a player in early position has already opened with a raise, a pair of nines quickly gets downgraded to a calling hand. After a raise and a reraise, it becomes a clear fold, barring some very unusual circumstance.

## The Big Pairs

For our purposes, big pairs are aces, kings, and queens. Any lower pair is a medium or small pair.

Big pairs are the best possible starting hands. Nevertheless, in no-limit hold 'em they can also be dangerous hands, particularly for beginners. The dark truth about big pairs is simply this: They tend to win lots of small pots, but when they get involved in a big pot, unimproved, they're usually the second-best hand.

Why should this be? The reason is actually pretty simple. The big pairs are usually the best hand preflop (always, in the case of aces), and they're usually the best hand on the flop. So if the hand ends preflop or on the flop, the big pair is generally winning it. But since the hand ended early, it's a small pot.

As the hand goes to the turn and the river, the pot gets bigger. But the other players in the hand are sticking around with something. Most players won't go deep into a hand unless they can either beat top pair or unless they're drawing to a hand that can easily beat top pair. With your unimproved big pair, the only hands you can beat late in a pot are pairs, and if the hand gets to the river with a big pot, it's a pretty good guess that your opponents won't be showing you just a pair. (If they do, cheer up. You're at a very weak table.)

So the preflop strategy for big pairs is pretty simple. You probably have the best hand, so you push the action along. You raise from early, middle, or late position. If someone opens in front of you with a raise, you reraise.

If you're reraising, how big should your reraise be? If the original raiser opened for three times the big blind, I like to reraise to nine times the big blind. That's actually slightly less than a pot-sized raise, which is a good amount. (If this isn't clear, look at how the pot is changing. The pot starts with 1.5 big blinds. The original raiser puts in 3 big blinds, making a pot of 4.5 big blinds. If I put in 9 big blinds, the first 3 call his bet, making a pot of 7.5 big blinds, and the last 6 are my raise to him, which becomes slightly less than pot-sized.)

Suppose the pot has been raised and reraised in front of you. Now my action depends a bit on what big pair it is. If my hand is aces or kings, I will continue to push the action and put in another raise. If it's queens, I need to consider the other players. With weak players or a low-stakes table, I can put in the third raise with queens because it's possible that I'm up against some combination of ace-king, ace-queen, jacks, tens, or a straight bluff. As my opponents get better and understand what values are necessary for reraising, I have to get more circumspect. Now queens become just a calling hand.

Should kings ever be folded? As I discussed in *Harrington on Hold 'em*, the practical answer is "No." It's true that you look like a genius when your opponent puts in a third raise and you show your kings and fold them, and he then shows his aces. But if you're willing to fold kings, I guarantee you that sometimes you'll be folding them to queens, or ace-king, or a total bluff, and over time, your willingness to fold kings will cost you money.

As part of a balanced strategy, you'll need to limp occasionally with these hands. Different players approach this problem in different ways. I will sometimes limp with aces, and very occasionally with kings. In early position, however, I'll only limp with aces. Despite its influence on my metagame, it's not part of my strategy to limp with kings and queens out of position. It's just too costly.

Johnny Chan is famous for limping with aces. Playing with Johnny, you sometimes feel that he limps more than he raises with this hand. Antonio Esfandiari is another top player who likes limping.

When you limp with aces (or kings) in early position, you often have a specific tactic in mind. You're hoping to start a cascade of limpers, followed by a big raise from late position, when some cowboy decides to take the limpers off the hand. Then the betting swings back around to you, and you can come over the top with another big raise. It's an effective play.

# Medium Pairs

For my purposes, a medium pair is anything from jacks down to about sixes. These hands are noticeably weaker than the big pairs, and within the group there is a rapid decline in strength as the pair gets smaller. If you're first to act with these hands, you will play all of them, but it's especially important to mix up your play.

Here are my quick rules for handling middle pairs when first to act:

- **Early position:** For the larger pairs, jacks through nines, you should mostly raise but sometimes call. Use a mixture of 70 percent raises and 30 percent calls. For the smaller pairs, eights through sixes, reverse the ratio and try 30 percent raises and 70 percent calls.

- **Middle position:** Middle position is safer than early position because several players have already folded, and there's less chance that someone behind you will pick up a hand. Now I want to mostly raise with all these hands. I'm trying to make sure that hands with a couple of overcards, like queen-jack or king-ten, will go away rather than stick around. Increase the raise-call ratio to 80-to-20 percent, and if you're varying your raise sizes, tend to pick a larger size with these hands, perhaps four to five times the big blind. Your goal here is to win the pot with these hands or get heads-up with position against one of the blinds.

- **Late Position:** Continue with the aggressive raise-call mixture of 80 percent raises and 20 percent calls. With the bigger pairs like jacks and tens, your limps are now a bit of a trap. If someone interprets your limp as weakness (which will often happen) and raises, you have the option of coming over the top with what is likely to be the best hand.

If the pot has been raised in front of you, and you'll have position on the raiser after the flop, these are all calling hands. (One exception: if either you or the raiser has a short stack, you can consider reraising with jacks, tens, and nines.) If your opponent raised with two unpaired cards you're the favorite, and the chance of hitting a set in a deep-stack game gives you massive implied odds.

If you see a raise and a reraise in front of you, throw all these hands away.

A raise followed by several callers is a different situation. Now you call, treating the pair as a straight drawing hand. You'll be getting some expressed odds and enormous implied odds if you hit your set. If you don't hit a set, you will mostly have to ditch your hand. If you do hit a set, you should be able to win a big pot.

If the initial raise comes from middle or late position, and your pair is a higher one, say jacks through eights, you're probably best. Consider tossing in a big reraise, at least four times the initial raise.

# Small Pairs

Small pairs are the pairs from fives through deuces. They're tricky to play. Before the flop, they may well be the best hand at the table. After the flop, their value declines rapidly if they don't make a set and overcards fall. Since small pairs are still pairs, you don't want to be in a hurry to throw them away. But since they're weak pairs, you have to play cautiously and be very cognizant of position.

The observant reader will notice that our advice in this section for handling small pairs differs somewhat from our advice in *Harrington on Hold 'em; Volume I*. There are two good reasons for this:

1. Proper play of small pairs is different in cash games than in tournaments.

2. Proper play of small pairs is different in strong, higher stake cash games than in weak, lower stake cash games.

Let's consider why this is so, then I'll get on to some specific advice for how to handle the small pairs. First, note that small pairs are, in essence, drawing hands. You're drawing to make a set. The odds against your making a set are a solid 7-to-1 against. You're almost never going to be in a situation preflop where you're actually getting those express odds. If you make your set, you need to win a pretty big pot to justify the call in the first place. So in analyzing the play of small pairs, we need to ask one important question: "What's likely to happen if we make our set?"

- **In weak, small-stakes cash games:** Players will usually refuse to fold hands like top pair, top kicker, or even medium pair. Instead, they'll go all the way to the river with those hands. In many cases, you'll see all-in bets on the river called with top pair. That's an ideal environment for playing small pairs, so in these sorts of situations you should make every effort to see a flop with a small pair. In such a game, I'd call a raise with a small pair even out of position.

- **In tournaments:** Small pairs are in much the same situations. If you flop a set, your opponents may have to go all the way with you because the blinds are rising so fast that they have to take a chance with a hand like top pair. (In the early stages of a tournament, when the stacks are deep, this doesn't apply for good players, although weak players may get their whole stack involved anyway.) Small pairs also have a second advantage in tournament play: direct all-in potential. Since a small pair is a slight favorite against any non-pair, you can push all-in with a small pair and a low M with a good chance that you're getting all your money involved as a favorite.

- **In cash games with strong players:** Small pairs have a real problem. Strong players don't think that top pair is a real good hand for getting all your money in the middle. They'd like something better. So if you flop a set with your small pair, and they have only a pair, you might pick up a bet, but probably not much more than that. However, if one of your strong opponents is willing to go to the river with you, the chances are that your set of fours or treys isn't going to be the best hand. Now the implied odds start working against you as your small set becomes good for winning medium pots, but losing big ones.

So the moral with small pairs in cash games is: Be very careful. Know your table (strong or weak), your opponents (passive or active), and your position. Play them when the situation is right or the game is easy, but when in doubt, let them go. Now let's look at more specific advice.

- **In weak, small games:** In early position, play your small pairs. You should mostly limp, but occasionally raise. In middle position, play the same way. In late position, mostly raise but occasionally limp. If players routinely defend their blinds with anything, mostly limp in all positions.

- **In strong games, or games with a lot of preflop raising:** In early position, fold the small pairs. In middle position, usually limp with fives and fours, usually fold the treys and deuces. In late position, raise with all these hands, although mix in some limps if the blinds seem willing to defend.

If you have position on a single raiser, you're usually not in a bad situation. The small pairs benefit greatly from having position. Use these two rules:

1. **In a weak game:** Always call with these hands.

2. **In strong games, or games with a lot of preflop raising:** Fold if there are several players yet to act behind you. You can't afford to get squeezed with these hands. Call if you have excellent position, or if there were one or two callers between you and the original raiser. In that case, you're getting pretty good expressed odds to go with your implied odds.

## Small Pairs and Implied Odds

Since small pairs are basically drawing hands, you need to be sure that the stacks of the players in the hand are large enough to give you the implied odds you need when calling a bet. You're a 7-to-1 underdog to make your set on the flop. In addition, when you hit your set, you don't have any guarantee that anyone else at the table will have a hand that will give you any action, or that the action will consist of anything more than a single bet. In order to compensate for all these dribbles of equity, you need to play these hands against players with good-sized stacks. When you do win their entire stack, you'll win enough money to balance the very frequent losses. I look for opponents who have a stack at least 25 times the size of the bet I have to call to see the flop. If I can't see that kind of payoff, I'd rather let the hand go and wait for a better opportunity.

When you do get the right situations and a little luck, small pairs can be very profitable. A long-time player I know likes to tell the story of a session where he was dealt eight pairs of deuces, drew to all of them, and made his set eight straight times! It was the biggest winning session of his life.

# Ace-King

Ace-king, also known as "Big Slick," is a peculiar hand. Most beginners, when picking up ace-king, think they've hit the jackpot. Experienced players are a little more circumspect. To see why, let's watch what happens when we match ace-king against a variety of hands, and deal down to the river.

First, let's pit ace-king against some smaller pairs:

- Against a pair of queens, it's 43 percent to win.
- Against a pair of deuces, it's 47 percent to win.

So against any smaller pair, ace-king is a small underdog.

Now let's match it against some smaller live cards (non-dominated):

- Against queen-jack offsuit, it's 64 percent to win.
- Against ten-seven offsuit, it's also 64 percent to win.
- Against seven-six suited, it's 58 percent to win.

- Against four-three suited, it's 60 percent to win.

Not so impressive. Ace-king is a solid, but unspectacular favorite in all these matchups.

When ace-king encounters some hands that it dominates, the results get better. Take a look at these pairings:

- Against ace-jack offsuit, it's 74 percent to win.
- Against ace-three offsuit, it's still 74 percent to win.
- Against king-queen offsuit, it's 70 percent to win.

Against dominated hands, ace-king is more than 70 percent to win in each case.

The only disaster for ace-king occurs when it runs into either aces or kings. Take a look:

- Against aces, it's 7 percent to win.
- Against kings, it's 30 percent to win.

Kings are bad, aces are terrible. Fortunately, these disaster pairings are extremely rare. Once you remove an ace and a king from the deck, only 1,225 two-card combinations remain. Of these, only three are a pair of aces, and three more are a pair of kings. That's six bad hands out of 1,225, so it's about 200-to-1 against any particular opponent having one of those two hands. If you have ace-king and you're sitting at a nine-handed table, the probability that anyone at the table has aces or kings is only about 4 percent.

With this information in mind, we can see why ace-king is an odd hand. It's not a big favorite against any hand, although it does pretty well in a domination situation. It's also not a big underdog to any hand, except the top two pairs.

These characteristics make ace-king an excellent hand in many tournament situations. With a smallish stack, you can move all-in with impunity, knowing that you'll often pick up the pot, and when you don't, you'll be a small favorite or a small underdog.

In cash games, however, ace-king doesn't play quite so well. You're not looking to get all your money in preflop, and when played normally, ace-king is a good, but not overwhelming hand.

Moreover, it has a significant weakness. It's another hand which tends to win a lot of small pots, but lose some big ones. When you make a hand, it's generally top pair, top kicker. Your opponents aren't going to get a lot of their stacks involved if they can't beat top pair, top kicker.

Having said all that, ace-king is still a very good hand, and it should be played aggressively. If you're first to act, here are my guidelines:

1.  **Early position:** Mostly raise, sometimes limp. A 75-to-25 percent ratio of raises to limps is good.

2.  **Middle position:** Even more raises, and very few limps. You're happy to win the pot right now with your ace-high hand.

3.  **Late position:** Same as middle position.

When the pot is opened in front of me, I'm playing my ace-king in almost all situations. If there are limpers, I will raise them. If there is a raiser, I will call. The only situation that causes a real problem is a raise followed by a reraise both in front of me, in which case I'll fold. There's too much danger that one of the hands in the mix is one of the two hands to fear.

# Ace-Queen

Ace-queen is a lot like ace-king, only weaker. While ace-king feared only two hands (aces and kings), ace-queen fears aces, kings, queens, and ace-king itself. So while ace-king is a big underdog to 6 hands out of 1,225, ace-queen is a big underdog to 24 hands out of 1,225: four times as many!

Having said that, I wouldn't play the two hands very differently preflop. With ace-queen my strategy will still be mostly raising when first in the pot, with a few limps for variety.

I would still tend to call a single raiser with ace-queen. If the raiser was in early position and there were several players left to act after me, ace-queen unsuited would hit the muck.

Ace-queen remains a good hand for attacking limpers, so I would raise if some number of players had limped in front of me.

I would certainly fold ace-queen to a raise and a reraise.

# Ace-Jack
# through Ace-Deuce

I'm grouping all the ace-x hands below ace-queen together, both suited and unsuited, because they share certain common characteristics. As a group, they are perhaps the most overrated and dangerous hands for beginners and intermediates to play. All these hands share a common and extremely troublesome characteristic in no-limit cash games: they tend to win small pots and lose big ones. As such, they are hands that have to be played very carefully.

What are some of the problems of these hands? Here's a partial list:

1. They are easily dominated by better aces.

2. Really good flops are few and far between.

3. When you make a big hand, it's hard to get action.

Let's look at each of these points in turn.

**Point No. 1: Easy domination.** Suppose you pick up ace-ten offsuit in third position and raise to open the pot. Everyone folds but the button, who calls. Now the flop comes ace-nine-eight. You hit your ace. Are you happy? Now you bet, and your opponent calls. The turn comes a five. Are you happy? You bet again, and now he raises. *What do you do?*

Consider this: if your opponent has an ace, what ace can you beat? You're losing to ace-king, ace-queen, ace-jack, tying ace-ten, losing to ace-nine, ace-eight, and ace-five, and beating only an ace with a seven, six, four, trey, or deuce. Your opponent saw you raise preflop, then bet twice after an ace came on the flop. Can you reasonably put him on a hand lower than a pair of aces at this point?

This example illustrates the big dilemma with ace-x hands. If an ace comes on the flop, you have to be very worried about being dominated by a better ace. If you don't really want an ace to come on the flop, however, you don't have that many flops that can help you. If you get a flop like ten-eight-four, you have top pair, top kicker, which is pretty good — for winning a small pot.

**Point No. 2: Few great flops.** A great flop for an ace-x hand is a flop that gives you two pair (or better). The bad news is that flops this good only happen about 5 percent of the time. The good news is that when they do occur you have a legitimate chance at a good pot, if anyone will stay with you.

**Point No. 3: Hard to get action.** Ace-x suited is a hand that many beginners and intermediates like, and they'll limp or call to see a flop with it, regardless of position, because they like the chance of hitting the nut flush. While the nut flush is a great hand, it's also a visible great hand. Once the third flush card appears on board, the action may (or should) dry up.

Contrast this with a hand like nine-seven offsuit which can make a completely concealed straight, and hence get great action from two pair hands and sets.

Now three last thoughts about the ace-x hands before we give specific advice on how to play them.

1.  **They benefit greatly from position:** The better your position, the more playable these hands become. If the hand is folded to you in the cutoff seat and no one has opened, the chance that you hold the only ace at the table rises dramatically. Now even an ace with a low kicker has an excellent chance to be the best hand at the table, and can be played aggressively.

    If someone opens the pot in front of you and you're on the button, and you call, you benefit from getting more information after the flop before you have to act. If an ace flops and your opponent checks rather than betting, you have some extra evidence (certainly not conclusive, but suggestive) that your opponent doesn't hold an ace and your hand may be best.

2.  **They play much better at short-handed tables:** Just as position favors the ace-small hands, so do short-handed tables. The fewer players at the table, the less likelihood that a dominating ace is present in another hand. Consequently, at five-handed and six-handed tables, these hands can be played much more aggressively.

3.  **They play much better at weak, low-stakes tables:** At a weak table, players are prone to play aces of any sort. Hence, if you play an ace-jack, you're much more likely to be in a dominating position after the flop. (At a strong table, players are keeping ace-king and ace-queen and often throwing the rest of the aces away.) In addition, your ace-x suited is much more likely to get paid off when you hit your flush since weak players are paying more attention to their hand and less attention to the board and the betting.

Here are my general recommendations for playing the ace-x hands at medium to strong tables when first to open the betting.

- **In early position:** Play only ace-jack suited with a mixture of raises and calls. Throw all other ace-x hands away with the exception of sometimes playing ace-ten suited.

- **In middle position:** Ace-jack through ace-seven become playable in middle position. Play these hands with a mixture of raises and calls, using a 75-to-25 percent raise-to-call ratio for the stronger hands, and a 50-50 ratio for the weaker hands.

- **In late position:** All the aces become playable. Taking the blinds is a good result, so use very high raise-to-call ratios, anywhere from 80-to-20 to 90-to-10.

At a weak table, you can play almost all your aces, although with some caution. I would, however, throw away hands below ace-nine unsuited in early position.

After a raise, throw all of these hands away unless you're against a known weak player. Against said weak player, use common sense and caution.

Against limpers, I would call with ace-jack or ace-ten and fold the rest. Many players limp with ace-x hands, and you don't want to be caught in a dominated situation.

One last word on the ace-small suited hands. These are best played in late position, after either several limpers or an early raise followed by a couple of calls. The more players in the pot, the better you like it. In those situations, you're getting good expressed odds to play the hand, and some reason to believe your implied odds may be there as well. As with the small pairs, you want both you and your opponents to have deep stacks. As a bare minimum, I want to see my opponents with stacks at least 25 to 30 times the money I need to call, and preferably much more.

# The Trouble Hands

The term "trouble hands" (which was first used by Doyle Brunson in his book *Super/System*) collectively refers to a group of five hands: king-queen, king-jack, king-ten, queen-jack, and queen-ten. Since the hands all contain high cards, they look like hands you want to play, and in many cases they *are* hands you want to play. In no-limit hold 'em, however, they require an extra measure of caution because they are easily dominated by ace-high hands or even by other hands in the group.

When you play these hands, hit the flop with one high card, and then get action, you won't know exactly where you stand. You may have top pair, with no obvious straights or flushes, and still have to let the hand go because of the implicit danger to your whole stack. They're difficult hands to play, even for top players, and hence the appellation "trouble hands."

Let's start with some general guidelines for playing these hands. As you'll see, with these hands I strongly believe in erring on the side of caution.

1.  The trouble hands are hands with which you want to either steal the blinds or win the pot with a bet on the flop. They are not hands to take to the river in a big pot. The exception obviously occurs when you flop a strong straight or flush draw, in which case they graduate from trouble hands to drawing hands.

2.  These hands play best against a single opponent. The more opponents you have, the less you like them.

3.  Don't call raises with these hands. There's too much danger that the hand which is raising is exactly the hand you fear.

Now let's look at some specific guidelines for playing when you're first in the pot.

- **In early position:** The only hand I'm happy playing in early position is king-queen suited which can be played by either raising or calling. At a weakish table, I might choose to limp with king-queen offsuit or king-jack suited. The other hands are too weak to be played here.

- **In middle position:** I'll play king-queen aggressively, mostly raising but sometimes limping. I'll also play king-jack and queen-jack with a mixture of raises and limps. King-ten and queen-ten, suited or offsuit, are still hands I would fold.

- **In late position:** I would raise with all these hands in late position, hoping to steal the blinds.

After a raise, throw all these hands away. After several limpers, I don't mind calling with king-queen and king-jack, suited or offsuited. Here your hand benefits from position since if there have been several limpers you must be in good position. I would still discard the other hands in this group. Even with king-queen and king-jack, however, I'll be very cautious after the flop. Against multiple opponents, I need a strong hand or a strong draw to continue.

## Suited Connectors

The suited connectors form an ideal group of hands for diversification and deception. Because they carry well-disguised straight and flush possibilities, I'm willing to use them in all positions when I'm first in the pot to disguise my play. Here's a quick rundown of my suited connector strategy when first to act.

- **In early position:** I'll raise with suited connectors in early position, but not too often. Why not? There are too many suited connectors for my purposes. If I were to raise with all the suited connectors I was dealt in early position, in addition to my premium pairs and ace-king, the bulk of my early raises would actually be with suited connectors! It wouldn't take my opponents too long to figure out that my early raises were mostly bluffs, and react accordingly. So I need to play just enough suited connectors to hit my opponents with the occasional unpleasant surprise, but not so often that they can be confident of what I'm doing. A good practical approach is to raise with somewhere between 15 and 25 percent of the suited connectors I'm dealt, folding the rest.

- **In middle position:** Since I'm playing more value hands in middle position, I can use more suited connectors as well. Here I'll play the larger suited connectors (jack-ten through seven-six), dividing them between raises and limps. At a tight table, I'll play some of the smaller suited connectors as well.

- **In late position:** Now I'm playing more hands, so I'll play all the suited connectors as well, mostly raising to steal the blinds.

With suited connectors, you need to be careful calling raises. The ideal situation for these hands is to play them in good position after several limpers, or after a raise followed by several callers. That way the suited connectors get three advantages:

1.  Better expressed odds from the larger pot.

2.  Better implied odds when they make a good draw since there are more opponents and hence more chances that someone else actually has a hand.

3.  Better winning chances from good position.

Consequently, my rules for suited connectors when not first in the pot are these:

1.  Don't call a single raiser.

2.  Call a raiser in position after at least one, and preferably two other callers.

3.  Limp in after two or more limpers.

Avoid playing these hands in the blinds unless there are already several people in the pot and the expressed odds are very good. Ideally, you'd like to play if you're getting 2-to-1 odds or better and you're facing a minimum of two opponents.

# Other Playable Hands

This group comprises all the remaining types of hands that are playable, including:

1.  Unsuited connectors (ten-nine offsuit, etc.)

2.  Suited and unsuited one-gappers (nine-seven, etc.)

3.  Suited and unsuited two-gappers (nine-six, etc.)

Hands even worse than these I just won't play in a cash game under any circumstances (although some players do).

In general, playing these hands requires a combination of circumstances to be right:

1.  Good position.

2.  A tight table with a lot of players folding to the first raise.

3.  A table with little or no reraising.

The latter is most important. When I play these hands, my purpose is to steal the blinds or because of the latent big-pot potential. In order for the big-pot potential to come into play, I have to actually see a flop! Hence, it's important not to get reraised after I've led out or called someone else's raise.

Even a tight-aggressive player needs to play these hands once in a while. Remember that one of the key goals in playing deceptively is to ensure that each flop contains a threat. Your opponent must feel that you play in such a way that any flop might have hit your hand. In order to achieve that goal, you'll need to play some of these hands some of the time. If a flop comes

your opponent needs to know that although you raised from middle position preflop, you could still have jack-nine or nine-six, and be sitting there with the stone cold nuts.

As we shall see later when we discuss loose-aggressive play, the big difference between the tight-aggressive player and the loose-aggressive player is how often they play these hands, and how aggressively they play them after the flop. If you're planning on playing a tight-aggressive style, I would recommend that you play these hands only occasionally. Remember that you only have to showdown one nut straight with a totally unexpected hand like nine-six to make a lasting impression on the table, and making that impression is what these hands are all about.

# Playing the Small Blind

When I'm in the small blind and the hand is folded around to me, it's only half a big blind to call, so I'm getting 3-to-1 odds. Those are great odds, so most hands become playable.

If I limp a lot in this situation, most players in the big blind will try to find out if they can push me out of the pot with a raise. To prevent that, it's necessary to limp with some of my very good hands so I can respond to his raise with a call or even a reraise. A couple of calls will be enough to discourage the big blind from raising without solid values.

With those thoughts in mind, here are my guidelines for playing the small blind in a big blind versus small blind confrontation:

1. Since you can get 3-to-1 odds to play, throw away only hands in the bottom 20 percent, i.e., the ten-four, nine-three, and eight-deuce type hands.

2. Of the remaining hands, raise about 30 percent of the time, limp the remaining 70 percent.

3. Save many of your good hands for limping, including some aces, some pairs, and some hands with two high cards. When the big blind raises you, you need some good hands to comfortably call or even reraise.

4. If you miss the flop, but you have high cards, don't feel you need to bet. Be willing to check the hand down so the big blind can see that a preflop limp on your part doesn't necessarily mean weakness. Also, at this point, your hand is good enough to catch bluffs.

Pay careful attention to what the big blind does at all times. Remember that you'll be in this relationship as long as you're both at the table, so what happens in these confrontations, and who can adjust better to the other, is important.

# Playing the Big Blind

The big blind is in a unique position compared to everyone else at the table.

1.  Because he is the last player to act preflop, he has more information available to him than any other player.

2.  Because he has already put some money in the pot, he has more favorable odds available to him than any other player. (Often, in fact, he'll see the flop for free.)

3.  Because he acts first or second on any subsequent betting round, his later position will be poor.

The first two conditions tempt him to loosen his standards and play more pots. The last condition slams on the breaks and says, "Be very careful."

In practical play, the big blind faces two recurring tactical problems:

1.  "My hand is weak but I'm being offered pretty good pot odds. What do I do?"

2.  "A player in stealing position has raised the pot. What hand do I need to call or raise?"

Let's take these two problems one at a time. First, consider the problem of a weak hand but good odds.

Let's imagine you're in the big blind in a $5-$10 game. In front of you there's a raise to $30 and three callers. The small blind folds. The pot is $135 and you only need to put in $20 to call. The pot is offering you almost 7-to-1. You look down and see

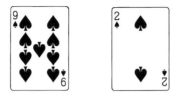

*What do you want to do?*

The pot odds, 7-to-1, sound pretty good. A lot of players look at two suited cards and simply toss a couple of chips in the pot. "How far off can the odds be? I'm playing."

So let's ask a good question here. What are the real odds for a hand like nine-deuce suited? Using PokerStove, we constructed some sample hand sets to see how nine-deuce suited really stands in practice. We also ran the same hand sets against nine-deuce offsuit to see how much edge the suited hand had. The results were a bit surprising.

**Set No. 1:** Here we're against a pretty average collection of hands: ace-king offsuit, jack-ten suited (but not in spades), a pair of eights, and a pair of fours. The ace-king made the raise and everyone else called. The nine-deuce suited is 15 percent against this set — not quite a 7-to-1 underdog, and an offsuit nine-deuce drops to 10 percent —a 9-to-1 underdog.

The nine-deuce offsuit is obviously in bad shape, but at first glance it looks like the nine-deuce suited is getting the odds needed. However, there are a couple of further problems. The big blind is out of position through the whole hand, which hurts its chances somewhat. And the percentages assume that the hand will be played to a conclusion with no further betting, which won't be the case. Most of the time, the big blind will be out of the hand after the flop, leaving some hard-to-quantify amount of equity on the table.

Let's look at a few other sets of plausible opposing hands and see what happens.

**Set No. 2:** Here we're against ace-king offsuit, a pair of tens, jack-ten suited, and a pair of fours. This is the same as Set No. 1 except one of the pairs is now higher than our nine. Now the chances drop precipitously. Nine-deuce suited is 12 percent — more than a 7-to-1 underdog, and the offsuit cards are 8 percent — an 11-to-1 underdog. Facing a pair higher than our highest card is a disaster.

**Set No. 3:** Now we face ace-king offsuit, a pair of jacks, ten-nine suited, and a pair of fours. With one of our nines out in another hand, our chances sink some more, to 8 percent for the suited cards and 6 percent for the unsuited cards.

**Set No. 4:** If our opponents are mostly playing high cards, we're all right. Against a set of ace-king offsuit, queen-jack offsuit, king-queen offsuit, and a pair of fours, we're 18 percent suited and 14 percent unsuited. Even out of position, we can probably squeeze out a call here, if we knew what they had.

The bottom line is that random cards combined with apparently big pot odds in the big blind doesn't equal a call. We need a semi-reasonable hand to compensate for our poor position and the sheer number of hands we need to beat. That's because the probability of winning the pot is going down faster than the size of the pot is going up.

Let's continue with this process and start substituting other reasonable hands for the nine-deuce suited and offsuit. We'll see how each hand does, played to the end, against the four sets of opposing hands we already defined.

| | Hand Sets | | | |
|---|---|---|---|---|
| | No. 1 (%) | No. 2 (%) | No. 3 (%) | No. 4 (%) |
| KT suited | 14.2 | 11.6 | 5.7 | 17.4 |
| KT offsuit | 10.4 | 4.8 | 4.6 | 12.1 |
| 75 suited | 15.5 | 14.6 | 16.7 | 23.2 |
| 75 offsuit | 10.7 | 12.7 | 12.1 | 20.3 |
| A9 suited | 14.5 | 9.2 | 9.6 | 17.1 |
| A9 offsuit | 9.6 | 6.1 | 4.4 | 14.3 |
| 54 suited | 14.8 | 16.3 | 13.6 | 25.1 |
| 54 offsuit | 11.8 | 12.1 | 10.5 | 19.6 |

As we look at this table, a few ideas pop out:

- The small suited and unsuited cards do surprisingly well because they usually aren't threatened with domination. Notice that king-ten, a hand likely to be dominated when multiple hands are in the pot, does worse than seven-five against all the hand sets in our example!

- The suited hands do *much* better than their unsuited counterparts. In a heads-up contest of two random hands, changing one hand from unsuited to suited usually adds only about 3 percent to the winning chances. But in the table above, changing a hand from unsuited to suited will usually add 30 to 50 percent to the winning chances. Why? Because for many of these hands, making a flush is actually the easiest way to win.

- Hands that can be dominated easily are surprisingly weak. King-ten offsuit, for example, isn't getting the odds it needs against any set of hands in our sample, even before we take position into account.

The moral here is that you can't call a raise in the big blind with random slop even though the pot odds seem very attractive. If you don't actually have a good hand you're happy to play, look for suited cards that aren't easily dominated.

Now on to the second big blind problem. We've been raised by someone in an obvious stealing position, say the button or the cutoff seat. How good a hand do we need to call?

Most players call in the big blind with too many hands. They're favorably influenced by the pot odds, which always seem favorable, and by the idea that "He's raising from a steal position, he could have anything." Sure, he might have anything, but one thing he certainly has is position. If you call with two unpaired cards, what will mostly happen is the following:

1. You miss the flop 70 percent of the time.

2. You check the flop.

3. He bets.

Now what? You've got nothing, you're out of position, and you've got a bet to call. You can lose an awful lot of chips in this scenario over the long haul.

I recommend a conservative approach, at least at the start of the session, to handle steal attempts. Play the following hands:

1. Pairs,
2. Aces,
3. Two high cards, and
4. Suited connectors down to seven-six.

Be willing to reraise with the better hands in this group remembering that preflop is the only part of the hand where your position is good.

As you play a session, the players in the button and cutoff seats will remain the same relative to you, so study them carefully. You're particularly interested in how often they raise when the hand is folded to them. As soon as you get some good information, act on it. If you see a player raise three times out of four in stealing position, widen your calling and raising ranges substantially and immediately. The evidence you've seen is the best evidence you have, so act. But don't broaden your range until you actually have evidence that your opponent has broadened his.

# Attacking Limpers

You're in late position and three or more players have limped in front of you. How strong a hand do you need to attack the limpers with a raise? How strong a hand do you need to just call?

Most players are actually too aggressive attacking limpers. While it's true that limping indicates some weakness (in general), and while you'll have position on these players after the flop, it's also true that you're now facing several players, so your hand may not be as strong as it appears. Don't be in a hurry to think of limpers' money as simply dead money to be swept up. Many players will defend their limps vigorously, and you don't want to take on a crowd without a premium hand.

The only hands where I'm completely comfortable raising a bunch of limpers (three or more) are the premium pairs, aces through tens, ace-king, and ace-queen suited. That's it. Everything else is situation-dependent. If the table is super-tight, and a lot of these players will surrender their limps to a raise, then I'll move my requirements a little bit and consider raising with ace-jack and ace-ten, and maybe a couple of the middle pairs. But to move my requirements any more, the situation will now be that I'm going to have a worse hand on average than the best of the limpers' hands.

# The Gap Concept in Deep-Stack Poker

The Gap Concept was introduced by David Sklansky in his book *Tournament Poker for Advanced Players*. The basic idea is pretty simple. Suppose the pot is opened in front of you by a player who has a solid, reliable opening range. You have a hand which is a minimum opening hand for your position. Should you call? The Gap Concept says no. In fact, you need a much stronger hand than the minimum opening hand to call for these reasons:

1. Your opponent opened in an earlier position than you, so his minimum opening hand is better than your minimum opening hand.

2. He didn't necessarily open with his minimum hand. He opened with a hand that, on average, was halfway between his best hand and his minimum hand.

In order to compensate, you need to call with a hand that's better than his minimum by some amount. The distance between the hand you actually need and the minimum hand for his position is what Sklansky termed "the Gap."

For instance, suppose a conservative opponent raised the pot in early position and the hand was folded around to you in late position. Knowing this opponent, you believe he would only have opened with one of these hands: a pair between aces and eights, ace-jack or higher, or king-queen. In order to call, you need a hand that's situated more toward the middle of his range: say a pair of tens or better, or ace-king or ace-queen.

The Gap Concept works very well in limit poker and in many tournament situations. In deep-stack poker, however, we have to make some adjustments. For deep stacks, let's restate the Gap Concept as follows:

> For hands designed to play small pots, the Gap Concept applies in full; you need a hand considerably better than the minimum hand your opponent would have used to raise in order to call.

> For hands which benefit from the massive implied odds present in deep stack poker, the Gap Concept doesn't apply.

To illustrate, suppose your conservative opponent opens in early position with a standard raise. In late position, you have ace-nine. Ace-nine isn't a suitable hand for playing a big pot, and it's weaker than the minimum hand your opponent would have used to raise, so the Gap Concept applies and you fold.

On the other hand, suppose in this situation you have nine-seven suited. This hand is objectively weaker than ace-nine, but it serves a different purpose. It's designed to win your opponent's whole stack by making a concealed monster. In this case, the Gap Concept doesn't fully apply and you can call with this hand as part of a balanced strategy. (You would not, however, call every time you had such a hand, or your strategy would become unbalanced very quickly.)

# The Problems

## Hand 3-1

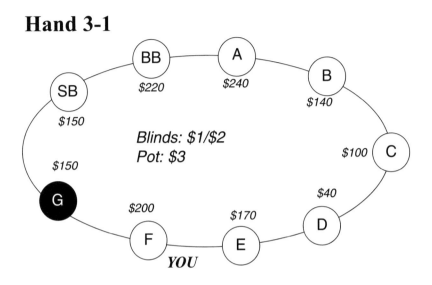

**Situation:** Small stakes online game. You sat down about 20 hands ago. Player D hasn't been involved in a hand until now.

**Your hand:** 3♥3♠

**Action to you:** Players A, B, and C fold. Player D raises to $8.

**Question:** *Do you fold, call, or raise?*
    **Answer:** It's 7-to-1 against improving your hand to a set. Your opponent bet $8 and has only $32 left in his stack. You can't win enough money when you improve to justify your call, and you won't be able to call a later bet with your treys if you don't improve.

    In addition, there are still three players to act behind you, and any one of them could raise you out of the pot. So fold.

**Action:** You fold.

# Hand 3-2

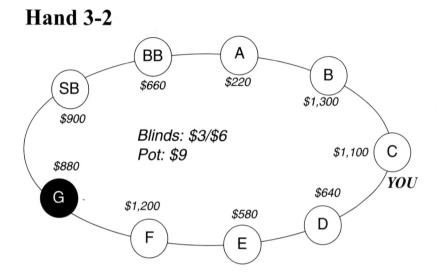

**Situation:** Medium stakes online game. You've played about 100 hands. Player B is tight and so far has always had the goods when he raises in early position. Players D, F, and G seem pretty aggressive.

**Your hand:** 6♥4♥

**Action to you:** Player A folds. Player B raises to $20.

**Question:** *Do you fold, call, or raise?*
  **Answer:** Unlike the previous problem, the stacks here are big enough for a speculative call with this sort of drawing hand. However, your position is poor. Six more players are still to act in the hand, anyone of whom could raise you off the pot. Again, you should fold.
    To make these plays, you want both big stack sizes and good position. During the course of a typical session, you'll get dealt far more of these sorts of hands (suited connectors, unsuited connectors, one-gap connectors, etc.) than you need to diversify your play. You can restrict yourself to playing

only those hands where the conditions are just right, and still have plenty of opportunities to get in there and mix up your game.

**Action:** You fold.

# Hand 3-3

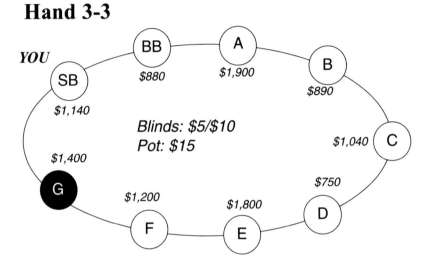

**Situation:** Medium stakes online game. You've been playing for about an hour. Generally tight table. Player F seems to raise more than his share when the table folds to him.

**Your hand:** 9♥9♠

**Action to you:** Players A, B, C, D, and E fold. Player F raises to $40. The button folds.

**Question:** *Do you fold, call, or raise?*
    **Answer:** Medium pairs are tricky to play preflop. While they're often the best hand at that stage, they are difficult to improve and difficult to play when a couple of high cards come on the flop.

Player F raised after five folds. From your previous observations, he doesn't need a premium hand for this raise. He could have a small pair, or two high cards, or ace-x, or even something weaker. He could, of course, also have a pair higher than yours.

Calling isn't a terrible play but it can put you in a pressure situation after the flop. If the flop comes queen-jack-seven, will you bet or check? If you check and he bets the turn, will you stick around? Either folding or calling might be a big mistake. Instead of playing out of position and waiting for the pressure to be applied to you, make a substantial raise and put the pressure on him. Even if he calls, he may have to fold to a continuation bet on the flop.

**Action:** You raise to $240. The big blind folds. After some thought, so does Player F.

# Hand 3-4

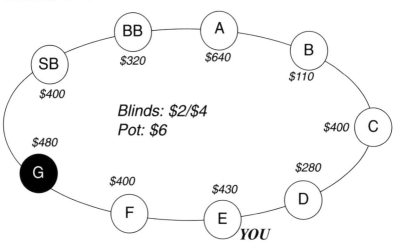

**Situation:** Medium stakes online game. You've only been playing a few hands, but you've already picked up a couple of pots. You don't have any information on the big blind.

**Your hand:** T♦9♦

**Action to you:** Players A, B, C, and D fold.

**Question:** *Do you fold, call, or raise?*
**Answer:** The players behind me would have to be extremely aggressive for me to lay this hand down after four folds. Since we don't have much information yet, I'm ruling out folding as an option.

Either limping or raising is an acceptable play. If your style is to raise whenever you're first to enter the pot, then raise to $10 or $12 here. My tendency is to limp or raise in about a 50-50 proportion.

**Action:** You limp for $4. Players F and G fold. The small blind limps for $2. The big blind raises $8 to $12. The pot is now $20.

**Question:** *What do you do?*
**Answer:** The big blind makes a small raise out of position. That's an unusual play since he's offering good pot odds to the other players in the hand. It might be a trap. On the other hand, it might just be a bad play. Don't assume your opponents are wizards until they've shown that's the case. You're in position, with suited connectors, getting 2.5-to-1 odds. In addition, both your stack and the big blind's stack are deep enough so the implied odds you need with a hand like this are present. You should call.

**Action:** You fold. The small blind folds. The big blind takes the pot.

Folding isn't a really bad play, and at a very aggressive table, it might be the right play. But your job in a no-limit cash game is to see a lot of cheap flops, and the flop here would have been cheap enough given your position and the pot size.

# Hand 3-5

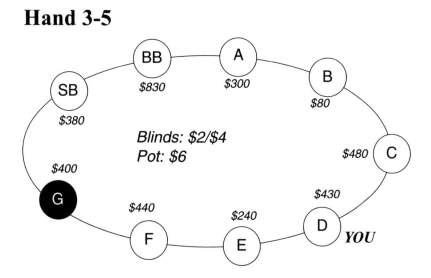

**Situation:** Same table as the previous example. You've now played about 50 hands. The table is generally tight. Players A and F are the most aggressive of the bunch, but they're not over the top. You've been playing quietly and are a little ahead at this point.

**Your hand:** 9♠8♠

**Action to you:** Player A raises to $16. Players B and C fold.

**Question:** *Do you fold, call, or raise?*
> **Answer:** This is a hand where complementary strategies and randomizing come into play. Nine-eight suited isn't a hand that's technically strong enough to call a first position raise, even from a player you've labeled as "somewhat aggressive." However, you can't simply restrict yourself to calling raises with pocket pairs or ace-king. Players at the table need to know that a flop that comes nine-seven-six might have hit you in some way.

I would make this call 25 to 35 percent of the time. Calls like this have the added merit (if your hand is eventually exposed) of showing your opponents that you're an action player, which helps you enormously when you hit a really good hand. Use your watch second hand as a randomizer, give it a quick glance, and make your decision based on that.

**Action:** You fold.

# Hand 3-6

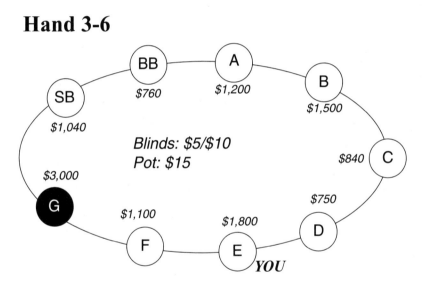

**Situation:** Medium stakes live game. You're familiar with some of the players. Player B is tight and aggressive. Player G is loose and aggressive. He's been pushing the table around, and has won some nice pots.

**Your hand:** T♦T♣

**Action to you:** Player A folds. Player B raises to $30. Players C and D fold.

**Question:** *Do you fold, call, or raise?*

    **Answer:** A pair of tens is a good medium pair. You can't consider folding just because someone raised in early position. You're a favorite against a lot of the hands they might be playing.

    But it's not a reraising hand either. For reraises, I want a genuinely big pair like aces, kings, or queens, or a hand like ace-king. A pair of tens just isn't good enough for this purpose. So simply calling is the right idea.

**Action:** You call $30. Player F folds. Player G, on the button, raises to $100. The blinds fold. Player B calls, putting another $70 in the pot. The pot is now $245, and it costs you $70 to call.

**Question:** *What do you do?*

    **Answer:** You call. "What?" some will object. You're obviously up against one big hand, perhaps two. "How can you call with just a medium pair?"

    Pot odds are the reason. Your tens are no longer a medium pair. Now they're a drawing hand. As a drawing hand, you're a 7-to-1 underdog to hit a set, and right now you're getting 3.5-to-1 expressed odds to draw. Your opponents both have big stacks, and the fellow behind you, at least, has shown he's willing to mix things up. If you hit a ten on the flop, you're going to win some more money, depending on just how you play the hand. One can never be precise about implied odds, but this is as favorable a situation as you're likely to see. Your call ends the betting, so you can see exactly the odds you're getting. Take the odds, call, and see the flop.

**Action:** You call $70. The pot is now $315.

**Flop:** 7♠6♥4♣

**Action:** Player B checks.

**Question:** *What do you do?*

> **Answer:** You check. Your call was predicated on seeing the flop, and you missed it, so you're done with the hand. Your preflop analysis was correct. One (or both) of these players probably has you beaten right now.

**Action:** You check. Player G bets $400. Player A folds. You fold.

This fold might seem excessively conservative to some players. After all, you have an overpair to the board, and Player G was supposed to be a loose-aggressive player who's been pushing the table around. *Isn't that enough to justify a call?*

Notice, however, two key points. First, even loose-aggressive players don't routinely reraise two players who've already shown an interest in the hand. There's easier money to be made than trying to steal from players who may already have big hands. Second, Player G's large bet starts to raise pot-commitment issues. If you call, your stack will be $1,300 and the pot will be $1,115. Any further action beyond this point could tie you to the pot, so this is the right time to make a firm decision on your real interest in the hand. While you have a hand, it's not good enough to take to the end, so let it go now.

# Hand 3-7

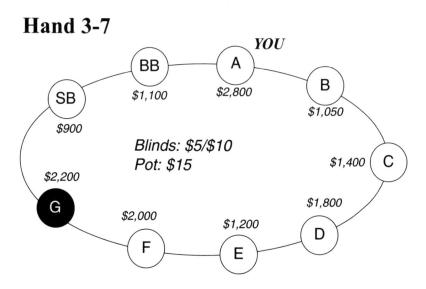

**Situation:** Medium stakes live game. You've been playing for awhile. The players like to see flops. Player G and the small blind are the most aggressive at the table.

**Your hand:** Q♥Q♠

**Question:** *Do you limp or raise?*
> **Answer:** I strongly think you have to raise with this hand. Queens just aren't suitable for limping. While balanced strategies are also important, this is an occasion where I would simply make the high-percentage play and raise to $30 or so. Playing queens normally in first position is a play that will show a long-run profit, but limping is more questionable. If you provoke a series of limpers followed by a big raise from late position, you're a lot less comfortable sticking in a big reraise with queens than you would be with aces or kings. You'll have plenty of other chances to diversify your play; this isn't one of them. Raise.

**Action:** You call $10. Player B folds. Players C and D call $10. Players E and F fold. Player G calls $10. The small blind calls $5 and the big blind checks. The pot is $60 and you will act third out of six players after the flop.

**Flop:** 8♣5♥4♦

**Action:** The small blind and the big blind both check.

**Question:** *What do you do?*

> **Answer:** That's a pretty good flop for you. There's no ace, no king, and no flush draw, all of which are a big plus. With five other players, this flop has probably given one or two players a pair, while a couple of others may have straight draws. Only someone with exactly seven-six has a straight, and as always, there's some possibility that a set or two pair is out there.
>
> Checking and hoping that someone else takes the lead is too dangerous. So many cards can come on the turn that will stop you from betting that you either have to make a move now or resign yourself to trying to check the hand down. I would make a pot-sized bet here of $60 and see what happens.

**Action:** You check. Players C and D check. Player G bets $45. The small blind folds. The big blind calls $45. The pot is now $150.

**Question:** *What do you do?*

> **Answer:** Last chance to make a move. The action is still not unfavorable for you. The last player in line, a very aggressive player, bet after everyone has checked. Probably means he has something, but doesn't signify yet he has much. The big blind calls, which again shows something, but not enough to

reraise. He might have something like a pair and an inside straight draw, or a pair and a backdoor flush draw.

Your queens are still good enough to raise. As we noted before, if you don't make a move for the pot now, the board will probably be too dangerous after the turn card arrives. I would raise to $200, a slightly smaller than pot-sized raise.

**Action:** You just call $45. Players C and D fold. The pot is $195, and three players remain.

**Turn: 6♥**

**Action:** The small blind checks.

**Question:** *What do you do?*

**Answer:** Anyone with a seven now has a straight. The highly connected nature of the board now makes many two-pair hands possible since players tend to limp with connected cards or one-gappers.

Betting now is too risky. Your best play is to hope that your hand is still best and you can check it down with the obvious straight possibility freezing the betting.

**Action:** You check. Player G checks. The pot remains at $195.

**River: 2♦**

**Action:** The big blind bets $100.

**Question:** *What do you do?*

**Answer:** The big blind took his last chance to bet and bet only half the pot. With the pot odds he's giving (you'd be getting 3-to-1 on your money) he's looking for a call. Your overpair isn't good anymore. Save your money and fold.

**Action:** You fold. Player G folds. The big blind wins the pot.

# Hand 3-8

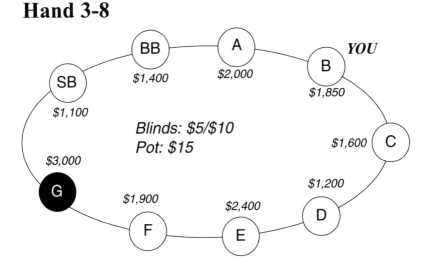

**Situation:** Medium stakes live game. You've been playing for awhile. The players seem tough and experienced. Players E and G are very aggressive, frequently raising from late position.

**Your hand:** 4♣4♦

**Action:** Player A folds.

**Question:** *Do you fold, limp, or raise?*
> **Answer:** You should fold. This is the worst possible situation for playing a low pair. It's a tough table, you're out of position, and you have aggressive players behind you who like to raise. You should only play small pairs when all the circumstances are right. Here they're not.

**Action:** You actually call $10. Players C and D fold. Player E raises to $40. Players F and G fold. The blinds fold. The pot is now $65, and it costs you $30 to call.

**Question:** *What do you do?*
    **Answer:** Small pairs don't play well out of position, so fold. Your opponent says he has a good hand. You have to hit a set to continue playing after the flop unless you plan to bluff out of position. You're 7-to-1 against hitting your set, and the pot is only offering 2-to-1. This is a good time to get out.

**Action:** You actually call $30. The pot is now $95.

**Flop:** A♥9♦4♠

**Question:** *Do you check or bet?*
    **Answer:** That's a great flop, and now you're in good shape. Since Player E took the lead in the betting preflop, and an ace came, which would have helped many of his possible holdings, you should check. Let him take the lead, and then you can decide if you want to check-raise or not.

**Action:** You check. Player E bets $70. The pot is now $165.

**Question:** *What do you do?*
    **Answer:** The ace didn't bother him, so his most likely hand right now is an ace with a good kicker, perhaps ace-king, ace-queen, or ace-jack. You can call or you can raise right now. Both plays have merit.
    If he has one of the hands you suspect, he doesn't have any immediate outs, although there are two-card combinations that will beat you. (You're a 98 percent favorite). If he has exactly ace-nine, he has four outs. (You're an 83 percent favorite). And if he happens to have hit a set of aces or nines, then *you* have one out (twice). (You're 4 percent to win.) You're in a way ahead/way behind situation, so you can afford to give him a card. The question is, do you want to?

If you raise right now, on a board devoid of draws, there are a limited number of hands you could be representing. You could have a set, you could have ace-nine or conceivably ace-four (although that was a pretty weak preflop call), you could have the best ace, ace-king, or you could be bluffing. That's about it.

1.  If he has a hand like ace-queen or less, he can only beat a bluff. With deep stacks, he's not going to want to get much more of his stack involved trying to figure out if you're bluffing. So he'll probably fold those hands.

2.  If he has exactly ace-king, he'll figure he may have a better ace than you, and call.

3.  In the less likely case that he has you beaten, he'll call or reraise. The way the hand has gone down, either action will tell you that you're probably beaten.

So raising is very informative, but probably won't make you much more money.

If you call, you won't know much about his hand. But he won't know much about yours either. You might have an ace that he can beat, or perhaps middle pair, and be calling to see if he'll bet at the pot again. This approach is more likely to make you another bet when you're winning, but could hurt you a lot if you're losing.

Since you're more likely to be winning than losing at this point, you decide to just call.

**Action:** You call $70. The pot is now $235.

**Turn: J♦**

**Question**: *What do you do?*
    **Answer:** The jack created another hand that you're beating but which could call another bet, namely ace-jack. Since you called on the flop to bet now, you should go ahead and bet.

**Action:** You bet $170. Player E raises to $500. The pot is now $905. It costs you $330 to call.

**Question:** *What do you do?*
    **Answer:** A raise is not what you expected, and it's a bad sign. Time to look at the stacks and see what's happening.
    You've invested $280 so far, so your stack is $1,570. If you call, you'll have $1,240 left and the pot will contain $1,235. Your opponent will have you covered. He can put you all-in on the river, and you'll be getting 2-to-1 odds with your bottom set.
    If you reraise now, it will take the rest of your stack to make a pot-sized raise. Will a non-set call? Not likely at a tough table.
    Your check-call on the flop followed by a bet on the turn showed real strength, but your opponent is showing even more strength. However, the pot's offering you 3-to-1 odds right now. You're only losing to sets, and you're being offered nice odds. My inclination would be to call now and make a small bet on the river, which looks like you're peddling the nuts. If that bet gets raised, you're probably up against the nuts and you should fold. If he raises you on the end, you fold, and if he shows you a bluff, start looking for a softer game.

**Action:** You reraise all-in. He calls. The river is the 2♣ and he shows you the 9♠9♥ for a better set.

# Hand 3-9

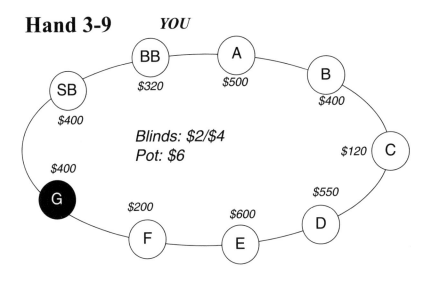

**Situation:** Medium stakes online game. You just sat down and don't have any information on the players.

**Your hand:** 5♣5♦

**Action:** Players A and B fold. Player C raises to $12. Players D and E fold. Player F calls $12. Players G and the small blind fold. The pot is now $30.

**Question:** *Do you fold, limp, or raise?*

    **Answer:** Fold. You only have to put in $8 to call, so your expressed odds of 3.5-to-1 aren't bad for this situation. However, your position is poor; you'll be first to act throughout the hand. Most important, though, are the stacks of your opponents. Player C, the player you're most likely to be facing throughout the hand, has a stack only 15 times the size of your call. Player F has a stack 25 times the size of your call. Player F's stack is the very minimum size I want to see in this situation. Player C's is much too small.

    When playing small pairs, you want the situation to be very good. Here it's not quite good enough, so let it go and wait for a better spot to get your money in. Remember that patience is key in deep stack play.

# Hand 3-10

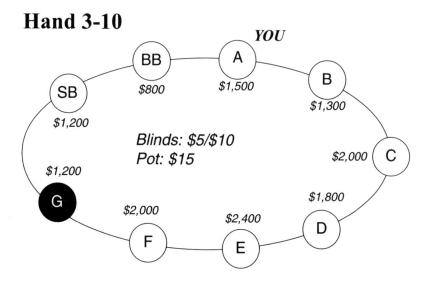

**Situation:** Medium stakes live game. You've been playing about an hour. The players like to play a lot of pots. They're generally loose-aggressive. Player C is particularly aggressive.

**Your hand:** A♠K♣

**Question:** *Do you limp or raise?*
 **Answer:** Raising is a bit more standard, but there's nothing really wrong with either play.

**Action:** You limp for $10. Player B folds. Player C raises to $50. Player D folds. Player E calls $50. Player F calls $50. The button and the small blind folds. The big blind calls $40. The pot is now $215. It costs you $40 to call.

**Question:** *Do you fold, call, or raise?*

    **Answer:** You certainly aren't folding. You could call and just see a flop, but you'll be out of position on the hand, so your prospects aren't all that good. But there's another move available to you —

**Action:** You raise to $700.

— and this is it. It's really an elaborate semi-bluff. You've pretty much established that no one else at the table has aces or kings. (Player C just might, but we know he's very aggressive and could have bet with a lot less.) Your play represents a player limping with aces and then coming over the top once someone raises. It's a hard bet to call, and you rate to take down the pot right here. But if someone does call or put you all-in, the resiliency of the ace-king hand comes to your aid. You should at worst just be a slight underdog to their pair.

**Action:** The other players all fold. You take the pot.

# Hand 3-11

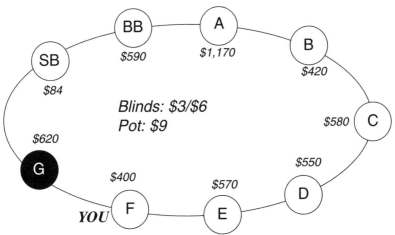

**Situation:** Medium stakes online game. The players have been very aggressive, especially Players B and the small blind.

**Your hand:** A♥K♠

**Action:** Player A limps for $6. Player B raises to $24. Players C, D, and E all fold. The pot is now $39.

**Question:** *Do you fold, call, or raise?*
   **Answer:** Just because an aggressive player attacked a limper is no reason to fold. With just an ace-king, however, you don't need to raise. Since you should have position in the hand, you can let your position work for you and play the pot small. I like just calling here.

**Action:** You call for $24. The button and the blinds fold. Player A reraises to $100. Player B folds. The pot is now $157. It costs you $76 to call.

**Question:** *What do you do?*
   **Answer:** The pot is offering you almost exactly 2-to-1 odds which means that the only hand that's really crushing you is a pair of aces. Your opponent is representing that hand, of course, but since you have one of the aces, he's a big underdog to have it despite his betting. You also have position for the rest of the hand, so you need to call.

**Action:** You call $76. The pot is now $233.

**Flop:** Q♥J♥7♠

**Action:** Your opponent bets $156.

**Question:** *What do you do?*

**Answer:** You missed the flop and your opponent doesn't seem to have lost his enthusiasm. You're losing to any pair and any hand that had a queen or a jack, so right now you can only beat a bluff. However, you do have some outs, so before folding let's look carefully at how you stand in the hand.

Right now you have $300 left in your stack, and your opponent has bet an odd amount — $156, a bit more than half your remaining stack. So his bet is offering you odds of $389-to-$156, or just about 2.5-to-1. If you call this bet but your opponent puts you all-in later, the pot odds will be $689-to-$144, or a bit less than 5-to-1.

If you think you're beaten now, how likely is it that you can improve to the best hand? The four tens are certainly outs, giving you a straight. It's also possible that the aces and kings are outs as well, giving you a maximum of ten outs. Your opponent limped and raised preflop, a very strong move, and then bet half your remaining stack on the flop. Let's look at some hands he might be holding and see just how likely it is that the aces or kings represent real outs:

- AA: no outs,
- KK: three outs,
- QQ: no outs,
- JJ: no outs,
- AK: split pot if you stay in, and
- AQ: three outs (the kings).

Unless he's holding exactly ace-king, any hand that fits his preflop actions leaves you with no outs or three outs concerning aces or kings. Thus, along with the tens, you either have four or seven outs and you can't get the odds that would make playing worthwhile. Time to fold.

**Action:** You fold.

# Hand 3-12

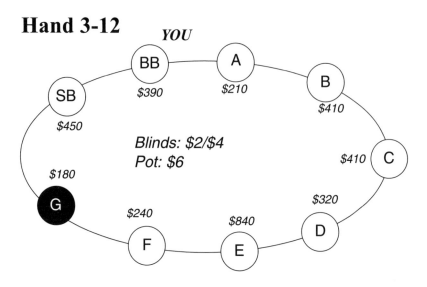

**Situation:** Medium stakes online game. The players have been tight and occasionally aggressive. Player G, on the button, is solid and tight.

**Your hand:** A♦J♥

**Action:** Players A and B fold. Player C raises to $16. Players D, E, and F all fold. Player G calls $16. The small blind folds. The pot is now $38. It costs you $12 to call.

**Question:** *Do you fold, call, or raise?*
  **Answer:** Three points to consider:

1. You're facing a raiser and a caller. The raise is indicative of some strength, the call of more strength.

2. Your hand, ace-jack offsuit, is a treacherous hand, especially out of position.

3. You're out of position.

Unless you flop a really big hand, you're not going to know how to proceed. If you hit an ace, you're in danger of facing a bigger ace. If you hit top pair with your jack, you're in better shape, but still vulnerable to an overpair. Anything else and you can't proceed.

Ace-jack is a trap hand which entices beginners. It's a hand you want to play in position, or at least as the preflop leader. Otherwise, let it go and save yourself a lot of *agita*.

**Action:** You fold.

# Hand 3-13

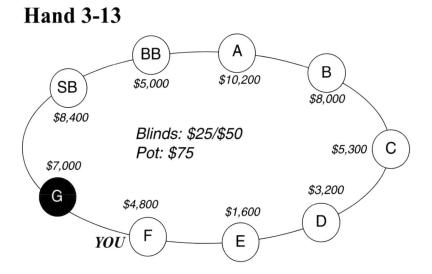

**Situation:** High stakes live game. The players are very experienced. Mostly tight and aggressive, but a couple of loose aggressive players in the mix. You're in over your head, but playing for the experience. The small blind is one of the tight-aggressive ones.

**Your hand:** A♥7♥

**Action:** Players A through E fold.

**Question:** *Do you fold, call, or raise?*

    **Question:** Raise. You're in late position, so a suited ace has a good chance of being the best hand at the table. You're basically stealing the blinds with a reasonable hand if you get called.

**Action:** You raise to $175. The button folds. The small blind raises to $700. The big blind folds. The pot is $950 and it costs you $525 to call.

**Question:** *What do you do?*

    **Answer:** Fold. Ace-small is not a hand for calling a raise from a good, tight player. You have position, but if you're dominated, the position won't do you any good. You were in the hand to steal the blinds and that didn't work. Let this one go quickly.

**Action:** You fold.

# Hand 3-14

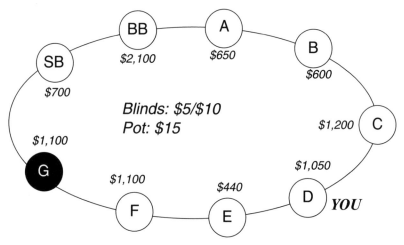

**Situation:** Moderate stakes live game. The table has been playing very tight-aggressive.

**Your hand:** Q♣J♥

**Action:** Players A through C fold.

**Question:** *Do you fold, call, or raise?*

**Answer:** Queen-jack is one of the weakest of the "trouble hands," but you can't just automatically throw it in the muck, so let's see what you should do.

The only mistake you can make here is limping, which, given the tight nature of the table, I don't like at all. This is a very marginal situation for the queen-jack, and either folding or making a standard raise is perfectly acceptable.

In one of the first three positions at a tight table I would certainly fold this hand. In one of the last three positions, given that I was first in the pot, raising would be my play. In middle position, with three players and the blinds still to act. I'm indifferent with this hand.

At a table that was playing more loose, I would let this hand go. Even at a loose table, however, my play is to raise from fifth position onward.

If someone reraises me I will fold, of course, and if there are a couple of callers after my raise, I'll be very careful after the flop.

**Action:** You raise to $30. Players E, F, and G and the blinds all fold.

# Hand 3-15

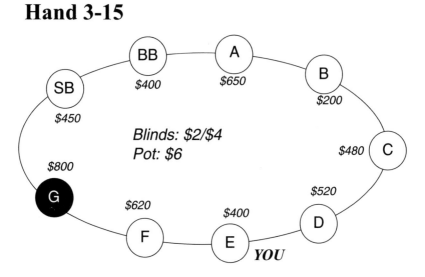

**Situation:** Moderate stakes online game. The table has generally been playing tight. Player A is a tight, conservative player who seems to play solid cards considering his position. Player G is looser, but has made some good moves and commands respect.

**Your hand:** K♥J♠

**Action:** Player A raises to $12. Players B, C, and D all fold.

**Question:** *Do you fold, call, or raise?*
>    **Answer:** You should fold. Player A's raise under the gun indicates, as far as you know, solid values. That almost certainly means a hand better than yours. Exactly how much better you don't know, but the trouble hands are not the cards you want to use to answer such questions. Let it go.

**Action:** You actually call $12. Player F folds. Player G calls $12. The blinds fold. The pot is $42 and you will be second to act after the flop.

**Flop:** K♣8♠7♠

**Action:** Player A bets $30.

**Question:** *What do you do?*

Answer: You have top pair, which is good, but a not terribly strong kicker, which is bad. Meanwhile, Player A has come out betting. What can he have?

If he has top pair as well, he almost certainly has a better kicker than yours. Not many tight players raise under the gun with king-ten, king-nine, or worse. So if he hit top pair, it's probably because he has ace-king or king-queen. In either case, he's better than a 5-to-1 favorite against you.

What other hands might he have? Against a pair of aces, you're about a 4-to-1 underdog. Against a pair of queens or jacks, you're about a 7-to-1 favorite. Against ace-queen, you're about a 5-to-1 favorite.

Is he just making a continuation bet with nothing? Perhaps, but the presence of Player G complicates the situation. Solid players are usually happy to make a continuation bet into a single opponent, but less eager to bet out into two players. This might be a continuation bet, but the probability has dropped some.

Speaking of Player G, we don't know much of anything about his hand yet. As a loose-aggressive caller after a raise and a call, he could have a fairly wide range of hands.

So what to do? It's hard to fold top pair in this situation after what looks like a pretty reasonable flop for you. The pot is now giving you 2.5-to-1 odds, and that's perhaps just about enough under the circumstances. I would call now, and reevaluate when more information comes in.

**Action:** You call $30. Player G calls $30. The pot is now $132.

**Turn:** J♣

**Action:** Player A checks.

**Question:** *What do you do?*
**Answer:** Three new pieces of information to evaluate. Player G called as well. Does he have some kind of draw, or two high cards? The turn gave you two pair, which is great news. And Player A checked, indicating that he may not feel his hand is worth putting any more money in the pot. He might have been bluffing after all.

Your hand is certainly strong enough to bet, and given the number of possible draws, you should try to chase the drawing hands away. I would make a substantial bet here. Against a single player I would bet about two-thirds of the pot. Against two players, bet a bit more, between three-fourths of the pot and the whole pot.

**Action:** You bet $100. The pot is now $232 and you have $258 remaining in your stack. Player G raises to $400, enough to put you all-in. Player A folds.

**Question:** *What do you do?*
**Answer:** As often happens, the death blow comes from an unexpected direction.

The pot was $232 and, with Player A out of the way, Player G has raised you the rest of your stack, another $258. So the new pot is $490 and it costs you $258 to call. You're getting just a bit less than 2-to-1 on your money.

What hands can Player G reasonably have? He's either betting for value, semi-bluffing, or bluffing. From what little we know of him, all these three courses of action are at least somewhat possible. If he has a value hand, it's almost certainly better than our two pair. Let's run through the possible value hands and see which makes sense in light of the cards and the betting:

- **A set of kings.** Very unlikely. He would have to have the last two kings in the deck, and would have just called after a raise and a call before the flop. A pair of kings would almost always reraise in that situation.

- **A set of jacks.** Also unlikely. The preflop call after a raise and a call makes sense because a raise would have seemed too speculative. But the call on the flop is suspect because the king on board inspired a bet and a call. A prudent player has to let the jacks go here.

- **A set of eights or sevens.** These fit the betting perfectly. The preflop call is for set value and implied odds, and the call on the flop is a trap because the king seems to have provoked some betting.

- **A straight.** Only a ten-nine holding makes a straight. It would be an aggressive call preflop, based on position and deception. On the flop, ten-nine would have made an open-ended straight draw. Ten-nine of spades would have had both a straight and a flush draw, and would have been a favorite against something like ace-king and king-jack in the other two hands.

While the first two value hands are unlikely, the last three fit the betting reasonably well.

The other possibility is a semi-bluff, based on a straight or flush draw (or both). If Player G has the K♠Q, for instance, he has 11 outs (eight spades plus three queens), and is about a 3-to-1 underdog in the hand. The straight draws are doing a little worse than this.

Folding top two pair is difficult, but the reason hands like king-jack are called "trouble hands" is precisely because they present you with many very difficult decisions. If Player G is betting for value you're up against a set or a straight, and you have at most four outs (the last two kings and jacks). There's some chance you have only three outs, since Player A may have folded a king. At best, you're about a 10-to-1 underdog. If Player G is running a semi-bluff, you're about a 3-to-1 favorite.

Putting those two numbers together means that if there's about a one-third chance that he's semi-bluffing, you have a marginal call with your 2-to-1 pot odds. You've seen Player G put together some moves before, so that's probably a reasonable number. You should reluctantly call.

**Action:** You call, and Player G turns over the T♠9♠ for a straight. The river is the four of hearts, and Player G wins the hand.

# Hand 3-16

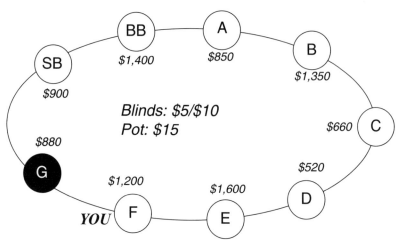

**Situation:** Moderate stakes online game. The table has been loose. Player C limps a lot but often folds without the nuts. Player E has been wild, raising and calling with below-standard hands. You've been tight and solid. The small blind has been even more wild than Player E.

**Your hand:** Q♣T♣

**Action:** Players A and B fold. Player C calls $10. Player D folds. Player E raises to $50. The pot is now $75.

**Question:** *Do you fold, call, or raise?*
    **Answer:** Fold. Hands like queen-ten, whether suited or not, are not hands for calling a raise.
    It's true that Player E has been wild, and your hand may be better than his, and you have position on the two players in the pot so far. But there are other aggressive players yet to act and you don't know what they have or what they'll do.

**Action:** You actually call $50. Player G folds. The small blind calls $40. Player C calls $40. The pot is now $205.

**Flop:** Q♠9♦6♦

**Action:** The small blind and Player C check. Player E bets $140. The pot is now $345.

**Question:** *What do you do?*
    **Answer:** You have top pair, but with a weak kicker. (A common occurrence with the "trouble hands.") Player E is known to be aggressive, but he's betting with three players still in the hand. He probably has something.
    With the pot offering you 2.5-to-1 and having position on Player E, it's too soon to fold top pair, even with a mediocre kicker. You should call and see what happens on the turn.

**Action:** You call $140. The small blind goes all-in with his last $850. Players C and E fold. The pot is now $1,335 and it costs you $710 to call.

**Question:** *What do you do?*

 **Answer:** The small blind is known to be the most aggressive player at the table, and the pot is offering you a little less than 2-to-1 odds. But you've already indicated some strength in the hand, Player E had indicated even more strength, and the small blind went all-in anyway. Aggressive players like to pick on weakness, not strength. It's safer. Assume that he has a real hand and it's better than your top pair, mediocre kicker. Even with a very good scenario, where you're facing a semi-bluff with something like A♦T♦, you're only a slight favorite, and against the bad scenarios you're a huge underdog. Fold.

**Action:** You fold.

# Hand 3-17

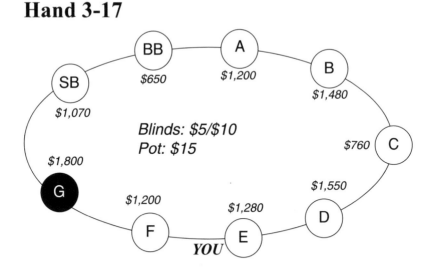

**Situation:** Moderate stakes live game. The table is a mixture of loose and tight players. Player C has been playing tight. Player G is generally tight, but can make a move at the appropriate moment.

**Your hand:** K♦Q♠

**Action:** Players A and B fold. Player C raises to $30. Player D folds. The pot is now $45.

**Question:** *Do you fold, call, or raise?*
> **Answer:** Fold. You don't want to call raises with the trouble hands, especially against tight players.

**Action:** You actually call $30. Player F folds. Player G raises to $150. The blinds fold. Player C calls $120. The pot is now $345, and it costs you $120 to call.

**Question:** *What do you do?*
> **Answer:** Time to rectify your mistake from before and fold. Player G may be making a move, but Player C definitely has something. You don't belong in this pot now.

**Action:** You fold.

# Hand 3-18

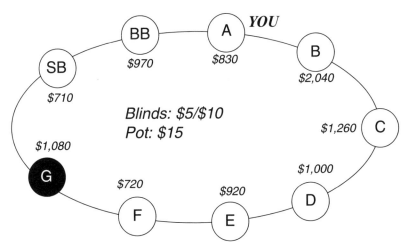

**Situation:** Moderate stakes online game. Player F has been very tight. In the last hour, you've only seen him show down a pair of kings. Player C is looser, fond of seeing cheap flops.

**Your hand:** 5♦4♦

**Action:** You are first to act.

**Question:** *Do you fold, call, or raise?*
  **Answer:** If you're trying to play a balanced strategy, you need to play some hands others than premium pairs and ace-king in early position. The suited connectors are ideal for this purpose. If you're known as a tight player, and you make a big hand with a suited connector from early position, it will usually be completely disguised to your opponents.
  Should you play all suited connectors in early position? Absolutely not. The reason, and it's a very important reason, is simply that there are too many suited connectors in the deck for your purposes. Suppose your plan is to raise with your premium pairs and ace-king in early position, and to balance these raises by raising with suited connectors. Let's look at the counts of these types of hands.

- Premium pairs (aces through jacks) = 24 hands

- Ace-king, suited or unsuited = 16 hands

Total = 40 premium hands.

- Suited connectors (king-queen through trey-deuce) = 44 hands.

There are more possible suited connectors than premium hands! The idea of playing the suited connectors is to balance your strategy and make you unreadable, not to cripple your strategy by forcing you to play primarily low cards. Instead, randomize by playing somewhere between one-fifth and one-quarter of your suited connectors. That way you have a deceptive mix, but one still heavily oriented toward good hands.

In this hand, your randomizer tells you it's time to play a suited connector.

**Action:** You raise to $30. Players C and F call. The others all fold. The pot is $105.

**Flop:** T♦5♥4♣

**Question:** *What do you do?*

**Answer:** That's a great flop for you. Bottom two pair, especially when the pairs are very low and subject to being counterfeited, is not a hand for slowplaying. Ideally, you'd like to make some money and wrap this hand up fairly quickly. So you're either going to start off with a bet, or check-raise. Either play is reasonable. The straight bet might be read as a continuation bet, while the check-raise indicates more strength.

I don't like to check-raise with hands that are extremely strong. If I had top set, for instance, which has the potential of winning my opponent's whole stack, I'd be afraid that a check-raise might chase my opponent off a decent hand, which would be a tragedy. That's not the case here. If I check-raise with bottom two pair and just win an extra bet, that's a pretty good result.

The problem with check-raising, however, is that I need some reason to believe that my opponent will actually bet. Here, I can't be sure of that. I led before the flop and one of my two opponents is known to be tight. If I check, there's at least a reasonable chance that both my opponents will check behind me. I don't want to give a free card to two players, so I like leading here.

**Action:** You bet $70. Players C and F both fold.

# Hand 3-19

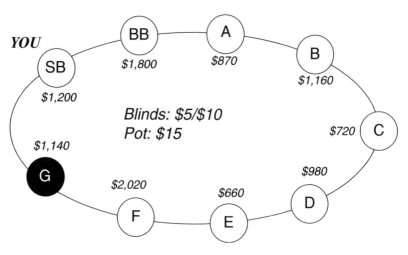

**Situation:** Moderate stakes online game. This is your first matchup against the big blind in a blind versus blind situation. So far he seems to be tight and conservative.

**Your hand:** A♦9♥

**Action:** Players A through G all fold.

**Question:** *Do you call or raise?*
> **Answer:** Your hand is objectively strong enough for a raise, and you may win the blinds as a result. It's also a good enough hand for calling if you call and he raises you. Since you want to establish that your calls in this situation don't signify weakness, use this hand to start building that framework. Call, and be prepared to call again if he raises.

**Action:** You call $5. The big blind checks. The pot is $20.

**Flop:** J♣7♥3♦

**Question:** *What do you do?*
> **Answer:** You could bet. It's entirely possible that your ace-high is still best. But I like checking and calling if he bets. Nothing has really happened to change your game plan which is to establish quickly that a check or call doesn't necessarily mean weakness.

**Action:** You check. He checks. The pot remains at $20.

**Turn:** 4♠

**Question:** *What do you do?*
> **Answer:** Continue in the same fashion, although it's a little less likely that your hand is best.

**Action:** You check. He checks.

**River:** 9♠

**Question:** *What now?*
> **Answer:** The nine gives us what is likely to be the best hand. Let's continue with our plan to the end and see if he will bet into us, perhaps trying to steal with a bluff if he still has nothing.

**Action:** You check. He checks. He shows Q♥7♣ for a pair of sevens, and you take the pot.

Both players showed they could check with a hand!

# Hand 3-20

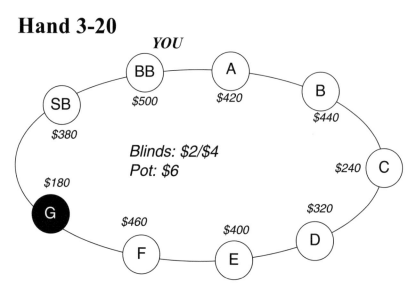

**Situation:** Moderate stakes online game. The table has been playing tight. Most of the players seem to be playing high cards when hands are shown down.

**Your hand:** A♦4♣

**Action:** Player A folds. Player B raises to $12. Players C and D fold. Players E, F, and G all call. The small blind folds. The pot is $54 and it costs you $8 to call.

**Question:** *Do you fold, call, or raise?*
> **Answer:** Fold. At this table, your ace is almost certainly dominated. Your cards aren't suited, which denies a key way of winning. You're probably a 10-to-1 underdog or worse, and you're out of position to boot.

**Action:** You fold.

# Hand 3-21

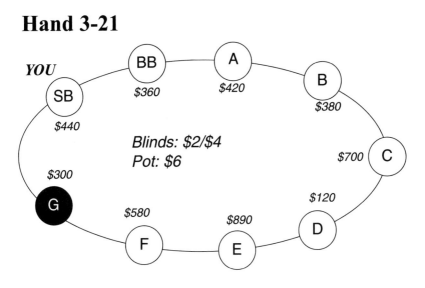

**Situation:** Moderate stakes online game. The table has been playing generally tight. Players E and F have been aggressive, playing more than their share of pots.

**Your hand:** A♥T♦

**Action:** Players A through E fold. Player F limps for $4. Player G folds. The pot is $10.

**Question:** *Do you fold, call, or raise?*

> **Answer:** Your hand is certainly strong enough to play against an aggressive, late-position limper. Since you'll be out of position after the flop, you have more interest in raising and winning the hand now rather than calling, so put in a solid raise.

**Action:** You raise to $20. The big blind folds. Player F calls. The pot is now $44.

**Flop:** A♠8♣5♥

**Question:** *Do you check or bet?*

    **Answer:** That's a fine flop for you and there's no reason to think you don't have the best hand. Since you raised preflop, it's unlikely that a check will elicit a bet from Player F. The pot is already a reasonable size, so bet now and see if you can take it down.

**Action:** You bet $30. Player F folds.

# Hand 3-22

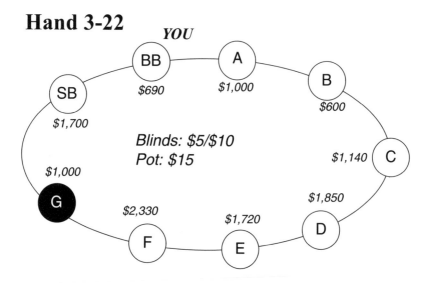

*YOU*

BB
$690

A
$1,000

SB
$1,700

B
$600

$1,000

G

Blinds: $5/$10
Pot: $15

$1,140 C

$2,330

F

$1,720

E

$1,850

D

**Situation:** Moderate stakes online game. The table has been playing generally loose. The small blind is extremely aggressive, playing almost half of all pots.

**Your hand:** A♥K♣

**Action:** Players A through E fold. Player F raises to $30. Player G folds. The small blind calls $25. The pot is now $70.

**Question:** *Do you call or raise?*

 **Answer:** You're certainly going to raise with your ace-king. This situation is one of the few where I recommend a raise slightly larger than the size of the pot. When I'm going to be out of position after the flop, and don't have a pair in my hand, I really like to try and end it now. A pot-sized raise here would be $110 — $20 to call and $90 to raise the new pot, so I'd put in about $150.

**Action:** You put in $150. Player F and the small blind fold.

 If you just make a normal raise and get called, about 70 percent of the time you miss the flop and find yourself sandwiched between an aggressive player and an unknown quantity with an ace-high hand. That's not an especially good situation.

 If you had a good pair, you could just make a normal raise to $100 or so, knowing that you'd be in reasonable shape whatever flop came. Also make sure you occasionally overraise with a big pair so your opponents can't put you on ace-king.

# Hand 3-23

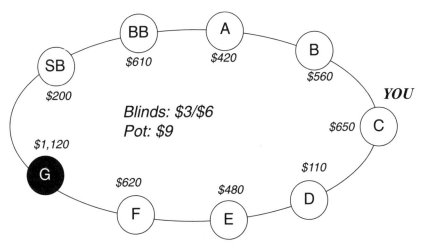

**Situation:** Moderate stakes online game. The table is a mixture of loose and tight players. The small blind has been playing tight but just suffered a bad beat to Player G. Your style is to play tight, but favorable circumstances have gotten you involved in a lot of hands recently.

**Your hand:** 9♦9♣

**Action:** Players A and B fold.

**Question:** *Do you call or raise?*
    **Answer:** I like a mixture of 70 percent raises and 30 percent calls with a pair of nines in middle position. It's a hand where you're happy to take down the blinds, and not especially eager to see a flop. If you get called, you'll mostly be playing the hand like a small pair from that point on.

**Action:** You raise to $18. Player D folds. Player E calls $18. Players F and G fold. The small blind raises to $54. The big blind folds. The pot is now $105.

**Question:** *What do you do?*
    **Answer:** First, let's note that folding is not an option. The pot contains $105 and it costs you just $36 to call, so your pair of nines are getting almost 3-to-1 pot odds. Only the five higher pairs are a favorite against you, and they're only a 4-to-1 favorite, so you almost have the correct odds to call them. Since the small blind had a short stack, you can't assume that you're a favorite to be facing one of those hands. So you're not folding.
    If you just call, however, two bad things happen. The pot becomes $141 and it costs Player E just $36 more to call, so he's getting 4-to-1 odds. Whatever hand he had that made him want to call before has even better reason for calling now. If he calls, the pot becomes $177 and the small blind

has only $146 left in his stack. It's now very likely that the small blind is pot-committed.

So calling forces a third player into the pot and leaves you pot-committed against the first player. That's not a good outcome with a pair of nines. Instead, you should simply raise enough to put the small blind all-in. That will likely drive out Player E and leave you heads-up against the small blind.

**Action:** You raise to $200. Player E folds. The small blind calls his last $146. The flop comes Q♠Q♥J♦, followed by the 2♣ and the 6♥. The small blind turns over A♣K♠, and your pair wins the pot.

# Hand 3-24

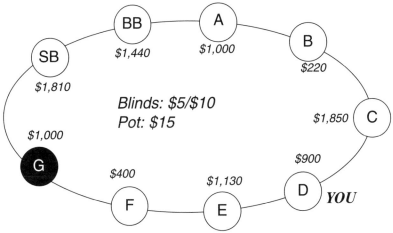

BB $1,440

A $1,000

SB $1,810

B $220

Blinds: $5/$10
Pot: $15

C $1,850

G $1,000

F $400

E $1,130

D $900

YOU

**Situation:** Moderate stakes online game. The table is loose with a lot of aggressive raising and reraising. You've been playing tight, but haven't picked up a lot of hands so far. Preflop, Player C raises almost every pot if he's first to act.

**Your hand:** 6♣6♥

**Action:** Players A and B fold. Player C mini-raises to $20. The pot is $35.

**Question:** *Do you fold, call, or raise?*
**Answer:** Your pair is almost certainly better than whatever Player C has. However, it's a weak reraising hand given that five players are yet to act. Just call.

**Action:** You call $20. Player E folds. Player F raises to $60. Player G and the blinds fold. Player C folds.

**Question:** *What do you do?*
**Answer:** Fold. Player F raised two players, so you have good reason to think he has a real hand. In addition, he has a relatively small stack. After his bet, you need to put in $40 to call, and he has only $340 left in his stack. That's not enough to make me interested.

When against a single player and I'm thinking of calling a raise with a small pair, I like to see that his stack is at least 20 to 25 times the amount needed to call. That might seem excessive to most players, but consider what needs to happen in the hand:

1. I need to hit a set — 7-to-1 against. If the set doesn't come, there will probably be a bunch of overcards on the flop, and I'm not going to be standing up to any large bets with my puny pair of sixes.

2. He needs to have something or hit something. That's a pretty safe bet since he's already announced he has something.

3. He has to go deep into the hand and lose a lot of money. That's not so likely. If he has a good-sized pair, I can get him for a bet on the flop. He might also go for a bet on

the turn, but maybe not. But I'm probably not going to get his whole stack unless he improves to something like two pair or better. (In which case he might be the one getting me.)

Remember too that position matters. You'll be out of position in the hand which makes playing the small pair even more difficult. (In position I would still fold, but it's a closer decision.)

In short, there's a lot than can go wrong when you call a bet with a small pair. Mostly I don't improve and lose the hand quickly, and mostly when I do improve there is only one more bet to be won, not enough to compensate for lots of small losses. Once in a while a small pair needs a really big win to make calling worthwhile in the first place, and that means I can only call when there's a big stack to shoot at. Hence we arrive at my rule of thumb: Both my opponent and myself should have a stack of 20 to 25 times the raise I'm calling. When I win that stack, I'll show a profit relative to all the times where my hand was discarded on the flop or I just pull down one small bet later.

Note that in a multi-player pot, my requirements get less strict. If I'm up against several players, there's a better chance that one of them can flop a hand and stay with me for a while when my set comes. In that case, I'm probably happy as long as everyone has at least 15 to 20 times the bet I'm calling.

**Action:** You fold.

# Part Four

# Tight-Aggressive
# Flop Play Heads-Up

# Tight-Aggressive
# Flop Play Heads-Up

# Introduction

After the players have completed the preflop betting with the hand still contested, the flop is dealt. Once the flop appears, you have much of the information you need to evaluate your hand.

Post-flop play depends heavily on the number of players still contesting the pot. The more players are involved, the more likely that one of them has actually hit a hand, and the more cautious you need to play. Accordingly, we've broken our discussion of post-flop play into two sections depending on how many players (besides yourself) have stayed to see the flop. In this section we discuss heads-up play where just you and one other opponent are still in the hand. In Part Five we'll talk about multi-way flop play.

Let's start now with the simplest case: you're heads-up after the flop. First, a few general observations.

Before any post-flop betting occurs, you want to orient yourself with regard to the information you already have. Here's a quick checklist:

- **Aggressor:** Whoever made the last raise preflop is the aggressor in the hand. For instance, if your opponent raised the blinds under the gun, and you called on the button with jack-ten suited, your opponent most likely has a better hand than you before the flop is dealt.

- **Position:** Do you act first after the flop or does he? It's an advantage to act after your opponent because he has to show you his intentions before you respond. Of course, he can try to mislead you by acting in a way opposite to the strength of his hand. However, he has to pay a price by doing so. If he has a strong hand and starts by checking, you may check behind him. In that case, no money goes in the pot and you get to see a free card to improve your hand. For this reason, most actions (but not all) are aligned with the strength of the hand.

- **Preflop Action:** The actions you and your opponent took preflop all tell a story about the relative strength of your hands. Suppose, for instance, he raised in fourth position at a nine-player table, you reraised from the button, and he called. The unspoken subtext goes as follows:

1. **Opponent:** Three players have already folded in front of me, and five are yet to act behind me. I'm raising because my hand is likely to be better than the five hands behind me. Even if I'm a conservative player, I don't need a monster hand to make this play, just a pretty good one. If I'm a conservative player, you can expect me to have a pair higher than fives, or a middle ace or better, or two high cards. If I'm a looser, more aggressive player, a few extra hands will figure into the mix, like the low pairs and suited or unsuited connectors. If I'm a wild man, I just want to take down the blinds and might have anything.

2. **You:** I'm reraising on the button to take the pot away from you. Whatever I think your range of hands might be, my hand is better than most of the hands in your range. It might be a high pair or a very strong ace. If you're loose, I might have a few more hands than that.

3. **Opponent:** The blinds have folded so it's just you and me. My hand isn't good enough to reraise you, so it's

not one of the top pairs or ace-king. But I'm not folding, so I've still got a pretty good hand, perhaps nines, tens, jacks, or queens, or one of the better high-card combinations.

4. **You and He Both:** I mostly tell the truth, but sometimes I lie.

● **Context:** Everything you know about your opponent in terms of style, level of aggressiveness, and betting patterns, goes into this category. Everything you think he might believe about you also goes here. In addition, everything that has recently happened between you and he helps determine the context. Your opponent might be a historically conservative player, but if you've chased him out of three pots in the last hour with big reraises, his aggression level may now be radically higher than normal.

● **Your Hand Strength:** Once the flop arrives, you have a pretty good idea of how your hand now ranks against other hands. Your hand will fall roughly into one of these six categories:

1. **Monsters:** If you were lucky, you might have hit a monster hand — a straight, a flush, a full house, or quads. The good news is that the hand is very likely to be the best hand at the showdown. The bad news is that it's hard for anyone to stand up to you if you show any strength. For instance, suppose you hold A♦T♣ and the flop comes A♠A♥T♦. You hold a full house, but there's only one ace and two tens left in the deck. Unless your opponent holds one of these three cards (not very likely), it's hard for him to do more than call one bet from you. You'd love to build a big pot with these hands, but it may be difficult to do so.

2. **Very strong hands:** These hands include sets and two pair. They're likely to win, but they occasionally run into trouble from a better made hand (set over set, for instance) or a draw that connects. Hands this strong, however, are worth betting on the flop and usually the turn as well. With these hands, you'll cooperate in building a big pot if the situation arises.

3. **Overpairs and top pairs:** These are your bread-and-butter good hands. They're worth a bet on the flop, and they'll frequently win the pot at that point. But there's a problem with them. Most players above the beginner's level won't invest much in the pot unless they (a) can beat these hands, (b) are drawing to a hand that can easily beat these hands, or (c) are planning a big bluff on a later street. If you have one of these hands and meet a lot of resistance after the flop, you're probably an underdog unless you're in a very weak game.

4. **Pairs below top pair:** These constitute the quintessential calling hands. Breaking even (or better) after the flop with these hands is a key skill for a no-limit hold 'em cash game player. They will often be the best hand on the flop, but you'll never be sure. How much of your stack are you really willing to jeopardize with second pair? Aggressive players make a lot of money by forcing tighter players with second or third pair to lay their hand down.

5. **Drawing hands:** A drawing hand is a hand that's currently worthless but can improve to a very big hand with a single card. They comprise straight draws, flush draws, and straight flush draws. The draw might be combined with an overcard or two which could make a pair better than the current top pair. Of the various types,

the straight draws tend to win the biggest pots because they are better concealed from your opponent. Playing drawing hands well is crucial in no-limit hold 'em because they offer the best chance to win your opponent's whole stack.

6. **Nothing hands:** Here you have no hand and no draw. A good player will win some of these from an opponent who also has nothing.

- **Your Opponent's Estimated Strength:** Depending on just what happened in the preflop action, you should have an intelligent guess as to how the flop helped his hand. If a conservative player raised in early position, and the flop came seven-six-four, it's a pretty good bet that the flop didn't help his hand.

Putting all of this information together should give you a very rough idea of where you stand after the flop. You're looking for answers to these four questions:

1. Am I probably ahead or probably behind?

2. If I'm ahead, how likely is it that my opponent is drawing to beat me?

3. If I'm behind but on a draw, how many outs do I have?

4. If I'm behind, is the hand winnable at a reasonable cost?

# Your Goal in the Hand

If you watch a lot of high-stakes cash game play, either on television or in real life, you'll probably be struck by the number of times players hit the flop, make top pair with a reasonable kicker, and check their hand. If you're used to tournament play where the blinds quickly get large relative to the stack sizes, cash game play with veteran players may seem unduly cautious.

But these players are cautious for a reason. They're acutely aware of the relationship between checking or betting the flop and the final pot size.

> Checking the flop is the path to a smaller pot size on the end.
>
> Betting the flop is the path to a larger pot size on the end.

Flopping a pair still hasn't given you a hand that wants to see a huge pot. When you flop a pair and bet, you're really hoping for everyone to go away. When they stick around, you have a problem on the turn, a problem which you might have to resolve by checking.

# Bet Sizing on the Flop

You can make a wide range of initial bets on the flop. In general, different bet sizes serve different purposes. Bets smaller than one-third of the pot are unusual, as are bets larger than the pot. Here's a brief summary of possible bet sizes within that range, and the usual meaning of each bet.

- **One-third of the pot:** These are small bets, usually probe bets or blocking bets. A *probe bet* is a bet to garner information, while enabling your opponent to throw the hand away if the flop has caused him to lose all interest. A *blocking bet* is intended to head off a possible larger bet from the opponent. It's usually employed in drawing situations where you feel your opponent may make a large bet if you check, but will just call rather than raise if you take any action at all.

- **One-half of the pot:** These are continuation bets, or value bets masquerading as continuation bets. Larger than probes, they're big enough to make your opponent lay down the hand if he has nothing or a very weak draw, while small enough to offer you favorable odds. If your opponent folds just one-third of your continuation bets, you'll at least break even on the move.

- **Two-thirds to three-quarters of the pot:** These are generally solid value bets, designed to get the opponent to put some significant amount of money in the pot if he decides to play.

- **Pot-sized:** These are serious bets which minimize your opponent's immediate expressed odds if he's on a draw. Pot-sized bets are usually seen when the board is obviously dangerous, with a straight and/or a flush draw. In these cases the bets usually represent either a value hand trying to charge a drawing hand, or a drawing hand making a semi-bluff.

Bets larger than the size of the pot are unusual and generally unnecessary. A pot-sized bet is large enough to accomplish anything that a bigger bet could accomplish. An exception occurs when one of the players has a very short stack, so that a pot-sized bet would effectively commit him to the pot. In that case the player may simply push all-in, or make a bet big enough to put his opponent all-in.

These bet sizes are only intended as rough guidelines. Obviously, you can't stick to a fixed bet size for any particular purpose, or your opponents will quickly discover what your bets mean. Instead, you need to vary your bets in a random pattern, with the idea that in general, your bets intended for a particular purpose need to average something like the amounts given here.

# Raising the Initial Bet

If your opponent bets at the pot, how big should your raise be to have the same impact as his initial bet? Many players are confused on this point, and habitually make raises that are too small, thus giving their opponent exceptionally good drawing odds.

Suppose that your opponent bets half the pot. How big a raise do you need to make to give your opponent the same calling odds he just gave you? In other words, what raise is the equivalent of a half-pot bet?

The answer is somewhat surprising: You have to put in triple the amount your opponent just bet to raise him half the pot! Let's see why.

Suppose the pot after the preflop betting is $40. Your opponent acts first and bets $20, a half-pot bet. If you want to confront your opponent with a half-pot raise in turn, you need to first put in $20 to call his bet, making the pot $80, and then put in an additional $40 to make the raise. The total amount you put in the pot was $60, three times the size of his bet.

If your opponent made a pot-sized bet and you want to make a pot-sized raise in return, you need to put in four times the amount of money he did. Again, suppose the pot after the preflop betting was $40. Your opponent bets $40, the size of the pot. When you call his $40, the pot becomes $120. A pot-sized raise requires you to put in another $120, or a total of $160. That's four times the size of his bet.

Here's a little table showing how much you need to put in the pot when raising an initial bet.

## Raising a Given Proportion of the Flop

| | | |
|---|---|---|
| **If your opponent bets half the pot** | To raise half the pot | Put in three times his bet |
| | To raise three-quarters of the pot | Put in four times his bet |
| | To raise the pot | Put in five times his bet |
| **If your opponent bets the pot** | To raise half the pot | Put in 2.5 times his bet |
| | To raise two-thirds of the pot | Put in 3 times his bet |
| | To raise the pot | Put in 4 times his bet |

While there are reasons for making small initial bets on the flop, most of those reasons don't apply to raises. Probing for information makes no sense since your opponent has already announced he's interested in the pot and has a hand. You can't make a blocking bet since he's already beaten you into the pot. And continuation bets don't apply by definition. So your raise is simply saying "I know you have a good hand and I have an even better one, so scram." Therefore your raises should mostly be in the range of two-thirds of the pot to the whole pot.

The same logic, of course, applies to reraises, although if you get around to reraising on the flop, issues of stack sizes and pot commitment will start to dominate. Here's a quick example:

.

# Sample Hand

You're playing in a $5-$10 game with a stack of $1,000. A reasonably tight player raises to $30 from early position. His stack seems to be about $800. Everyone folds to you on the button. You have

and elect to call putting $30 more in the pot. The blinds fold. The pot now has $75.

The flop is

giving you the nut flush. First to act, your opponent checks. You bet two-thirds of the pot, $50. Your opponent puts in another $200, calling your bet and raising you an additional $150, a slightly less than pot-sized raise. In the past, you've only seen him make a play like this when he holds a big hand like a set. You decide to raise again, hoping he will interpret your raise as a semi-bluff with a single heart. How big should your raise be?

Let's first note that your opponent bet $30 preflop and another $200 so far on the flop. With an initial stack of $800, that means he has about $570 left. If you did nothing but call his bet, you'd have to put in $150, creating a pot of $475.

$$\$475 = \$75 + \$50 + \$200 + \$150$$

If you elect to raise rather than call, you have some choices. You could push all-in, raising him another $570. Or you could raise a smaller amount, say $300. If your opponent called that bet, the pot would rise to $1,075 and he'd have only about $270 left in his stack.

Does the smaller raise commit him to the pot? If so, which raise is better? To answer the pot commitment question, let's look at what can happen on the turn.

1. **A fourth heart comes:** If he has a set of kings, and he believes you have a flush, then he has a mandatory call if you put him all-in. You'd be betting his last $270, the pot would then be $1,345, and he'd be getting about 5-to-1 on his call. With a set of kings, he's about 3.5-to-1 to improve to a full house on the river.

2. **The board pairs:** You still have the nut flush but now you're afraid he just made a full house. He bets his last $270, and now you're getting 5-to-1 on your money. Can you lay down your flush? Probably not.

So if he has a set as you suspect, betting $300 is really the same as pushing all-in since you're both pot-committed on the turn. Are the two bets really therefore equivalent?

Not really. There's actually a practical reason for betting the smaller amount if you know you have the best hand. No matter what hand your opponent holds, he's more likely to call the smaller amount than the bigger amount, and that's what you want. Just because *you* know that his bet commits him to the pot doesn't mean *he* knows it, so raise him $300. When faced with a good player, reverse the thinking. Raise the larger amount, and he will think you are trying to move him off the hand.

# General Guidelines for Flop Play

Before we get into the detail of playing individual hands and flops, let's consider some general concepts of play after the flop when heads-up.

**Concept No. 1: If you were the aggressor preflop, you will generally take the lead post-flop.** The aggressor (the last player to raise preflop) has advertised that he has a strong hand. His opponent has acquiesced, in a sense, by just calling, rather than raising on the end. So the preflop betting has told a clear story regarding who stands better and who stands worse. In general, the aggressor needs to stick to the script. If you raised with a good pair, you should bet when first to act. If you raised with two high cards and hit one on the flop, you should bet. If you raised with two high cards and missed the flop, you should mostly make a continuation bet representing that you in fact had a good pair.

Of course, you can't always do any of these things. A good frequency for continuation betting is 65 to 70 percent of the time post-flop. To protect those bets, you need to employ a roughly similar frequency of betting with your made hands. That way your checking sequence also contains some made hands so your alert opponents can't profit by assuming that a check means weakness.

**Concept No. 2: If you were not the aggressor preflop, and you are first to act, you should almost always check to the aggressor.** This follows from the previous principle. If your opponent is supposed to bet in his turn, you should check and let him do it without first giving him any information about the strength of your hand. Don't worry that you may flop a big hand, check, and he checks behind you. You still have two streets left to get some money in the pot.

**Concept No. 3: Be prepared to exploit the bluffing flops.** Three kinds of flops are particularly susceptible to bluffing in heads-up situations:

1.  Three to a suit.
2.  Three to a straight.
3.  A paired flop.

These flops look dangerous, and mostly they will miss your opponent. That makes them prime bluffing flops. The player who first bets at these flops will usually take them down. Make sure you are that player. If one of these flops appear and your opponent acts first and bets, you should raise a larger than usual percentage of the time when you have nothing.

One caveat. These bluffs are "raise and run" situations. If your opponent bets at one of these flops, you raise, and he sticks around, you're dead. Let the hand go.

**Concept No. 4: Be prepared to semi-bluff.** A semi-bluff is a bet made with a drawing hand like an open-ended straight draw, a flush draw, or some combination of the two. The number of cards which complete the straight or flush are called outs since hitting one of them will probably make a winning hand. The draw might also be combined with an overcard or two which might provide extra outs.

Semi-bluffs combine the characteristics of both strong hands and bluffs. They're bluffs because they are hands which currently are losing to any made hand. But when they hit their draw they improve to monsters, hence the term semi-bluff.

Semi-bluffs are effective bets because they have two ways to win. Your opponent can fold to the bet (called *folding equity*) or he can call, and you can hit your hand and win. You don't need much folding equity to be a favorite in the hand. For example, if you have 11 true outs, good enough to be about 40 percent to hit your hand with two cards to come, then 20 percent folding equity is enough to make you a net favorite in the hand if you can see both the turn and the river card. (You win 20 percent of the time when he folds, plus plus another 32 percent [(.40)(.80) = .32] when he calls.)

The last sentence, however, illustrates the weakness of the semi-bluff. You need to be able to see both the turn and the river cards at no extra charge. If your opponent suspects you're semi-bluffing, he can confound your strategy with a big bet on the turn, ruining your odds. Semi-bluffs are best made in position so that your opponent will have to act first on the turn. Since he has to fear that your flop bet was made with a genuinely big hand, he may check the turn, giving you a chance to check behind him.

**Concept No. 5: Don't be afraid to be aggressive.** In a heads-up post-flop situation, you only have one player to beat and he probably missed the flop. Exploit that knowledge. Continuation bets are strong in part because they are an aggressive, rather than passive, variation. When both players miss the flop, which commonly happens, the first player to bet will mostly win the pot.

Suppose, for instance, that you have a reputation as a tight player and you raise from middle position with

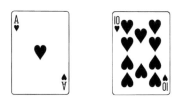

Your opponent, respecting your reputation, calls from late position with

The flop comes

You've both missed the flop, but he still has you dominated. When you make a continuation bet, your opponent will mostly lay down his hand, a hand where right now he's almost a 5-to-1 favorite.

# Handling a
# Single Pair on the Flop

The case where you flop a single pair against one opponent in a no-limit hold 'em cash game occurs often and is misunderstood by many players. If you watch a lot of televised cash games, you'll see that in many cases players check their pair, even when it's top pair, top kicker, although it seems clear they very likely have the best hand at that point. This behavior seems confusing at first. Why not be aggressive and bet an obviously strong hand? Let's try to clarify by looking at some of the issues involved when you hit a single pair on the flop.

Let's start with a concrete example. You and the player on the button both have stacks of about 150 big blinds. He's a reasonable player and so are you. You raise 3 big blinds preflop in early position with

The button calls, and everyone else at the table folds.

The flop comes

You have hit top pair, top kicker. Based on what you know so far, your hand is extremely likely to be best right now. You can check or bet. How often should you bet?

If you're a tournament specialist just moving to cash games for the first time, this question must seem a little puzzling. "Bet? Well of course I bet! I've got a great hand. In tournaments I mostly just push all-in here. Oh, wait, it's a trick question. I check, so I can check-raise. Yeah, that's the answer!"

Our tournament specialist isn't entirely wrong. In tournaments top pair top kicker is an easy hand to play precisely because the stacks are usually small compared to the blinds. With the blinds steadily increasing, you have to take reasonably good hands, push them hard, and hope they hold up. If you don't, the blinds will quickly pulverize you. Top pair top kicker is plenty good enough for that purpose.

But here our stacks are very big, and that changes the problem completely. The relative strength of our hand isn't the main issue anymore; what we care about is our ability to show a profit in the long run. Picking up the blinds when no one has a hand and losing our whole stack when someone picks up a set behind us won't make us money over time, so we have to be more careful in our play.

To start, let's review the goals of a bet and see just how well they apply in this hand.

**Goal No. 1: You make weaker hands put money in the pot.**
Can that happen here? Yes, at least on this street. Someone who called with a pair between kings and sevens will stick around. Someone who called with a pair below sevens might play. Someone who called with king-queen or king-jack won't fold their hand for a single bet, even though they might be dominated.

A few other hands, like ace-queen, might stick around, but most hands that completely missed the flop will go away. Still, that leaves a fair number of hands that will put in a bet.

**Goal No. 2: You make stronger hands go away.** That won't happen here. The stronger hands are a pair of aces (unlikely), two pair (also unlikely), and sets, and none of those hands will fold to a bet.

**Goal No. 3: You charge drawing hands to call.** The only possible drawing hand on this flop is six-five, which will stick around for a bet, but this isn't a draw-heavy board.

The arguments for betting are obvious, and they hold up pretty well. There are a fair number of weaker hands that will call a bet, although there aren't any better hands that will go away (partly a function of the fact that our hand was pretty strong to begin with). Now let's look at the possible reasons for checking and see how they look.

**Reason No. 1: Balance.** You're sometimes going to be checking when you miss your hand. Hence, you need to occasionally check when you hit your hand so that checking is not simply a sign of weakness.

**Reason No. 2: Small hand, small pot.** You have top pair, top kicker, which is a good hand right now. But it's not a mysterious hand, a hand your opponent can't see. Will your opponent put a lot of money into this pot with a hand that can't beat top pair, top kicker? Probably not.

**Reason No. 3: Stability of the hand.** You have five cards to improve your hand on the turn. If your opponent holds a smaller pocket pair, like tens or nines, he has only two cards to improve to a better hand than yours. If he has middle pair with a hand like ace-seven, he has four cards to improve to a better hand (two of which are disastrous for him). In short, if you have him beaten now, it's not likely he can draw out on the turn, and if he has you beaten, you probably won't draw out on him. The hand right now is *stable*; whoever is currently ahead will very likely be ahead on the turn. Since you're not looking to build a big pot with this hand, betting now is not very different from checking now and betting the turn.

**Reason No. 4: Allowing improvement.** Will checking allow your opponent to improve to a hand with which he'd be willing to call a bet? Quite possibly. Suppose he has a dominated ace, like ace-queen, ace-jack, ace-ten, or ace-nine, all hands that might easily have called the preflop bet. Right now he has nothing. He might call a flop bet, he might not. But say he has ace-ten, you check, and an ace comes on the turn. You'll win at least one bet for sure, and perhaps a second bet on the river. The same probably holds true if a ten comes.

**Reason No. 5: Deception.** The balance principle requires you to play in a diversified manner to make your play hard to read throughout the session. The deception principle says that playing in a manner opposite to the strength of your hand may make you more money right now. Your check on the flop plants the notion that you don't have a king, so all sorts of scenarios become possible for later profit, especially against a relatively weak or straightforward player.

When we look at the arguments for and against betting, we can see that simply betting your top pair isn't the clear cut decision it seemed at first. There are good results that can come from betting, but there are also good results that can come from checking.

Is betting, in general, correct? Yes. If someone came to me and said "I'm a tricky player and I bet my top pair, top kicker hands less than 50 percent of the time," I'd be certain that he was making a mistake and leaving some money on the table. If a different player came to me and said "I bet top pair, top kicker more than 90 percent of the time," I'd also be certain that his play was less than optimal. Checking that hand a solid percentage of the time is necessary for a balanced strategy. What's the "correct" percentage? In a normal game, absent any other information, I'd peg the number at 65 to 70 percent. That leaves plenty of room for deception while making a solid number of value bets. It also ensures that you're betting good hands enough to provide cover for your continuation bets. Once I've played in a game long enough to become familiar with the players, I might scale that number up or down a bit. At a tight table, where people are more likely to have a real hand to call it goes up, and down at a loose table where people play more junk, and are more likely to try and take me off the hand after a check, it goes down.

# Betting
# Monsters on the Flop

Assume, for purposes of discussion, that both you and your opponent have stacks in the range of 100 to 150 big blinds. What should your general strategy be when you flop a monster, a hand so strong that you are now extremely likely to win the pot no matter what happens on the turn or river?

As always, we're not looking for an approach that we're always going to employ. Whatever the "best" approach seems to be, let's remain aware that we will vary our approach across all reasonable strategies. What we want to know is simply this: What approach rates to make the biggest profit assuming our opponent is unaware of any tendencies we may have?

In order to make the problem manageable, we're going to make a whole bunch of simplifying assumptions. As we go along, I'll explain what our assumptions are and why they should be reasonable.

**Assumption No. 1: Stack sizes.** We'll do our calculations three times, first assuming that we each have a stack of 100 big blinds, then assuming we have 150 big blinds, and finally assuming we have 70 big blinds. The first stack size is the most common in both online and live play. The second size will let us see if a deeper stack game calls for a different strategy. The third size will give us an idea of how to adjust for smaller stacks. For simplicity, we'll assume that the pot after the preflop betting is 10 big blinds.

**Assumption No. 2: Ignoring drawouts.** Only some straight flushes on the flop are immune to draws. No matter what other hand you have, your opponent could be on a draw to beat you. Rather than try to factor in the effect of only being a 90 or 95

239

percent favorite in reality, we'll just ignore this effect and see what approach works best if we indeed win every hand.

Next we need some strategies to test against one another. Here are three that seem reasonable:

**Strategy No. 1: Bet the pot on the flop.** If called, bet the pot on the turn. If called again, bet the pot on the river. If betting the pot on the river requires a bet of more than 70 percent of our stack, push all-in.

**Strategy No. 2: Bet 60 percent of the pot on the flop.** Repeat on the turn if called. Bet the pot on the river or push all-in, as above.

**Strategy No. 3: Check the flop. Bet the pot on the turn.** Bet the pot on the river or push all-in, as above.

Our next assumption is pretty straightforward.

**Assumption No. 3: Passive opponent.** Our opponent won't bet if we check, and won't raise when we bet. If our opponent is willing to actively bet, it makes less difference what strategy we adopt. We're likely to get all the money in by the river anyway. We want to know what's best against a passive opponent who is nonetheless willing to stick around for awhile.

Now we have to make some assumptions about how often bets get called. In my experience, a continuation bet (50 percent of the pot) gets called about half the time on the flop. Bigger bets will get called less often, so here's my best guess regarding calls on the flop:

**Assumption No. 4: Calling frequency on the flop.** A pot-sized bet will get called 30 percent of the time on the flop. A bet of 60 percent of the pot will get called 40 percent of the time.

On the turn, some of the players who called on the flop will now fold, partly because they didn't hit a draw and don't want to chase the last card at bad odds, partly because they had some sort of hand and wanted to see if you would keep betting.

**Assumption No. 5: Calling frequency on the turn.** A player who called your flop bet will call 50 percent of your bets on the turn. If you checked the flop, your turn bet will get called 40 percent of the time.

On the river, you'll again lose some callers when they don't make the hand they wanted.

**Assumption No. 6: Calling frequency on the river.** A player who called your turn bet will call 30 percent of your big river bets.

What we've done is construct a very simplified model of flop, turn, and river action when you have a good hand and bet strongly. While the particular numbers depend on the playing style of the table and to some extent the stake, they're all reasonable. If this method demonstrates that one of our strategies is noticeably better than any other, we can have some confidence in the result.

Let's work through the calculations for one sample case, where the stack sizes are 100 big blinds and we use Strategy No. 1. Then we'll show the table for all cases and strategies, and draw some conclusions.

# Example: Strategy No. 1 and Stacks of 100 Big Blinds

To start, we have a pot of 10 big blinds after the preflop betting, and each of us has stacks of 100 big blinds. Since this is Strategy No. 1, we make a pot-sized bet of 10 big blinds. Our opponent folds 70 percent of the time (Assumption No. 4), and we win 10 big blinds when our opponent calls the other 30 percent, the pot becomes 30 big blinds, and we go on to the turn. The stacks are both 90 big blinds.

On the turn, we bet the pot again, 30 big blinds. Of the 30 percent of the time we're still playing, our opponent calls half and folds half (Assumption No. 5). Of the 15 percent of the time he folds, we win 20 big blinds (10 from the preflop pot and 10 more from his call on the flop). When he calls in the last 15 percent of the hands, the pot becomes 90 big blinds, and our stacks are down to 60 big blinds each. In these 15 percent of the hands, we go on to the river.

On the river, we push all-in since our stack (60 big blinds) is less than the pot (90 big blinds). By Assumption No. 6, he's going to call (and lose) 30 percent of these bets, or 4.5 percent of our original sample, and fold the other 10.5 percent. So 10.5 percent of the time we win 50 big bets (10 from the preflop pot, 10 from his call on the flop, and 30 from his call on the turn). When he calls to the end, however, we win 110 big blinds (10 from the preflop pot plus his entire stack, which was 100 big blinds.)

Now let's sum up what has happened.

- 70 percent of the time we won with our flop bet. Our profit was 10 big blinds.

- 15 percent of the time he called the flop but folded the turn. Our profit was 20 big blinds.

- 10.5 percent of the time he called the flop and turn but folded the river. Our profit was 50 big blinds.

- 4.5 percent of the time he called all three streets. Our profit was 110 big blinds.

To calculate our expectation from this series of bets (pot-sized bet on the flop, pot-sized on the turn, all-in on the river) we multiply the probability of each by our profit in big blinds.

- We win on the flop. Expectation = (70%)(10 big blinds) = 7 big blinds.

- We win on the turn. Expectation = (15%)(20 big blinds) = 3 big blinds.

- He folds on the river. Expectation = (10.5%)(50 big blinds) = 5.25 big blinds.

- He calls on the river. Expectation = (4.5%)(110 big blinds) = 4.95 big blinds.

Our total expectation for this line of play is 20.20 big blinds.

$$20.20 = 7 + 3 + 5.25 + 4.95$$

We can perform the same calculation for the other combinations of strategy and stack sizes. We won't give the play-by-play for the other examples, but the results are summarized in the following interesting table.

## Results of Three Different
## Strategies and Three Stack Sizes

|  | 70 BB | 100 BB | 150 BB |
|---|---|---|---|
| **Strategy No. 1**<br>Pot-sized bets | 18.85 BB | 20.20 BB | 22.45 BB |
| **Strategy No. 2**<br>60% of pot on<br>flop and turn | 18.06 BB | 17.58 BB | 17.58 BB |
| **Strategy No. 3**<br>Check flop, then<br>pot-sized bets | 17.6 BB | 17.6 BB | 17.6 BB |

Each entry in the table shows the expectation, in big blinds, for that combination of strategy and stack size. The middle entry in the first line, for instance, is the result we just calculated.

First, a couple of notes about the results in the table. In Strategy No. 3, the entries are all the same because the aggressor only gets to make a pot-sized bet on the river no matter what the starting stack size. After checking the flop, the turn bet is 10 big blinds and the river bet is just 30 big blinds.

A similar situation occurs with Strategy No. 2. When the stacks start at 70 big blinds, the pot on the river is 48 big blinds and the remaining stacks are 51 big blinds, so the aggressor makes an all-in move of 51 big blinds. At stacks of 100 and 150 big blinds, however, the pot is 48 big blinds, but the stacks are 81 big blinds and 131 big blinds respectively. So the river bet is just a pot-sized bet of 48 big blinds, and that's why the average profit with Strategy No. 2 is actually bigger with the smallest stack.

With Strategy No. 1, the aggressor is able to make an all-in move for all three stack sizes, so his profit rises steadily across the table.

Now for the real question: *What conclusions can we draw from this table?* The most important point to notice is that Strategy No. 1 dominates for all stack sizes, and the bigger the stacks, the more it dominates. Although the smaller betting strategies tend to keep the opponent in the hand a little more often, and as a result do a little better collecting an extra bet or winning a medium-sized pot, the big betting strategy more than compensates by collecting the whole pot at the end. Given our assumption, that result (winning the opponent's whole stack) occurs less than 5 percent of the time with the big-bet strategy, but that's still enough to make it a dominating strategy.

This result, however, confirms one of the basic tenets of deep-stack poker. When you have a hand so strong that your opponent's entire stack is at risk if he chooses to play the hand, you need to play the hand in such a way that you can put him all-in on the river without needing to make a bet so large that it's out of line with the action that has occurred so far.

# An Interesting Variation: The All-In Semi-Bluff

When we talked about semi-bluffs a little bit earlier, we pointed out a weakness in the semi-bluff maneuver. In order for the arithmetic of the semi-bluff to work properly, the bettor needs to be able to see both the turn and the river cards at no extra charge. If the turn card misses the draw, and his opponent sticks in another bet on the turn, the semi-bluffer has some problems.

One way to fix this problem is to move all-in with a semi-bluffing hand. Now if his opponent calls, he can't make another bet on the turn, so the semi-bluffer indeed gets to see his two cards.

That's the upside. The downside of moving all-in with a semi-bluff on the flop is that, unless you have a really big draw, like a flush and straight combined (typically 15 outs), you're an underdog for all your chips to anyone that calls you.

Having said that, the all-in semi-bluff is an interesting move. Here's how it's typically implemented in practice:

1. **Control your stack size:** A stack of 40 to 60 big blinds is ideal. More than that, and you're risking too many chips when you get called.

2. **Create a big target:** Rather than be the first into the pot on the flop, you'd rather make this move as a raise or a check-raise after your opponent has led off with a good-sized bet. Having position after the flop is very helpful.

3. **Teamwork:** Semi-bluffs can't carry the load alone. Pair them with some all-in moves from your monster flops (two pair,

sets, straights, and flushes) so your opponents can't easily read what you're doing.

The all-in semi-bluff is an intriguing maneuver, but be aware it contains a couple of key weaknesses.

1. **Balance:** Over the course of a typical session of a few hundred hands, you're not going to see a lot of monster flops. Committing several of them to complement the semi-bluffs means not enough monsters left to complement your other betting sequences.

2. **Stack size:** The strategy requires you to limit your stack size, which hampers all your other betting sequences. Pot commitment will arise more often and more quickly and limit your flexibility in other areas.

# Various Flops
# and How to Respond

The rest of this chapter is divided into four sections. The division reflects what position you have relative to your opponent, and who the aggressor was preflop. The sections are:

1. You were the aggressor preflop, and you are out of position.

2. You were the aggressor preflop, and you now have position on your opponent.

3. Your opponent was the aggressor, and you are out of position.

4. Your opponent was the aggressor, and you now have position.

In each section we'll give a number of hands you might commonly hold in that situation, and show how you should respond to various flops.

In responding to flops, we're not going to simply say "You should raise" or "You should call." Instead, we're going to define what actions are the most reasonable, and give rough percentages for how often you should take one action as opposed to another. This description will seem awkward and peculiar to many readers, especially beginners and intermediates, but there are very good reasons for dealing with the flop in this fashion, especially in a heads-up confrontation.

Back in Part Two, we defined the Metagame Principle as one of our fundamental elements of no-limit hold 'em. The Metagame Principle requires that you play in a generally deceptive manner so that your actions give minimal clues as to the identity of your hole cards. It's tempting to think that you can make such plays on the spur of the moment; "Let's see, I raised the last three times I flopped a set, so now I'll check." But, in real life, that doesn't really work.

As humans, our brains aren't really wired to make good probabilistic decisions. (Actually, this is a huge understatement; many of us never fully grasp the ideas of probability and expectation at all.) We may think that we can play in a random and deceptive manner, making the occasional deviation from our standard strategy, but we can't. What actually happens is that we quickly fall into very predictable patterns of behavior. The conservative player mostly makes the play that he thinks is "right" in the given circumstance while making other plays much less frequently than he should. The aggressive player makes the deviant play much more frequently than he should, and only occasionally resorts to the natural "value" play.

The solution is to mechanize the randomization process. In Part Two I described one method of getting random numbers at the poker table. Now we're going to put that method to full use. Here's how.

Let's start with a concrete example. On the button, we have

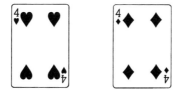

The conservative player in third position makes a standard raise of three big blinds. Everyone folds to us and we call. The blinds fold. We're heads-up, in a hand that falls into the fourth section of this chapter — our opponent is the aggressor, and we have position post-flop.

The flop comes

We have bottom set on a flop that is likely to have missed our opponent if he had two high cards, or to have given him an overpair if he started with a high pair. In addition, the flop has some draws, but not a huge number. We're not worried about the draws because it's unlikely that our conservative opponent opened in early position with jack-nine or nine-seven. Instead, we're looking at the flop through our opponent's eyes, and he's asking if it's possible we have a draw on that flop, and his answer is "Possible but unlikely."

He now bets 70 percent of the pot. We're not folding, so — do we raise or do we call?

*Rather than try to decide exactly what to do, let's instead decide that we'll make each play part of the time.* Then we just need to figure out which play we'll make more often, and roughly what the proportions should be between the two plays.

Here, for instance, I mostly want to call rather than raise. It's highly likely my hand is best, it's highly unlikely that my opponent is drawing to beat me, and it's also highly unlikely that, if I raise, my win will be much more than the one bet my opponent has already put into the pot. If I call, my opponent may put me on a draw, and if a card comes that doesn't help any possible draws, he may decide he can bet for value on the end, or failing that, call a bet of mine.

Since I prefer calling to raising, and I'm sure it's right by a solid amount, let's assign a heavy weight to calling — say 80 percent calls and 20 percent raises. Then I'll use my watch for my randomizing agent and check out the second hand. If it's between 0 and 48 seconds, I call. If it's between 48 and 60, I raise.

This randomizing approach solves, in an easy and clear-cut fashion, most of the problems associated with diversifying your play. Rather than wrestling with insoluble problems like "What hand does my opponent have?" you replace them with an even more easily soluble problem: "Given what I've seen so far, am I most likely to be ahead, well ahead, behind, or well behind?" Once you assign some percentages to your possible actions, the desired balance in your play follows automatically.

You'll mostly be making a value-oriented play, but you're guaranteed to be creating scenarios where some of your strongest hands are scattered among your passive betting sequences. This in turn ensures that your opponents have to fear that each of your possible sequences of checks, bets, calls, and raises may conceal the nuts. And since the exact betting sequences are determined by an essentially random process, they won't be able to determine any useful information from analyzing your betting patterns.

How far does this randomizing process extend? For the most part, I focus on randomizing play preflop and post-flop. By the time the hand reaches the turn or the river, the pot is getting larger, and the possible gain from randomizing starts to be outweighed by the goal of winning this particular pot.

As we work our way through the examples in the sections that follow, keep in mind that the idea is not to memorize the exact percentages I'll suggest, but to focus on the method used for analyzing the situation. The exact numbers themselves aren't nearly as important as the general idea of diversifying your play in a random but rational manner.

# Preflop Aggressor Out of Position

**You were the aggressor preflop. You are out of position after the flop. For these examples, assume you raised three big**

blinds from third position and were called only by an opponent on the button. You act first after the flop.

# Hand A: You Raised with K♠K♣

**Flop No. 1:** K♥7♣2♠

**Strategy:** Bet 30 percent of the time, check 70 percent.

**Analysis:** You have flopped a very strong hand, top set on a board without any draws. Your problem now is making some money on the hand. Obviously, it's very difficult for your opponent to have a hand that's legitimately strong enough to call a bet, if you choose to bet. However, you need to bet some of the time, so you can't be read as a player who routinely checks his strong hands and bets when he misses the flop. Not only do your weak betting sequences need to contain strong hands, but your strong betting sequences need some as well! Hence checking predominates in our strategy, but not overwhelmingly so.

One good by-product of checking is that our opponent may figure we had ace-x, didn't bet when we missed the flop, and are now hoping for a free card. That may induce him to stick in a bet with nothing.

How much should we bet when we do bet? Right now the pot should contain 7.5 big blinds, so I'd bet about 4 big blinds, a bet that looks much like a continuation bet.

If we know something about our opponent, we can modify our strategy from the 30 percent bet, 70 percent check ratio. If he's a tricky, aggressive opponent who likes to call and take pots away on a later street, we need to lead out more often. Now a 50-50 ratio makes more sense. If he's tight and passive, a player who won't stab at the pot without some kind of hand, then we need to give him a chance to catch something. Now 15 percent bets and 85 percent checks looks more reasonable as he probably doesn't have anything yet.

Now suppose we bet and get raised. (A happy thought!) Now our play deviates a little based on what we know about our opponent.

If he's a tight player who needs solid values to raise, then he probably has a smaller set. What else can he have? Ace-king? He called us preflop, and only one king remains in the deck. Did he call us with king-seven or king-deuce or seven-deuce? Not likely for a tight player. If he called us with a pair of queens or jacks or tens, and he's a tight player, he's not going to raise us with an overcard on board. So the most likely case is that he called us with a pair of sevens or deuces, and he hit his own set. So we reraise the pot and hope he's willing to commit his whole stack with a strong hand that's not the absolute nuts.

With any other read on our opponent, we need to mostly call. We have the best hand, we hope he has something, and we don't want to ruin our chances of picking up another bet down the road. Hopefully he'll interpret our call as weakness. Perhaps we raised initially with jacks and now fear the king which he is representing. So I would call 90 percent of the time and reraise 10 percent here. (Remember, we almost never take any action 100 percent of the time unless it's crystal clear.) On the turn in this scenario, I would bet half the time and check the other half.

---

## Flop No. 2: A♣T♠4♠

**Strategy:** Bet 20 percent of the time, check 80 percent.

**Analysis:** An ace has come on the flop. This is the situation every player dreads after raising with kings. If your opponent called with an ace in his hand, he correctly thinks he's probably winning, while if he didn't have an ace, he thinks you probably did and now he's beaten. It's hard to make money in this situation.

I recommend a bet-to-check ratio of 20 percent bets, 80 percent checks. You need to bet sometimes, of course, but the number should be small because the situation is very unfavorable. On the last flop we mostly checked because we wanted to lure our opponent in; now we're just trying to save money.

**Variation No. 1:** We bet. He calls. On the turn, either make a small bet or check and call only a small bet. You're done trying to extract value; your hope is to keep the pot small, ideally checking the hand all the way down.

**Variation No. 2:** We bet. He raises. We fold barring some very unusual read on our opponent. He saw us raise preflop and bet the flop and he still likes his chances, so give him credit for a big hand.

**Variation No. 3:** We check. He bets. Unless he's made some huge overbet, we call. On the turn, we'll mostly check and see if he's willing to bet again. If he does, we'll have to give up the hand.

**Variation No. 4:** We check and he checks behind us. His check means he probably doesn't have an ace. On the turn, we'll bet 50 percent of the time and check 50 percent. If that bet gets called, we'll be looking to keep the pot small, mostly checking the hand down. Remember, there's little reason to bet if you don't think your bet can get called by a hand you can beat. If he doesn't have an ace, he doesn't have much reason to call any bet, so our passivity can't cost us much.

---

**Flop No. 3:** T♦9♣8♣

**Strategy:** Bet 60 percent of the time, check 40 percent.

**Analysis:** A very tough flop. You probably still have the best hand, but a lot of his potential preflop calling hands are now beating you with either a straight, a set, or two pair. In addition, other hands now have value plus a draw. Jack-ten, for instance, has become top pair plus an open-ended straight draw.

Your hand is much too good to simply check and go away, but you need a reasonable strategy to avoid losing a lot of money when your hand is worst. My recommendation is to make more bets than checks, and to make a large bet to reduce the potential drawing odds. If the pot at this point was 7.5 big blinds, I would bet 6 to 7 big blinds. There's a reasonable chance your opponent is also scared of this flop. He might have ace-king, ace-queen, or a small pair, so a bet can sweep up those pots.

**Variation No. 1:** We bet and he calls. We're mostly done here. The pot is now getting large (if we bet 7 big blinds, the pot is now 21.5 big blinds) and our hand and position make our situation mediocre. That's a poor recipe for making a profit.

**Variation No. 2:** We check. He bets. Call 70 percent of the time and fold 30 percent. We can't simply go away with an overpair, but setting the folds to 30 percent begins the process of extracting ourselves from the hand.

---

**Flop No. 4: T♣7♥2♥**

**Strategy:** Bet 70 percent of the time, check 30 percent.

**Analysis:** This is a favorable flop with just a few drawing threats. We're very likely to have the best hand, but the drawing threats mean that we can't be quite as trappy as with Flop No. 1. The majority of our plays should be bets, and I would bet about 50 percent of the pot. (Four big blinds into a pot of 7.5 big blinds.) Hands like this provide good balance to the continuation bets we make when we miss our hands and have to act first.

**Variation No. 1:** We bet and get called. I would use the same 70-to-30 percent ratio of bets to checks on the turn. This continues to be a good situation for us, and I would hope to be facing a hand like ace-ten which might be willing to lose a couple of bets before giving up.

**Variation No. 2:** We check. He bets. Again, we're very likely still best. I would now raise 30 percent of the time, call 70 percent. The relatively small raising percentage reflects my unwillingness to try and build a really big pot with just an overpair. However, we rate to be beating most of the hands that bet, so some raising is indicated.

# Hand B: You Raised with A♥Q♥

**Flop No. 1: A♣9♥4♠**

**Strategy:** Bet 70 percent of the time, check 30 percent.

**Analysis:** This is a straightforward situation which is good enough to bet and not good enough to trap, so most of our plays are bets.

**Variation No. 1:** We bet. He raises. Now there are two sub-variations. Against a known tight player, whose raising hands are likely to be ace-king or two pair, or a set, we have to start folding. I would use a mixture of 40 percent folds, 60 percent calls. Against anyone else, we call 100 percent of the time, but proceed cautiously thereafter.

**Variation No. 2:** We bet. He calls. Now we're back into small pot mode with a hand that doesn't really want to see a big pot. On the turn, our ratio of bets to checks will be more like 20 to 80 percent. In this case, we'll modify our randomizing strategy and for greater profit aim our bets at opponents who appear to be calling stations.

**Variation No. 3:** We check. He bets. Now we have one of the situations where I'll only make one play, which is to call. Folding with top pair good kicker to a single bet is inconceivable, and raising builds too big a pot for the strength of our hand. On the turn, I would also check.

**Variation No. 4:** We check and he checks behind us. This is a good variation, indicating that he didn't hold an ace. Now I would bet the turn 90 percent of the time, checking the rest as a trap.

---

**Flop No. 2: Q♣J♦7♥**

**Strategy:** Bet 70 percent of the time, check 30 percent.

**Analysis:** This is an ideal flop for our hand since we eliminate the variations where our opponent has top pair, better kicker. As in the last instance, we're going to bet the majority of our hands for value, checking our standard 30 percent for balance and trap potential. The bets we make here help to complement the continuation bets we will make when we miss the flop.

**Variation No. 1:** We bet. He raises. This sequence is unlikely but curiously dangerous because of the presence of the jack. Unless he's a very loose player, there are not many hands that he could consider raising which you can beat. Consider this short list:

- Raising hands that beat you: QQ, JJ, 77, and QJ (suited or unsuited).

- Raising hands that beat you but which would have raised preflop: AA, KK.

- Raising hands that you beat: KQ.

- Raising hands that you tie: AQ.

- Semi-bluffs that you beat: AK, T9.

The real problem is that the raising hands that beat you (except for aces and kings) are hands that fit his two actions (preflop call of early raiser, post-flop raise of bettor), while the hands you beat are much shakier. Would he really raise holding king-queen? Most players would call with that hand. The same holds true with the semi-bluffs.

His raise has put you in one of those post-flop situations where you really want to draw on any other knowledge you have about the table and how play has proceeded. Have you been on a run? Have you been pushing the table around? Those become good reasons to call since he may be taking a stand with a weak hand like king-jack. Have you been quiet and steady? Then he's probably got what his bet says he has, and you need to fold.

In the absence of any such information, I would start the extraction process with a mixture of 30 percent folds and 70 percent calls.

**Variation No. 2:** We bet. He calls. This is a good sequence since there are lots of callings hands we can beat.

Much now depends on the turn card. If a blank comes, bet 90 percent of the time and use a half-pot bet, a bet relatively easy for him to call. If a king comes, however, we must check. That's the most dangerous card since it doesn't help us and turns king-queen and king-jack, two of his mostly likely holdings, into winning hands.

**Variation No. 3:** We check. He bets. Here we call 100 percent of the time. Again, a fold is out of the question and a raise grows the pot too quickly. If a good card comes on the turn, anything below a nine, we usually bet. If the jack pairs, however, we check and proceed with extreme caution.

**Variation No. 4:** We check and he checks. Now we are very likely to be best, and we bet any card on the turn.

---

**Flop No. 3:** 8♥8♠2♦

**Strategy:** Bet 40 percent of the time, check 60 percent.

**Analysis:** This is a safe flop, unless he had a pair. However, a tight player would call with most pairs preflop, and a loose player would call with all pairs, so we must proceed with some caution. A bet to check ratio of 40 to 60 percent seems about right.

**Variation No. 1:** We bet. He raises. We fold 100 percent of the time. That's a very strong move on his part, we don't have anything but an ace-high hand, and we're out of position. Putting more money into the pot is a waste, so we get out.

**Variation No. 2:** We bet. He calls. This is also a strong move on his part considering our preflop raise. If we don't hit an ace or a queen on the turn, we're done.

**Variation No. 3:** We check. He bets. We call against anyone we don't know to be tight and solid. Otherwise we fold. His bet may just be a steal in response to our check, so we're mostly sticking around. However, if we know he's tight, his bet probably represents real value, and in that case we don't have enough outs to continue.

**Variation No. 4:** We check and he checks. Now we need to know a little more about our opponent. If he's tricky or inclined to bluff, then we need to bet fairly often on the turn, perhaps 60 percent bets, 40 percent checks. We're trying both to bluff and to head off a bluff on his part which would be difficult to call. Against a more conservative player, our hand is good enough to check down and see if we have the best hand. In that case, I'd go with 30 percent bets, 70 percent checks on the turn.

---

### Flop No. 4 T♣8♠4♠

**Strategy:** Bet 60 percent of the time, check 40 percent.

**Analysis:** This isn't a terribly dangerous flop right now, but we want to prevent him from picking up a straight or flush draw. We should bet a bit more than half the time; we may have the best hand, we're making a continuation bet, and we're trying to chase away hands that might make a draw on the turn.

# Hand C: You Raised with T♣T♠

### Flop No. 1: A♦9♣3♥

**Strategy:** Bet 80 percent of the time, check 20 percent.

**Analysis:** If your opponent called with an ace, he hit his hand and you're losing. Otherwise, the first player in the pot has a significant advantage. ("First in the pot wins" is a common saying to describe these flops with an ace and no draws.) Another strong argument for betting is that so many cards can come on the turn that hurt you. Any king, queen, or jack may beat you, and you'll be hard-pressed to call a bet with two overcards on board. So the bet to check ratio for this hand is close to the maximum for a post-flop play with no action yet from my opponent — 80 percent bets and 20 percent checks. The amount of the bet should be large. For a pot of 7.5 big blinds, I'd bet 6 big blinds. You would really like to end this pot right now. The more strength you can force him to show in response to your bet, the more confidence you can have in letting the hand go later.

**Variation No. 1:** You bet and he raises. Fold 100 percent of the time. He says he can beat the good ace, which you've represented, with an even better ace. Your hand isn't as good as you've represented and you have only two outs, so you fold.

**Variation No. 2:** We bet. He calls. He's representing an ace with a weak kicker, or perhaps a middle pair. We can beat the latter but not the former. On the turn we'll bet about 30 percent of the time, check about 70 percent, depending on the turn card.

**Variation No. 3:** We check. He bets. We call 100 percent of the time. His bet may be just a response to our refusal to bet, in which case our call should slow him down. We'll check the turn and see what happens.

---

**Flop No. 2: K♦Q♥4♠**

**Strategy:** Bet 60 percent of the time, check 40 percent.

**Analysis:** With two overcards to our tens, this is a very dangerous flop. As with the previous flop, you need to bet the majority of the time since this is your best moment to win the pot. Since I'm less confident of actually having the best hand, I'd bet a smaller amount, however — perhaps 50 percent of the pot.

**Variation No. 1:** We bet. He raises. We fold 100 percent of the time.

**Variation No. 2:** We bet. He calls. We're no longer very interested in the hand. True, he could be calling with a queen in his hand, and we might be able to push him off the hand by representing a king, but getting that information will be very expensive. When playing "First in the pot wins" hands, remember that if you get in first and don't win, you're losing.

**Variation No. 3:** We check. He bets. Now you need some assessment of the opponent. Against a loose, tricky, trappy opponent, call 70 percent of the time and fold 30 percent. By representing a queen or a weak king, you may be able to save the hand against a player who feels he may not be able to push you off. Against a tight opponent, just fold. This flop hit a lot of the hands he might have played.

**Variation No. 4:** We check. He checks. That's a favorable result, so we're very interested in the hand now. On the turn, I would bet 50 percent of the time and check 50 percent.

---

**Flop No. 3: A♥T♦9♣**

**Strategy:** Bet 70 percent of the time, check 30 percent.

**Analysis:** We've hit middle set, which of course is very good. An ace has come, so a bet could draw a call or a raise from a strong ace. The board is somewhat dangerous, with a lot of possible straight draws floating around.

The possible draws and the fact that a bet has a good chance of being called both argue for a solid preponderance of bets to checks, hence our 70-to-30 percent ratio. A bet here also helps to balance the continuation bets which we're frequently making when we miss our hand.

**Variation No. 1:** We bet. He raises. Now we're trying to balance reraising with calling. Although reraising gives the strength of our hand away to some extent, we do need to reraise with some percentage of our hands to cover the bluff-reraises we'll occasionally make with weaker hands. Here I like 20 percent reraises and 80 percent calls.

In general, reraising post-flop is a bit of a rare event. If we have a real good hand, we want to keep our opponent around and make more money on later streets. I mostly like to use my reraises to shut my opponent out of these quasi-dangerous drawing flops.

**Variation No. 2:** We bet. He calls. His call most likely means an ace or some kind of draw. (We know he almost certainly doesn't have middle pair, and it's a very optimistic call with a pair of nines.) Much depends now on whether a potential straight card comes on the turn.

If a straight card comes on the turn (a king, queen, jack, or eight), we must bet to prevent a free card on the river that could complete his hand. Here I'd bet 90 percent of the time and check 10 percent, with my bets mostly being pot-sized.

If a weak card comes on the turn, we're still in comfortable control. Now I would bet 50 percent and check 50 percent, with the bets mostly being half-pot bets.

**Variation No. 3:** We check. He bets. I like to raise 40 percent of the time and call 60 percent. If he calls my raise I will lead out on the turn. If I just called his bet, I'll bet 70 percent on the turn and check the rest.

**Variation No. 4:** We check and he checks. On the turn I'll bet 80 percent of the time and check 20 percent. We need to start getting money in the pot, but we're still saving a few well-concealed sets for a river bet.

---

## Flop No. 4: 7♦6♣5♣

**Strategy:** Bet 80 percent of the time, check 20 percent.

**Analysis:** Here we have a very strong desire to bet because we have a good hand, and because so many scary cards can come on the turn. We'll be scared of cards higher than our tens since they could make a higher pair, and we'll be scared of low cards which could make a set or a straight. So our bet to check ratio is very high: 80-to-20 percent.

**Variation No. 1:** We bet. He raises. We're in a tough spot. He could be making a value bet with a set, or a straight, or two pair. He could be semi-bluffing with lots of outs. Or he could be on a pure bluff. Although I don't like the situation, our hand is too good to just concede, so I'll call 50 percent of the time and fold the rest. Against an A-B-C type player, however, I would just fold. He's not going to be kidding here.

**Variation No. 2:** We bet. He calls. Future action here hinges on the turn card. If a club comes, check. If a straight card comes, check. If an overcard comes that isn't an ace, bet 60 percent of the time and check 40 percent. Make a solid bet, about 70 percent or more of the pot. You'd really like to win the hand as soon as possible.

**Variation No. 3:** We check. He bets. Here I would call 100 percent of the time.

**Variation No. 4:** We check and he checks. That's a green light to bet the turn. Whatever card comes, I would bet 80 percent of the time and check 20 percent.

# Preflop Aggressor in Position

**You were the aggressor preflop. You are in position after the flop. For these examples, assume you raised three big blinds from the cutoff seat, and were called only by the big blind. You act after him on the flop.**

Before we go on to the hands, let's make a couple of brief notes about playing the big blind after the flop. In particular, how often should you take the lead in the betting?

While most players are very conservative with the big blind, I think a little more aggression is required. Since the big blind gets a favorable price when he calls, he can call with a wider range of hands. Therefore, he can represent a credible threat on a wider range of flops than a player who had to play full price to call. Here are my rules for playing with the big blind in a heads-up situation:

- With a super-strong hand after the flop, bet more often than normal. Your hand is less likely to be recognized as a real threat.

- Against a tight or passive opponent, mostly lead out in the betting whether you hit your hand or not. The fact that you could be playing a wide variety of hands weighs more heavily on the mind of a tight opponent, and may be enough to claim the hand right there.

- When three low cards come, bet. These are the cards your opponent doesn't have and thinks you may have, so your bet puts enormous pressure on him. If he just calls, bet again on the turn.

# Hand D: You Raised with A♠A♣

**Flop No. 1: A♦8♥5♣**

**His action:** He bets 3 big blinds.

**Strategy:** Raise 10 percent of the time, call 90 percent.

**Analysis:** This is an ideal situation. We have top set on a board with no draws, and our opponent is betting into us! The vast bulk of our plays must be calls here. Our opponent is representing an ace, and our call represents a weaker ace or middle or small pair. We should give our opponent every chance to steal the pot or make what he might think are value bets later, mixing in a few raises only for balance.

**His action:** He checks.

**Strategy:** Bet 25 percent of the time, check 75 percent.

**Analysis:** The maxim of "big hand big pot, small hand small pot" breaks down when it's hard for the opponent to have a hand to play. In these cases you have to forgo the idea of winning a big pot and just concentrate on winning something more than the pot you have. Here our actions are heavily skewed toward checking, again with a few bets tossed in for balance.

In general, flopping middle set is a bigger money-maker over time than flopping top set. When you flop middle set, your opponent might have top pair with a good kicker, and be willing to go some distance with you. When you have top set, it's hard for him to have much more than a draw.

**Variation No. 1:** He checks. You bet. He calls. Now the plan for the turn is to raise if he bets, and bet if he checks. His call on the flop indicates there's some chance he has a hand that he's willing to back. Once you know that, it's time to push the action. If by some miracle he has a smaller set or two pair, you need to set the stage for winning his whole stack on the river. Any realistic possibility of winning his whole stack dwarfs the odd bet that you might forfeit by chasing him away prematurely. But notice that you waited for a show of strength from him before making that decision. Absent any show of strength, remain focused on winning that odd extra bet.

**Variation No. 2:** He checks and you check. The plan for the turn is 70 percent bets, 30 percent checks.

You have two strong reasons for betting the turn. The first is obvious: get more money in the pot. The second is less obvious.

Each card that comes off has two possible effects on your opponent. The card might hit his hand and give him a holding he feels might be best. Or the card could miss him but make an even more dangerous-looking board, "freezing the action" as we say. *The more cards on board, the more likely that the next card is a freezer rather than a helper.* Hence, the standard strategy for most professionals with a very big hand is to give a free flop card, then bet on the turn, rather than waiting all the way to the river to bet.

Why not bet all your hands here for that reason, rather than just betting 70 percent of the time? We need to balance our strategy by making sure that some of our monsters are checked all the way to the river. That way our opponents learn that we can still have a huge hand after a sequence of checking the flop, checking the turn, and making what appears to be a steal on the river.

---

**Flop No. 2: T♦9♥8♥**

**His action:** He bets 3 big blinds.

**Strategy:** Raise 10 percent of the time, call 90 percent.

**Analysis:** We're definitely scared of that flop, with possible sets, straights, and two-pair combinations floating around. But we can't fold to a single bet, so our actions are heavily skewed toward calling with just a few raises for balance. When the turn comes and he takes another action before us, we'll have a clearer idea of what to do.

**His action:** He checks.

**Strategy:** Bet 75 percent of the time, check 25 percent.

**Analysis:** His check makes life a bit easier for us. Because of the extreme dangerousness of the flop, we need to take the lead in the betting and bet a significant amount, aiming to win the pot right here if possible. At the very least, we need to make him pay a significant price to draw. I want to bet somewhere between 80 percent of the pot and the full pot. With a pot of 6.5 big blinds, I'd bet somewhere between 5 and 7 big blinds.

**Variation No. 1:** He checks. We bet. He calls. Now much depends on the turn card. If a blank comes, my hand should still be good, and I would bet 60 percent of the time and check 40 percent. If a straight card (jack or seven) or a club comes, we have to check.

Eights and nines are interesting cards because each has the possibility of giving us a better two pair than him. For instance, if he has ten-nine and an eight falls, our aces up dominate his two pair of tens and nines. The same holds true if he has ten-eight and a nine falls. Balanced against that is the smaller possibility that he just made trips or a full house, so we're still mostly checking those situations down if we can.

**Variation No. 2:** He checks. We bet. He raises. We're in another very tough situation where any knowledge of our opponent's tendencies is useful.

The first question to answer is: Can he be bluffing? Very few players can pull off a check-raise bluff on a dangerous board while out of position. Unless he's a known maniac or a really good cash game player, we've got to downgrade the possibility of a pure bluff in this situation to nearly zero.

If he's not bluffing, he either has a made hand — a straight or a set — or a semi-bluff. We're usually a small favorite against the semi-bluffs, but a huge underdog to the made hands. Our formerly imposing hand is now a weak one, and we have to reorient ourselves. Our new question becomes, "What pot odds are we getting?" If they're good, we can call more often. With poor odds, we're mostly folding.

The minimum pot odds I require in a situation like this is about 2-to-1. With smaller odds than that, I'm willing to let the hand go. Consider a typical sequence where the pot was 6.5 big blinds before the flop. (Our 3, his 3, and 0.5 big blinds from the small blind.) If he checks and we bet 5 big blinds, slightly less than the pot on the flop, the pot becomes 11.5 big blinds. To make a pot-sized raise, our opponent would have to put in about 20 more big blinds. That would leave a pot of 31.5 big blinds, and require us to put in 15 big blinds to call, for odds of a bit better than 2-to-1. Most experienced players will size their check-raise semi-bluffs to be at least pot-sized or even a bit larger, for exactly this reason.

When I get the minimum odds I want, I'll call 30 percent of the time and fold the rest. If I get better odds (because my opponent's check-raise was too small) I'll call more, perhaps 40 or even 50 percent. Be very aware, however, that once you get check-raised your aces become a weak hand. You're calling to let your opponent know that he can't chase you away with just a semi-bluffing hand.

---

**Flop No. 3: 9♥9♣6♠**

**His action:** He bets 3 big blinds.

**Strategy:** Raise 40 percent of the time, call 60 percent.

**Analysis:** This is a good flop for you with very few draws available. If he called preflop with a pair, he's realizes that he's well-positioned to have the best hand. If he has a nine, of course, you're going to lose some money.

**Variation No. 1:** He bets and you call. On the turn, your plan depends very much on how he proceeds. If he bets again, you'll just call. Despite your pair of aces, you still just have an overpair to the board, not a hand where you really want to risk your whole stack. Notice how quickly your perfect preflop holding descends into "small hand small pot" mode. If he checks on the turn, you'll bet 50 percent of the time and check 50 percent, with your bets being half-pot bets.

**Variation No. 2:** He bets. You raise. He reraises. You represented a big hand and he reraised you. Not many hands lacking a nine will do that. Fold 80 percent of the time and call 20 percent, with the calls demonstrating that you can't be pushed out of a hand automatically.

**Variation No. 3:** He bets. You raise. He calls. Again, very few hands can make this play. He may have a nine and be trapping, or he could have a pair, an eight-seven, or a bluff. The turn play is complicated and depends on the card that appears and his action. In general, you want to stay in the hand, but keep the pot small.

**His action:** He checks.

**Strategy:** Bet 60 percent of the time, check 40 percent.

**Analysis:** His check indicates that you're likely to have the upper hand, so you want to mostly bet.

**Variation No. 1:** He checks. You bet. He raises. Although he might be check-raising with trip nines, many players in this spot would believe that a pocket pair, especially a pair higher than the nines, would be good. They're check-raising just with the idea of picking up an extra bet on the flop. This is also a common spot for check-raise bluffs.

I would call here unless against a very tight player who is certainly not bluffing and is unlikely to make a check-raise with anything other than a nine.

**Variation No. 2:** He checks. You bet. He calls. This betting sequence could represent a variety of hands, almost all of which you're beating. If he checks the turn, bet about 40 percent of the time and check 60 percent. If he bets, call.

---

**Flop No. 4: K♥Q♠J♠**

**His action:** He bets 3 big blinds.

**Strategy:** Raise 10 percent of the time, call 90 percent.

**Analysis:** Here's another very difficult flop to play. You may be beaten already, and the board is loaded with draws, so semi-bluff bets will be common. In addition, you can't even be sure that hitting an ace is good for you. It might instead cost you a big chunk of your stack.

Calling 90 percent of the time looks about right here. You can't fold your overpair yet, and you do have a draw to the nut straight. The 10 percent raises are not value bets; they're just randomizing bluffs.

**His action:** He checks.

**Strategy:** Bet 80 percent of the time, check 20 percent.

**Analysis:** This play is similar to other bets we've made on very dangerous flops. We're trying to extract the apparent value of our hand quickly, before someone makes the nuts. The bets should be large, 80 to 100 percent of the pot.

**Variation No. 1:** He checks. We bet. He raises. This is the worst possible sequence. Still, we can't yet fold all our hands because of the strong semi-bluffing possibilities. Instead, call 30 percent of the time and fold 70 percent, and see what happens on the turn.

**Variation No. 2:** He checks. We bet. He calls. We're hoping for a blank on the turn and a chance to check the hand down.

**Variation No. 3:** He checks and we check. On the turn, the bad card is a nine, giving him a possible straight we can't match. The weird card is an ace, after which we don't know where we stand, and we're locked into more betting.

Against most turn cards, we'll bet 75 percent of the time and check 25 percent. We need to start extracting some value from the aces if they are, in fact, the best hand.

# Hand E: You Raised with A♥Q♥

**Flop No. 1:** A♣9♥4♠

**His action:** He bets 3 big blinds.

**Strategy:** Raise 20 percent of the time, call 80 percent.

**Analysis:** This recommendation may seem unduly conservative to some. We have top pair and an excellent kicker; why not raise more often? But top pair hands are the quintessential example of the "small hand small pot" maxim. Outside of very small stake, weak games, getting into a raising war with these hands simply means that the hands that can't beat top pair go away and the better hands keep playing. Once the first bet goes in the pot and gets called, a good player gets very cautious with ace-queen.

Having said that, we will make a small number of raises. These raises are hard to categorize precisely. They share characteristics of value bets, bluffs, and metagame plays, all rolled into one package.

**Variation No. 1:** He bets. We raise. He reraises. We fold. Too tight? Well, what can he reasonably have? A pair of kings? A weak ace? Not very likely. His reraise says he has ace-king, aces, or a smaller set. All those hands leave us crushed and gasping for air. If he's bluffing he has the heart of a lion.

**Variation No. 2:** He bets. We raise. He calls. This is an interesting variation but we can't really formulate a plan yet. We'll wait for the turn card and his response to it. His failure to reraise means we may have the best hand, but whether we'll invest much more money is unclear.

**His action:** He checks.

**Strategy:** Bet 80 percent of the time, check 20 percent.

**Analysis:** This is pretty straightforward. We have top pair, good kicker and he didn't bet. Our bet will probably win the pot, which is a fine result.

**Variation No. 1:** He checks. We bet. He raises. This is a much better variation for us than when he reraised our raise. We might have simply been betting in response to his check, so his raise could represent some sort of medium to small ace up against an underpair. We should call 80 percent of the time and fold 20 percent, aiming our folds at the players we know to be tight.

---

**Flop No. 2: Q♣J♦7♥**

**His action:** He bets 3 big blinds.

**Strategy:** Raise 40 percent of the time, call 60 percent.

**Analysis:** This is a very favorable situation, only slightly complicated by the possible straight draws around the queen-jack. He probably has a weaker queen or a jack. If so our raise should win the pot.

**Variation No. 1:** He bets. We raise. He reraises. Your response here depends on your read, if any, of your opponent and his characteristics. Against a good, tight player, you fold. He wouldn't make this move without a hand that beats yours. Against a weak player you can call and continue. You might be up against king-queen, queen-ten, or even king-ten. Against a wild, trappy player who makes moves here and there, you'll keep slogging. If he really has a hand, he'll get all your money.

**His action:** He checks.

**Strategy:** Bet 70 percent of the time, check 30 percent.

**Analysis:** This is a standard value betting situation. You'd be happy to take the pot down right away with your top pair, top kicker; the checks provide balance, ensuring that some good hands get pushed through to the turn.

**Variation No. 1:** He checks. You bet. He raises. This check-raise is more likely to represent a very strong hand than the check-raise in the previous flop. Many players will check-raise with simply a good ace in their hand; not so many players get very excited about a good queen or even a good jack.

I would call 40 percent of the time and fold 60 percent. Rather than randomizing, try to aim your folds at the tighter or unknown players, and the calls at the loose-aggressive players.

**Flop No. 3: 8♥8♣2♠**

**His action:** He bets 3 big blinds.

**Strategy:** Raise 20 percent of the time, call 60 percent, fold 20 percent.

**Analysis:** This is a premium bluffing flop, and frequently prompts a game of chicken between the two players, with each player raising or reraising to represent an eight. Good players tend to excel in these scenarios because they're much better at judging when to push the envelope, against whom to push it, and how to tell when an opponent's psychology has changed from aggression to fear.

Here are some rough, general guidelines for these situations (medium pair plus a low card on board):

1. An average to weak player has a set 40 percent of the time when they raise your initial bet.

2. A tight but unimaginative player, someone who's just trying to grind out a profit, will only raise your bet with something. He'll have a pair 80 percent of the time, and a set 20 percent of the time.

3. A good player could have anything.

The initial bet (as opposed to the raise of a bet) is player-specific and doesn't necessarily mean much. Lots, if not most, players will lead at a flop like this heads-up. However, you don't have anything except an ace-high hand with six outs, so you should fold a small percentage of the time. Try to aim your folds at the tightest players at the table.

**Variation No. 1:** He bets. You raise. He reraises. Fold 100 percent of the time. You don't have a pair and if you continue you're jeopardizing your entire stack. You don't want to do that with an ace-high hand. "Small hand, small pot," remember.

**His action:** He checks.

**Strategy:** Bet 60 percent of the time, check 40 percent.

**Analysis:** This is a classic continuation bet play. You actually have less incentive than normal to make a continuation bet here since your ace-queen is probably best, and in that case you're about a 4-to-1 favorite in the hand. There's not much need to put money in a pot your winning anyway, unless you're pretty sure your opponent will call with a worse hand. But here that's likely since your bet will often be interpreted as a steal.

Your bet achieves another goal however, which is to stop him from betting on the turn. With this kind of flop, that's a good achievement.

**Variation No. 1:** He checks. You bet. He raises. 50 percent of the time fold, 40 percent call, and 10 percent reraise. You have to fold some number here since he could be raising you with a pair. You also have to reraise a few because he could be trying to chase you away with nothing. I would target the reraises, however, against the wildest players at the table.

**Variation No. 2:** He checks. You bet. He calls. He probably has a non-paired hand with two high cards, perhaps even a hand you dominate. If a high card (that doesn't hit you) comes on the turn, mostly fold to his bet, and mostly check behind his check. If a low card comes, you can call his bet and check behind him if he doesn't bet. The general idea is to keep the pot small and see if your hand is good enough to win a showdown.

**Flop No. 4: T♣8♠4♠**

**His action:** He bets 3 big blinds.

**Strategy:** Raise 20 percent of the time, call 40 percent, fold 40 percent.

**Analysis:** The flop is murky. It missed you, and it might or might not have hit your opponent. He may be betting with a real hand, or betting because it's his only real chance of winning the pot.

Since you don't really know where you stand, your strategy here combines a little of all three actions. You fold sometimes because you don't have anything and he's betting. You raise sometimes because he may be bluffing. And you call sometimes because you might hit an ace or a queen on the turn, and even if you don't, you'll have the opportunity to take the pot away from him at that point. Your actions are completely balanced and your opponent won't really be able to get a handle on what you're doing.

**His action:** He checks.

**Strategy:** Bet 75 percent of the time, check 25 percent.

**Analysis:** We're mostly making a standard continuation bet here. The flop is more dangerous for us than the previous flop (because with three different ranks, there are more chances our opponent hit something) but also more dangerous for him (for exactly the same reason). We want to be first into such pots, so mostly we bet. Our bet size should be about half the pot. Note that we only need to make pot-sized bets on really dangerous, connected boards like ten-nine-eight where it's essential that we chase our opponent away as soon as possible. Normal boards allow normal bets.

**Variation No. 1.** He checks. We bet. He raises. Fold 80 percent of the time, call 15 percent, reraise 5 percent. We're mostly beaten here, but he might be bluffing, so we continue playing in a few cases.

# Hand F: You Raised with 9♠9♣

**Flop No. 1:** A♥8♣4♦

**His action:** He bets 3 big blinds.

**Strategy:** Raise 20 percent of the time, call 80 percent.

**Analysis:** This might seem unduly aggressive with an ace on board, but consider just what your opponent's bet means. Most players who just paired their ace would check to the preflop aggressor. Hence, his bet mostly indicates a player who's bluffing or else betting a lower pair to see if it's any good. Your nines rate to be the best hand in these variations, particularly since they are higher than the middle card in the flop, so don't be in a hurry to get out of the pot. The 20 percent to 80 percent raise to call ratio seems about right.

**Variation No. 1:** He bets. You raise. He reraises. Fold 100 percent of the time. Now he's told you emphatically that he's not fooling around.

**Variation No. 2:** He bets and you call. Now your play depends on the turn card and his response. Here are a few cases:

1. A high card comes (king through ten) and he bets. Unfavorable. Now it's hard to credit him with a pair lower than your nines, and it's even harder to think he has nothing. Call 20 percent of the time, fold 80 percent.

2. A high card comes and he checks. Favorable. Your nines are even more likely to be best, and he should have few outs on the river. Bet 70 percent of the time, check 30 percent. Your bet could chase away a pair of tens and eliminate some other hands that could draw out on the river.

3. A low card (seven or below) comes and he bets. Each bet on his part increases the chance that in fact he holds an ace. Call 20 percent of the time, fold 80 percent.

4. A low card comes and he checks. Bet 70 percent of the time, check 30 percent. You are probably best, but a bet won't make any better hand fold, so you're hoping to make money by getting a weaker pair to call, while protecting yourself against a high card on the river.

**His action:** He checks.

**Strategy:** Bet 80 percent of the time, check 20 percent.

**Analysis:** You're probably best, but you need to bet a high percentage of the time because so many cards can come on the turn to hurt you. (Any king, queen, jack, or ten is bad news.) As your pair gets higher, two interesting things happen. Fewer turn cards are troublesome, so you don't need to bet as much to protect your hand. But the chances increase that your opponent can hold an underpair that can call your bet, so your desire to bet and get more money in the pot grows. With a pair of kings in this situation, for example, you have hardly any need to bet for protection, but you have a strong desire to bet for value because many pairs under your kings will have to call.

**Variation No. 1:** He checks. You bet. He raises. This is a particularly bad variation, but he might be bluffing, so you need to call sometimes. Fold 70 percent of the time, call 30 percent.

Note that the check-raise presents a situation where any knowledge of your opponent's tendencies can cause you to adjust these folding/calling percentages dramatically. Against a known tight player, the calling percentage might drop to 5 to 10 percent (but never to zero). Against a loose player, you could reasonably call 40 to 50 percent of the time.

---

### Flop No. 2: K♥Q♦3♣

**His action:** He bets 3 big blinds.

**Strategy:** Raise 10 percent of the time, call 40 percent, fold 50 percent.

**Analysis:** Two overcards plus a bet equals an unhappy situation, but it's too soon in the hand to just assume we're beaten. Folding half the time seems about right, while the 10 percent raises are enough to counteract the times he's just bluffing.

**His action:** He checks.

**Strategy:** Bet 70 percent of the time, check 30 percent.

**Analysis:** If we're currently ahead, we still need to bet a lot because there remains plenty of overcards that can hurt us — aces, jacks, and tens. If we're behind, we'll have to find out sooner or later. Besides, our preflop raise indicated that we should be pretty happy with this flop, so let's bet it.

**Variation No. 1:** He checks. We bet. He raises. Since we did raise preflop, and since the flop should have hit us, it's very hard for him to bluff here. Let's call 10 percent of the time and fold 90 percent, calling only against the loosest and most aggressive players.

**Flop No. 3: A♥K♣9♦**

**His action:** He bets 3 big blinds.

**Strategy:** Raise 5 percent of the time, call 95 percent.

**Analysis:** No one leads at this flop without a pretty good hand. The only straight draw that's possible is a gutshot draw to the nut straight, and there are no flush draws. So he has something, probably a pretty good ace.

Our goal is not to raise him off the hand. If he has a good ace, he'll be willing to commit another bet, but probably not willing to get his whole stack involved. So we proceed with caution, starting mostly with a call on the flop. We stick in a few raises for balance since we've been willing to raise other hands essentially as bluffs.

**His action:** He checks.

**Strategy:** Bet 60 percent of the time, check 40 percent.

**Analysis:** Once he checks, you have to ask if there's anything he can catch to give you action. It's certainly possible, based on his preflop call, that he has an ace or a king, but chose not to bet it. In that case, a bet now will get called and will start the process of getting money in the pot. If he called preflop with a low pair, that flop is just too scary and you won't be able to make any money on the hand.

If he has a draw, it's to an inside straight with something like jack-ten. He won't call your bet, but when you check, you won't make any money on the turn if he misses and you'll lose a lot when he hits, so you have no reason to let him draw.

**Variation No. 1:** He checks. You bet. He raises. Reraise 30 percent of the time and call 70 percent. The ideal scenario is that he called you with ace-king and is now willing to commit a good chunk of his stack. The nightmare scenario is that he slowplayed aces or kings and will now win your whole stack. When you call, expect him to lead out on the turn no matter what comes.

---

**Flop No. 4: 6♦5♠4♠**

**His action:** He bets 3 big blinds.

**Strategy:** Raise 30 percent of the time, call 70 percent.

**Analysis:** You can't fold here. He may have hit a pair and thinks it might be good if you were playing two high cards. He probably doesn't have a draw unless it's something like seven-six since his bet has raised the possibility of your taking him off the hand. So you can put him on one pair, two pair, a set, or a bluff. It's too soon to fold, and a small number of raises are indicated with your overpair.

**His action:** He checks.

**Strategy:** Bet 80 percent of the time, check 20 percent.

**Analysis:** When he checks, draws become much more likely. Now we need to go into offense/defense mode, making big bets most of the time to charge the draws. I would bet at least 75 percent of the pot.

**Variation No. 1:** He checks. We bet. He raises. We need to respect his check-raise, but not too much. Since we were the preflop aggressor, this flop should have missed us. Therefore our bet looks like a bluff and his check-raise may be a bluff as well. We're not inclined to reraise ("small hand, small pot") but we'll stick around most of the time. Call 80 percent of the time, fold 20 percent.

# Non-Aggressor Out of Position

Your opponent was the aggressor preflop. You are out of position after the flop. For these examples, assume he raised three big blinds from the cutoff seat, and you called in the big blind. You act before him on the flop.

With our opponent as the preflop aggressor and in position, our betting percentages, even when we make a hand, will be lower than in the two previous sections. When we have a weak hand we're less likely to push the action since he has already told us he has a strong hand. When we have a strong hand we're more inclined to trap. Even so, we will still bet, although at a lower rate, to balance our play.

# Hand G: You
# Called His Raise with J♥J♦

**Flop No. 1: A♣J♠T♦**

**Strategy:** Bet 30 percent of the time, check 70 percent.

**Analysis:** The flop is good for you, of course, since you have middle set. It's also dangerous since anyone with a king or a queen is drawing to a straight. On the bright side, your opponent may well have an ace and be inclined to play.

We'll start off betting 30 percent of the time on the theory that he'll bet after most of our checks. Either way, we shouldn't have much trouble getting a lot of money in this pot.

**Variation No. 1:** We bet. He raises. The raises will usually indicate one of three hands: ace-king, ace-queen, or ace-ten. The first two have top pair, great kicker, and an inside straight draw. The latter has top and bottom pair. In all cases we're a big favorite. We're also a big favorite if he happens to have a pair of tens for bottom set.

We reraise 40 percent of the time, call 60 percent. We're trying to vary our play while at the same time getting a lot of money in the pot. Either sequence may do the job depending on our opponent and his predilections, so varying between them is both balance and good technique.

**Variation No. 2:** We bet and he calls. On the turn we will mostly bet again. The bet might chase him away, but when our opponent is showing an interest in a pot that could cost him his whole stack, we have to continue maneuvering toward that goal.

**Variation No. 3:** We check. He bets. We raise 80 percent of the time, call 20 percent. This is a pretty standard check-raise, but the texture of the flop may trap our opponent for his whole stack.

**Variation No. 4:** We check and he checks. On the turn, we'll bet 80 percent of the time and check the rest, creating a few variations where we have checked to the river with a very strong hand.

---

**Flop No. 2: A♣9♠8♥**

**Strategy:** Bet 20 percent of the time, check 80 percent.

**Analysis:** You're unhappy to see the ace, but he may be as well. There's a very reasonable chance your jacks are good, although being out of position makes your job more difficult. You should mix a few bets with a preponderance of checks.

**Variation No. 1:** You bet. He raises. His raise is a strong move with an ace on board. Call 50 percent of the time, fold 50 percent. It's too soon to give up entirely, but you need to start extracting yourself from the hand.

**Variation No. 2:** You check. He bets. Call 100 percent of the time. You still have no solid reason to think you're beaten, so continue playing.

---

**Flop No. 3: T♣9♠8♠**

**Strategy:** Bet 60 percent of the time, check 40 percent.

**Analysis:** Now it's you that has the open-ended straight draw. You have a strong hand. Against a pair of aces, you're only a 60-to-40 underdog. With both a made hand and a draw, you should mostly bet.

**Variation No. 1:** You bet. He raises. Call 50 percent of the time, reraise 30 percent, reraise all-in 20 percent. When you have reasonable prospects of making a huge hand, you don't need to fear the occasional big pot. You finally have a hand that's suitable for playing very aggressively, so go ahead.

**Variation No. 2:** You check. He bets. Call 50 percent of the time, raise 50 percent. A lot of your raises are going to win the pot right here. When you don't win immediately, you're still in fine shape.

**Variation No. 3:** You check and he checks. Bet 80 percent of the time on the turn no matter what comes.

---

**Flop No. 4: 7♣7♠5♦**

**Strategy:** Bet 30 percent of the time, check 70 percent.

**Analysis:** You're in good shape with what is likely to be the best hand. It's unlikely that he has more than a few outs, so pushing the betting hard isn't required. Leading out 30 percent of the time seems about right.

**Variation No. 1:** You check. He bets. Raise 70 percent of the time, call 30 percent. As we've seen before, a lot of players see this flop as a license to steal. This is a good time to lower the boom on those players.

**Variation No. 2:** You check. He bets. You raise. He reraises. Now we have a totally different situation — "Small hand, small pot." The pot is getting very outsized for the strength of your hand. You mostly have to go away here, but call a few as bluff-catchers. Fold 70 percent of the time, call 30 percent.

# Hand H: You Called His Raise with 3♣3♥

**Flop No. 1: A♦T♥6♣**

**Strategy:** Bet 10 percent of the time, check 90 percent.

**Analysis:** Calling with small pairs is an implied-odds play designed to win a big pot when you flop a well-hidden small set. When you miss the flop, there's not much you can do but toss in the occasional bluff.

**Variation No. 1:** You check. He bets. Fold 90 percent of the time, call 5 percent, raise 5 percent. Again, you're using what's almost a worthless hand to get some of your bluffs working.

---

**Flop No. 2: J♦T♥3♠**

**Strategy:** Bet 30 percent of the time, check 70 percent.

**Analysis:** You have bottom set, but the board is a little dangerous with two middle cards opening up some straight draws. You can't entirely sit back and let him take a free card, hence the 30 percent betting frequency.

**Variation No. 1:** You bet. He raises. Call 30 percent of the time, reraise 70 percent. The hand is just a little too dangerous to allow a bunch of cheap cards to come off. If he wants to see more cards, let him pay a high price.

**Variation No. 2:** You check. He bets. Raise 60 percent of the time, call 40 percent. The calls are traps and you'll be aiming for bets or check-raises on the turn.

---

**Flop No. 3: 9♥7♣2♠**

**Strategy:** Bet 30 percent of the time, check 70 percent.

**Analysis:** Your treys have a reasonable chance of being best here, but your unfavorable position reduces their value. Even when you're ahead, you'll have difficulty calling any significant raises. Betting less than half the time and checking the rest is prudent.

**Variation No. 1:** You bet. He raises. Fold 100 percent of the time. You can't get a lot of money involved with this hand and this flop. If you call, what's your plan for the turn?

**Variation No. 2:** You check. He bets. Call 60 percent of the time, fold 40 percent. You have a pair and need to call one bet a fair percentage of the time. On the turn, just wait and see what happens.

# Hand I: You Called His Raise with K♣J♠

**Flop No. 1: A♥K♠T♣**

**Strategy:** Bet 20 percent of the time, check 80 percent.

**Analysis:** A very difficult flop. You have middle pair and a gutshot straight draw, but an ace is on board and you're out of position.

Your hand isn't strong enough to be very aggressive, but the flop might have scared your opponent as well, so you need to mix in some bets. However, I like playing this hand cautiously, so I'll keep the betting percentage down to 20 percent.

**Variation No. 1:** You bet. He raises. Fold 100 percent of the time. The situation is much too dangerous to be playing a large pot out of position. Notice as well that hitting your jack may simply complete a straight for your opponent. While the strategy here will seem excessively tight to many players, this is a hand where you need to cut your losses very early.

**Variation No. 2:** You check. He bets. Raise 10 percent of the time, call 90 percent. The raises are more bluff than semi-bluff, of course, and you need to bluff sometimes at a dangerous flop. Randomizing your play helps ensure that you make the right percentage of bluffs over time. The high call percentage shows that you shouldn't be willing to fold second pair to the first bet.

---

**Flop No. 2: T♥T♣4♠**

**Strategy:** Bet 40 percent of the time, check 60 percent.

**Analysis:** This is a good bluffing flop, so our bet percentage gets closer to 50 percent.

**Variation No. 1:** We bet. He raises. His raise mostly means he has a pair, although an ace would beat us as well. Our chances of winning the hand out of position are slim. Fold 100 percent of the time.

**Variation No. 2:** We check. He bets. Raise 10 percent of the time, call 10 percent, fold 80 percent. The high fold percentage is dictated by the likelihood that we're just losing here. The high raise percentage relative to our calling hands reflects the good bluffing nature of the flop. Without the randomizing strategy, we might never remember to bluff in situations like this which is obviously a clear error, but an easy one to make when you're trying to judge each play separately rather than as part of a well-defined strategy.

---

**Flop No. 3:** T♠9♠8♠

**Strategy:** Bet 60 percent of the time, check 40 percent.

**Analysis:** An open-ended straight flush draw is a very strong hand. Exactly how many outs we have is unclear. If our opponent has the A♠, K♠, Q♠, our draw may cost us our entire stack, but that's somewhat unlikely. (However, if a significant amount of money goes in the pot after a fourth spade hits the board, it becomes more and more likely. Our highest-quality outs are the sevens, giving us a jack-high straight, and the queens, which give us a king-high straight. (In that respect, we're actually ahead of someone holding ace-jack.)

If all our outs were good, we'd have 15 outs, with some possibility that our king is an out as well. Since the value of our flush draw is unclear, probably 12 to 13 outs is a better estimate.

(Of course, this is assuming we're behind in the hand at present, which might not be the case.)

Our hand is clearly strong enough to bet, and to bet aggressively. I like starting with 60 percent bets, and the checks are just an invitation to a check-raise.

**Variation No. 1:** We bet. He raises. If the stacks are about 100 big blinds, call 50 percent of the time and reraise all-in with the other 50 percent. If the stacks are more in the neighborhood of 200 big blinds, all-in is too much of an overbet. In that case call 70 percent of the time and reraise to about 50 big blinds the remaining 30 percent of the time.

This is another example of the nuances of very deep-stacked play. If the stacks are very deep, and your raise to 50 big blinds gets reraised, the play indicates more strength than you'd like to see. On that flop, there are very few holdings that can confidently put in the third raise. His most likely hand in that case is something like A♠K♠, or maybe the A♠ with one of the remaining jacks.

**Variation No. 2:** We check. He bets. Raise 70 percent of the time, call 30 percent. The check-raise was the point of most of our initial checks. The calls just create balance, allowing us to reach the turn or river with a deceptively strong hand.

# Hand J: You
# Called His Raise with 7♥6♥

**Flop No. 1:** A♥7♦2♥

**Strategy:** Bet 30 percent of the time, check 70 percent.

**Analysis:** We flopped a good hand, a pair plus a flush draw. Our plan is to lead out with some bets, while check-raising with some of our other hands.

**Variation No. 1:** We check. He bets. Raise 60 percent of the time, call 40 percent. We probably have 14 outs, which is good enough for a healthy majority of check-raises. The calls leave our opponent in the dark as to the real nature of our hand.

**Variation No. 2:** We bet. He raises. Reraise 60 percent of the time, call 40 percent. With the ace on board, the reraise is misleading. Our opponent is more likely to put us on a good ace than a flush draw. This is a leveraged bet where a good card on the turn or the river could win a huge pot, while a bad card allows us to exit the hand for a minimal cost.

---

**Flop No. 2: K♣Q♠9♦**

**Strategy:** Bet 10 percent of the time, check 90 percent.

**Analysis:** The bets are bluffs. Otherwise we're just giving up on the hand.

---

**Flop No. 3: T♥T♣4♦**

**Strategy:** Bet 40 percent of the time, check 60 percent.

**Analysis:** Again, we make a healthy number of bets into an obvious bluffing flop, partly to discourage our opponent to take the lead in the bluffing.

**Variation No. 1:** We bet. He raises. Fold 90 percent of the time, reraise 5 percent, call 5 percent. Obviously we have no value here.

The reraises and calls just serve as bluffs to balance our value raises and calls in other situations.

**Variation No. 2:** We check. He bets. Fold 80 percent of the time, raise 10 percent, call 10 percent. His bet is more likely to be a bluff than in Variation No. 1, so we increase our raising and calling frequencies somewhat.

# Non-Aggressor in Position

**Your opponent was the aggressor preflop. You are in position after the flop. For these examples, assume he raised three big blinds from third position, and you called on the button. You act after him on the flop.**

## Hand K: You
## Called His Raise with T♥T♣

**Flop No. 1: K♠T♦5♣**

**His action:** He bets 3 big blinds.

**Strategy:** Raise 30 percent of the time, call 70 percent.

**Analysis:** You've flopped middle set. As we've seen before, that's a great hand because your opponent can make top pair and play along with you for awhile. We'll mostly call, but put in a raise with a few hands.

**His action:** He checks.

**Strategy:** Bet 50 percent of the time, check 50 percent.

**Analysis:** This is a slightly higher bet-to-check ratio than one might at first expect. To see why, let's look at the flop more closely. If he doesn't have any high cards, there isn't much money for you to win no matter what action you take. If he does have high cards, the flop is slightly dangerous. If he has a king, the flop is ideal for you, and he will certainly call your bet and may raise it. But if he doesn't have a king, then he probably doesn't have a ten as well (since three tens are accounted for), which leaves him with possible holdings of ace-queen, ace-jack, and queen-jack. Those are bad combinations for you since he can't call if you bet, but by checking he gets a free card to fill a straight and beat you. That's the worst possible situation for you, and you want to increase your betting percentage when that's floating in the air.

A second reason for betting is that you're in position, and therefore your bet looks more like a steal after he checks, so he's more likely to call it.

---

**Flop No. 2: 9♦7♠4♣**

**His action:** He bets 3 big blinds.

**Strategy:** Raise 40 percent of the time, call 60 percent.

**Analysis:** You have an overpair, so you're likely to have the best hand even after he bets. Raising 40 percent of the time seems about right.

**Variation No. 1:** He bets. You raise. He calls. If a blank comes and he bets again on the turn, you have to face the possibility that he has a better pair than yours. In addition, the pot is getting pretty big for a hand which is just the smallest possible overpair. Call 30 percent of the time, fold 70 percent. If he checks, you should check behind him. Your problem now is that very few hands worse than yours will call the third bet, while not many hands better than you can fold. Keep the pot small and try to check it down.

**His action:** He checks.

**Strategy:** Bet 80 percent of the time, check 20 percent.

**Analysis:** You're probably best, but you don't have a monster hand by any means. Make your bet and get some money in the pot from someone with top pair or middle pair. Someone with two high cards will mostly go away, but might stick around for a bet, so be sure to charge them to draw at an overcard.

**Variation No. 1:** He checks. You bet. He raises. Fold 80 percent of the time, call 20 percent. He's probably not raising you with top pair, which puts you in a dangerous situation. Calling 20 percent is enough for catching bluffs and keeping him honest.

---

**Flop No. 3: A♠Q♦5♠**

**His action:** He bets 3 big blinds.

**Strategy:** Call 50 percent of the time, fold 50 percent.

**Analysis:** It's an unfavorable flop, but you have position and you can't be sure he has an ace or a queen in his hand. He may simply be making his best move to win the pot. Folding half and calling half is the right balance.

**His action:** He checks.

**Strategy:** Bet 40 percent of the time, check 60 percent.

**Analysis:** Checking is a bit unusual since he was the aggressor preflop and could be expected to make a continuation bet even if he missed his hand. It perhaps represents a slight bit of evidence that your hand is good, but not much more than that. You should bet out a healthy amount since this may be your best chance to win the hand.

**Variation No. 1:.** He checks. You bet. He raises. Fold 100 percent of the time. Check-raising out of position is a strong move. Let the pair go.

# Hand L: You
# Called His Raise with 4♠4♦

**Flop No. 1:** T♣8♠4♥

**His action:** He bets 3 big blinds.

**Strategy:** Raise 20 percent of the time, call 80 percent.

**Analysis:** You flopped bottom set on a board which isn't particularly dangerous and which is likely to have missed him. If he has a pair higher than tens, your call may be interpreted as top pair, mediocre kicker or middle pair, or even some sort of draw. In any case, calling should collect at least another bet or two down the road. Raising a small amount is necessary to balance some of the bluff raises we've made with nothing.

**His action:** He checks.

**Strategy:** Bet 30 percent of the time, check 70 percent.

**Analysis:** When the preflop aggressor doesn't even bother to make a continuation bet on an innocuous board, you don't have much clear indication as to the strength of his hand. He may be trapping a big pair, or he might just be balancing his own play. Here we're making a few bets to balance our play, and checking to let him know that the flop didn't help us either.

---

**Flop No. 2: A♣J♦6♠**

**His action:** He bets 3 big blinds.

**Strategy:** Fold 80 percent of the time, call 10 percent, raise 10 percent.

**Analysis:** We're in bad shape, so we throw in a few calls and raises for diversification, and otherwise just get out of the hand.

**His action:** He checks.

**Strategy:** Bet 30 percent of the time, check 70 percent.

**Analysis:** As in other cases, we bet 30 percent of the time because the hand may be winnable right now.

**Variation No. 1:** He checks. We bet. He raises. Fold 100 percent of the time.

A brief note: Watching televised poker, even *High Stakes Poker,* gives you a skewed idea of just how much action is in the average hand. No-limit cash game poker contains far more checking and calling than you might expect because raising, although the best way to pull down a particular pot, exposes you to potentially massive reraises and bluffs, and brings up issues of pot commitment.

**Flop No. 3: 7♦6♦3♥**

**His action:** He bets 3 big blinds.

**Strategy:** Call 80 percent of the time, raise 20 percent.

**Analysis:** That's an innocuous flop for a preflop aggressor, so mostly you will have the best hand here. Why so few raises? "Small hand, small pot." You only have a pair of fours, after all. Stick around, but don't go crazy trying to build a big pot here.

**His action:** He checks.

**Strategy:** Bet 70 percent of the time, check 30 percent.

**Analysis:** His check, plus the texture of the flop, indicates that your hand rates to be good. Most cards that can come on the turn will make your situation worse, so concentrate on winning the pot now with a high betting percentage.

**Variation No. 1:** He checks. You bet. He raises. On this flop, his check-raise smells like a bluff. Call 50 percent of the time and fold 50 percent. You may still have the best hand, six outs if you don't, and you have position.

# Hand M: You
# Called His Raise with K♠Q♠

**Flop No. 1:** Q♥J♥T♥

**His action:** He bets 3 big blinds.

**Strategy:** Call 70 percent of the time, raise 30 percent.

**Analysis:** You have a strong hand with top pair and the open-ended straight draw. While it's true that your opponent could have a flush or a flush draw, you can't allow a mere threat to force you to lay down a very good hand for just an opening bet. So folding is out of the question, and you have to balance calling and raising. I like to get aggressive with good draws, but not overly aggressive, so about 30 percent raises seems right to me.

**Variation No. 1:** He bets. We raise. He reraises. We fold 70 percent of the time and call 30 percent. The reraise moves us to a new level of danger. He's saying he has a set at the minimum. We're hoping that's the case since we're in big trouble against a made straight or flush. Now we're mostly folding rather than drawing to a hand that may already be beaten. But we can't always lay down. Our draw may be good, or it may be better than his draw, or we might have the best hand right now and he could be on a flush draw. So we'll call 30 percent of the time and see what happens.

**His action:** He checks.

**Strategy:** Bet 70 percent of the time, check 30 percent.

**Analysis:** This is a natural bet with a strong hand against his check. We mostly need to bet because he may be on a draw as well. The checks are for balance.

**Variation No. 1:** He checks. We bet. He raises. The check-bet-raise sequence indicates less strength than the bet-raise-reraise sequence, so we play more strongly as well. Now we should tend to mostly call. Call 60 percent of the time, fold 40 percent.

---

**Flop No. 2:** 9♥9♣4♦

**His action:** He bets 3 big blinds.

**Strategy:** Call 20 percent of the time, raise 10 percent, fold 70 percent.

**Analysis:** You don't have anything except two overcards and you could be beaten by a lot of hands: a small pair, a single ace, and so forth. You mostly need to fold when you have nothing and your opponent takes the lead. But since it's a natural bluffing flop, we'll mix in some calls and raises for balance.

**His action:** He checks.

**Strategy:** Bet 60 percent of the time, check 40 percent.

**Analysis:** Now we get to bet at the natural bluffing flop, so we mostly do.

---

**Flop No. 3: A♠Q♥6♣**

**His action:** He bets 3 big blinds.

**Strategy:** Call 100 percent of the time.

**Analysis:** You have middle pair, but an ace has appeared. Note that if your hand is best right now, you don't have to fear any overcards. (Another ace won't hurt you since if he holds an ace you're already beaten.) For that reason you can always call the first bet.

**His action:** He checks.

**Strategy:** Bet 50 percent of the time, check 50 percent.

**Analysis:** If you have the best hand, he doesn't have many outs, so you don't need to fear a free card. Your check may induce a bluff on the turn.
 If you are worst, your check will save a bet.

# The Problems

## Hand 4-1

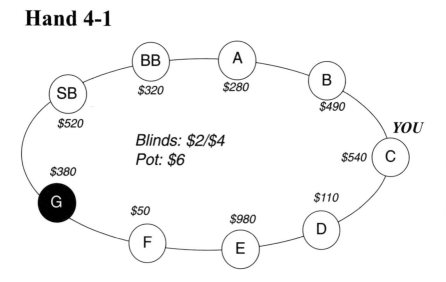

**Situation:** Medium stakes online game. You've been playing for about an hour. Player A is generally tight and conservative, playing solid values for his position.

**Your hand:** T♠T♣

**Action to you:** Player A calls $4. Player B folds.

**Question:** *Do you call, or raise?*

   **Answer:** Preflop, I like raising 80 to 90 percent of the time with this hand, calling the rest of the time. Raising has several advantages to calling:

1.   Raising may win the hand right away, not a bad result here.

2. Raising may discourage hands with two overcards to my hand, like king-jack, from calling.

3. Raising may discourage players from entering the pot with position on me.

4. Raising may leave me heads-up against the initial limper (if he decides to call) with my having position.

That's a lot of solid reasons for raising, hence my very high raising frequency. Calling is a balancing play which is sometimes required. When calling, I'm willing to let other hands in behind me. As a result, I'll be treating my pair of tens like a low pair for the most part, hoping to flop a set and win a big pot, while otherwise being willing to let the hand go if overcards appear and players start betting.

When raising, I'll make a larger than usual raise, probably to five big blinds or so. I need to make this larger raise because of the limper that's already in the pot, and it's best to discourage action behind me.

**Action:** You raise to $20. Players D through G fold. The blinds fold. Player A calls $16. The pot is $46.

**Flop: K♠7♣2♦**

**Action:** Player A checks.

**Question:** *What do you do?*
  **Answer:** This situation is similar to an earlier hand where you held a pair of nines and an ace was on board. As we explained there, the higher your pair, the more interested you are in value betting because more underpairs can call you. In addition, the king is a less dangerous card than the ace since

fewer players would call a raise preflop with a king-high hand, and fewer players would check a king on the flop.

Put these two facts together and I would bet 85 to 90 percent of the time, checking the rest to induce a bluff on the turn. The bet doesn't need to be especially big; one-half to two-thirds of the pot is plenty.

**Action:** You bet $24. Player A folds.

# Hand 4-2

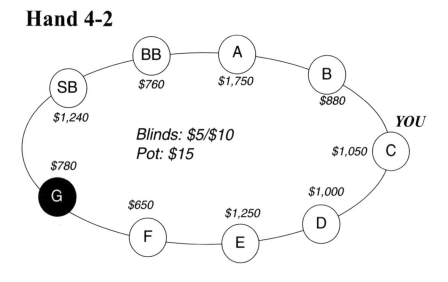

**Situation:** Medium stakes online game. You've been playing for about two hours. Player F has recently lost three tough hands and is fuming and muttering in the chat box.

**Your hand:** Q♣Q♦

**Action to you:** Players A and B fold.

**Question:** *Do you check or raise?*

**Answer:** When first to act in the pot, queens are a raising hand. You don't want to let players with hands like ace-eight or king-jack limp into the pot cheaply and then catch an overcard on the flop. My limping percentage with queens is very low, only about 10 percent. When calling with queens, be very careful after the flop when overcards appear.

When raising with queens, raise something near the high end of your range (assuming you choose to vary the size of your raises). Three to four big blinds is usually about right.

**Action:** You raise to $35. Players D and E fold. Player F calls. Player G and the blinds fold. The pot is $85.

**Flop:** K♠Q♥6♥

**Question:** You act first. *What do you do?*
  **Answer:** This is a great flop. You have middle set, and the high overcard means there's a chance your opponent has top pair and can give you action.
  Should you bet out or slowplay? Here are my general guidelines for handling this problem post-flop.

1. Don't slowplay a flop with a lot of draws. This isn't an extremely dangerous flop, but your opponent could have either a flush or straight draw available to him. I would certainly tend to bet this flop rather than slowplay. (The ideal slowplaying flop would be something like king-nine-deuce, three suits.)

2. Don't slowplay if there is a good chance your bet will get action. A good example is a hand where your opponent showed strength preflop, you called with a pair of sixes, and the flop comes ace-king-six. There's no need to slowplay this since it's very likely your opponent has made a hand. If he instead has a hand like a pair of jacks, you can't make any money anyway because he'll probably read you for an ace.

3. Be more willing to slowplay weak players. If they hit an overcard later in the hand, they'll bet it strongly, believing they're way ahead.

4. Don't slowplay steamers. When a player on tilt makes a hand, he'll often go all the way with less value thán he would normally require, believing that equalizing justice is now on his side.

In this case, with some drawing potential on board, an overcard to my set, and a steamer at the table, I would bet out the vast majority of the time, 85 to 90 percent.

**Action:** You bet $45. Player F raises to $150. The pot is now $280. Player F has $465 in his stack, while you have him covered.

**Question:** *What do you do?*
**Answer:** Put him all-in. It's only a normal pot-sized raise, and a steamer with a king won't fold in this situation.

**Action:** You push all-in and Player F calls. The turn and river are the 8♦ and the 2♣. He turns over K♥Q♠, and you win his stack.

# Hand 4-3

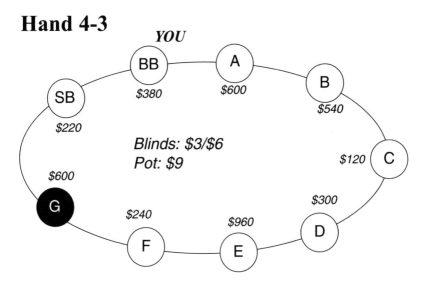

*YOU*

BB
$380

A
$600

B
$540

SB
$220

$600

G

Blinds: $3/$6
Pot: $9

$120 C

$300

$240

F

$960

E

D

**Situation:** Medium stakes online game. You've been playing for about an hour. The table is pretty tight. Player D is also tight and plays solid values. You've been playing tight as well and have shown down some good hands, but have lost a couple of bad beats.

**Your hand:** A♣T♣

**Action to you:** Player A folds. Player B calls $6. Player C folds. Player D calls $6. Players E, F, and G all fold. The small blind calls $3. The pot is $24.

**Question:** *Do you check or raise?*

    **Answer:** You've seen two limps, one from early position and one from middle position, followed by a discount-rate limp from the small blind. Now you have to evaluate just how good your ace-ten suited rates to be.

    Ace-ten suited is a good, but not great hand. If no one has limped with a medium or small pair, you probably are best right now. If you're facing a small pair out there somewhere, you're not currently best, but the small pair won't be looking to call many substantial bets unless he flops a set.

Beginners and some intermediates tend to overestimate the strength of hands like ace-ten, and are happy to put in a raise here. I won't rule out a raise, but it's not a play I'll make most of the time. My preferred distribution here is something like 80 percent checks and 20 percent raises. Here, however, the second hand on my watch says "raise," so —

**Action:** You raise to $40. Player B folds. Player D calls $34. The small blind folds. The pot is $92. You will act first after the flop.

**Flop:** T♥8♥7♦

**Question:** *What do you do?*
**Answer:** Your raise was strong enough to drive out two of your three opponents. You did get one call, from a player known to be tight. When he called, he was getting about 2-to-1 on his money and he knew he would have position after the flop.

It's usually a good idea to quickly run through the hands your opponent might hold before the flop arrives. Start with the four main groups of hands and see how many are consistent with his actual play so far.

1. **Group 1: High pairs.** Inconsistent. A high pair would have raised rather than limped preflop after an initial limper. A high pair might have called your raise as a trap, although a reraise would have been reasonable.

2. **Group 2: Medium to low pairs.** Very consistent. A small pair would have limped, and would most likely have called your raise as well, figuring that the implied odds would be there if the flop hit.

3. **Group 3: Two high cards.** Not terribly consistent for a good, tight player. The best high card combinations (ace-king and ace-queen) might have raised preflop after a limper. The weaker high card combinations would mostly have folded to your raise out of fear of being dominated. However, many loose players like to see a flop with high cards even after a raise, so this possibility can't be ruled out.

4. **Group 4: Suited/unsuited connectors.** This group includes all the nine-seven suited and jack-ten type hands. Most of these hands would not have called your raise, but they can't be ruled out.

While all these hands are still somewhat possible, the small pairs represent the likeliest group of hands for the action we've seen.

Meanwhile, the flop gave us top pair and top kicker, a good result. However, it is a draw-heavy flop with two hearts and three cards that could fit into a straight. If our opponent called with a nine, he now has at least an open-ended straight draw.

Putting all this information together gives us a strong reason to lead off with a large bet. They are:

1. We have a good hand now, but little chance that it will improve.

2. The board creates many possible draws.

3. We must act first.

I would bet about 90 percent of the time, checking only 10 percent. My bet would be slightly smaller than the size of the pot. With a $92 pot, $70 to $80 sounds about right.

**Action:** You bet $70. Your opponent folds.

Most likely he had the hand we expected, a pair lower than sevens. Any other pair would have called or raised our bet.

# Hand 4-4

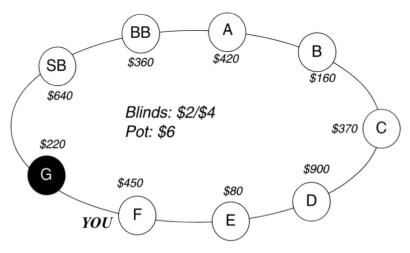

**Situation:** Medium stakes online game. Although the table has been tight, the big blind is moderately loose and tends to defend his blind.

**Your hand:** Q♥T♦

**Action to you:** Players A through E fold. The pot is still $6.

**Question:** *Do you fold, call, or raise?*

> **Answer:** Queen-ten in the cutoff is good enough to raise to take the blinds. Although you know the big blind likes to defend, you don't need a stronger than usual hand to attack. Remember, he'll mostly be out of position after the flop with a weaker than usual hand; that's not a situation you need to avoid.

**Action:** You raise to $12. The button and small blind fold. The big blind calls $8. The pot is $26.

**Flop:** Q♠8♥3♣

**Action:** The big blind checks.

**Question:** *What do you do?*

    **Answer:** You have top pair, medium kicker on a board with hardly any draws against a player who commonly defends his blinds. That's a much above average situation and entitles you to consider checking and allowing your opponent to try and catch a card that will enable him to bet or call. Betting out, on the other hand, will probably win the existing pot but no more. I would make a half-pot bet about 30 percent of the time, checking the other 70 percent.

**Action:** You check behind. The pot remains at $26.

**Turn:** 8♦

**Action:** The big blind bets $15.

**Question:** *What do you do?*

    **Answer:** Unless your opponent holds an eight in his hand, that's a good card for you since the board is still essentially free of draws. You could raise, but top pair moderate kicker on the turn isn't really strong enough to seriously push the action. I would raise 20 percent of the time and call 80 percent. The calls may entice a further bet out of my opponent on the river.

**Action:** You call $15. The pot is now $56.

**River:** J♥

**Action:** The big blind bets $35. The pot is now $91.

**Question:** *What do you do?*
    **Answer:** Call. You probably have the best hand and you're getting substantial pot odds to boot. Raising, however, is questionable. If your top pair is best and you raise, you might get called if the big blind has a pair. Otherwise, he'll either fold (and you'll make no money) or put in a bluff-reraise which you may have trouble calling. If your top pair isn't best, raising won't chase him away and will cost you a lot of money.

**Action:** You call $35 and the big blind shows J♣9♠. You win with your pair of queens.

# Hand 4-5

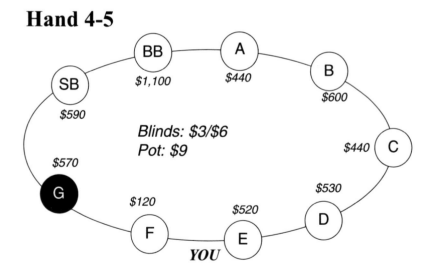

**Situation:** Medium stakes online game. You've been playing for about an hour. The table is tight. Player C has played well and seems like a very good player.

**Your hand:** 9♠9♣

**Action to you:** Players A and B fold. Player C limps for $6. Player D folds.

**Question:** *Do you call or raise?*
**Answer:** This situation is similar to the previous one save for two minor differences:

1.  The nines are a lower pair than the tens. Thus you should raise a little less and limp a little more.

2.  More players have folded. Thus raising is a little safer than before.

The net effect is a wash and I would stick to the previous recommendation: 80 percent raises and 20 percent calls.

**Action:** You raise to $24. Everyone folds but Player C who calls for another $18. The pot is now $57.

**Flop: J♥5♥2♥**

**Action:** Player C checks.

**Question:** *What do you do?*
**Answer:** Although you have missed the flop, it's likely your opponent has as well. Flops with three of a suit make for good bluffing flops as it's very hard to call a bet unless you have at least one card in the suit, and even there you have to be worried that you're drawing dead against someone with a higher suited card.

These hands are most often won by the player first to bet. In this case, since your opponent has checked you should make that bet. So I would bet 90 percent of the time, and check just 10 percent.

**Action:** You bet $24. Player C calls $24. The pot is now $105.

**Turn:** T♣

**Action:** Player C checks.

**Question:** *What do you do?*
**Answer:** The check-call sequence from your opponent was not a favorable development. He has something because he passed on the opportunity to make a bluff or a semi-bluff when first to act. On a flop like this, there are only a limited number of hands he might be holding:

- A made flush,
- A pair of jacks plus a flush draw,
- A pair of jacks without a flush draw, and
- A flush draw.

While you might be able to chase away the flush draw with another bet, the other three hands are likely to stick around. After all, if you flopped a made flush, would you really be betting this hard? Probably not. You made your flop bet and it didn't win, so now you have to see if your pair of nines are going to win the pot while investing as little money as you can. Check 100 percent of the time.

**Action:** You check. The pot remains at $105.

**River:** 3♠

**Action:** Player C bets $60.

**Question:** *What do you do?*
**Answer:** The pot is offering you an attractive 2.7-to-1, but can your nines possibly be any good? Your opponent can

have a flush, a pair of jacks, or a pair of tens, all of which beat you and all of which square with his betting action so far. Is it reasonable to think that he offered you good calling odds with a hand weaker than any of those? If he did, he's a very, very fine player indeed. Save some money and fold.

**Action:** You call $60. Your opponent shows A♥3♥ for a made flush and pulls down the pot.

Your opponent read the situation perfectly. He trapped on both the flop and the turn, and made only one small bet on the river. Had he pushed harder, he wouldn't have won that much. Make a note that he's a good player.

# Hand 4-6

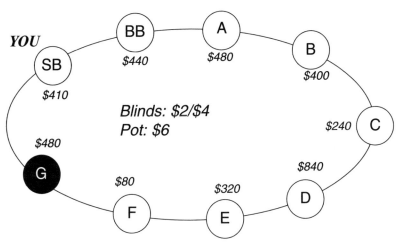

Blinds: $2/$4
Pot: $6

**Situation:** Medium stakes online game. You've played just a few hands. Player F has not played a hand since you sat down.

**Your hand:** A♥T♦

**Action to you:** Players A through E all fold. Player F limps for $4. Player G folds.

**Question:** *Do you call or raise?*
**Question:** Ace-ten is a reasonably good hand, and right now there's no reason to believe that you don't have the best hand at the table. In addition, you'll be out of position after the flop, so checking is less desirable. I'd raise 80 percent of the time and call the other 20 percent, and I'd make a good-sized raise of about four big blinds.

**Action:** You raise to $20. The big blind folds and Player F calls $16. The pot is now $44.

**Flop:** A♠8♣5♥

**Question:** *Do you bet, and if so, how much?*
**Answer:** You now have top pair with a good kicker, so again you should assume you have the best hand until your opponent says otherwise.

Both betting and checking to give your opponent an extra card are reasonable plays. Betting will probably take the pot down right now given the ace on board and your preflop raise. Checking is a little more complicated. The board is free of draws unless your opponent happened to call with exactly seven-six. If he called with two high cards like king-jack, he can't catch anything that will give him the best hand, but if he hits a king or a jack on the turn, your check on the flop might induce him to call a bet at that point. If he called with a low pair other than eights or fives, he only has two outs to beat you. My quick rule of thumb is that I'm happy to let my opponent draw to a two-outer if I think there's a good chance to win another bet that I wouldn't otherwise get.

Overall, I think checking is a little more likely to make some extra money than betting. I'd divide my choices into 40 percent bets, 60 percent checks. The real question is how much to bet when I decide to bet. Since our opponent started on a short stack, we need to consider his stack size carefully.

Player F started with $80 and put in $20 preflop, leaving him with $60 at this point. The pot, meanwhile, is now $44. If I'm going to bet on the flop, my goal is not to bet too much. For reasons given earlier, draws are not an issue, so I'm not concerned with figuring out what bet size would make drawing a mistake. Instead, it's best to make an attractively small bet which is easy to call but will get a little more money in the pot and keep a little less in his stack. That way, if he has anything at all, I'm giving myself a shot at getting his whole stack. In this case, a bet of about $16 sounds right. That bet gives him about 4-to-1 pot odds, and if he can't call a bet that small, there wasn't any money to be made.

Playing short-stacked is inherently a little dangerous for players at all levels. There's a tendency to forget that every dollar lost is as important as every other dollar lost. In the real world, players tend to undervalue their stack when it's short, and push their last few dollars in with hands they normally wouldn't play. When you're against a short stack, you want to grease the skids for them.

**Action:** You bet $24, and Player F folds.

With a pot size of $44, a $24 bet was perfectly appropriate against an opponent with a normal-sized stack, but here it was just a bit too much.

# Hand 4-7

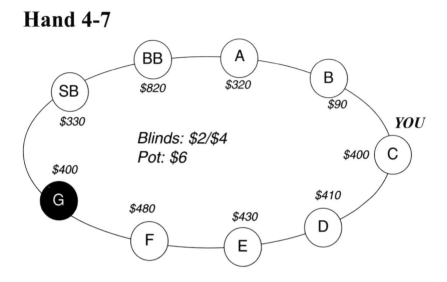

Blinds: $2/$4
Pot: $6

**Situation:** Medium stakes online game. You've played just a few hands. Player B lost a big pot a few hands ago when his aces got cracked.

**Your hand:** J♦J♠

**Action to you:** Player A folds. Player B calls $4.

**Question:** *Do you call or raise?*
    **Answer:** I usually raise with jacks in this position since they're susceptible to a lot of overcards on the flop. The fact that it's a short stack who limped and may be steaming makes me even more interested in getting some money in preflop. Players on tilt are prone to make desperate plays, particularly when they already have some money invested in the pot. It's likely I'm getting called no matter what he limped with, so let's start getting some money in the middle.
    In a more normal situation I would raise here 80 to 90 percent of the time with my jacks, calling the rest. This,

however, is a special situation, and I wouldn't bother trying to trap. Just raise.

**Action:** You raise to $16. Everyone folds around to Player B who calls another $12. The pot is $38.

**Flop: T♣9♠6♥**

**Action:** Player B moves all-in for his last $74.

**Question:** *Do you call or fold?*

**Answer:** If you play a lot of poker you'll see this exact situation many times. A player loses most of his stack in a hand where he was a big favorite. He goes on tilt, calls with a marginal hand, then shoves in the rest of his chips when he hits a piece of the flop. Your jacks are a huge favorite to be the best hand. Don't even think about folding.

**Action:** You call. The turn and river are the 3♥ and the 7♦. He shows K♥9♥ and your jacks beat his nines.

As predicted, he limped with a weak hand, king-nine suited in second position, and then compounded his error by making a bad call of your raise. When he hit middle pair on the flop, he got all his money in.

The psychology of this move is a little interesting. He got all his money in, not because he *thought* he had the best hand, but because he *wanted* to have the best hand. He didn't wait because he didn't want a bet from you to tell him that perhaps he didn't have the best hand. His bet was a preemptive strike to avoid the news he desperately didn't want to hear.

# Hand 4-8

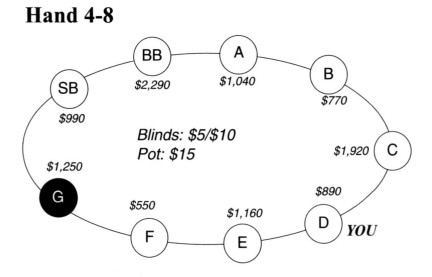

**Situation:** Medium stakes online game. You've played about an hour and a half. The table is a mixture of loose-aggressive and tight-aggressive players. You've played tight so far.

**Your hand:** K♦T♦

**Action to you:** Players A, B, and C all fold.

**Question:** *Do you fold, call, or raise?*

> **Answer:** King-ten suited is a marginal hand in fourth position. My strategy would involve a mixture of folds, calls, and raises, something like 40 percent folds, 20 percent calls, and 40 percent raises. I'd underweight the calls simply to disguise the hand somewhat. Since the hand is subject to domination, I don't really want to get in a pot against several players. By overweighting raising, I'm giving myself a better chance to get heads-up.

**Action:** You raise to $20. Player E, a solid player, calls. Everyone else folds. The pot is $55.

**Flop:** A♦K♠4♦

**Question:** *What do you do?*
    **Answer:** You have middle pair plus a draw to the nut flush. That's a great hand, and I would play it very strongly. Check 70 percent of the time (intending to check-raise) and bet 30 percent. If betting, I would make a strong bet of $35 to $40.

**Action:** You check. Player E checks behind you. The pot remains at $55.

**Turn:** 4♥

**Question:** *What do you do?*
    **Answer:** Your draw is now weaker with just one card to come, but his check indicates your pair of kings is probably best. It's time to start building the pot with a good hand. Make a smallish bet and see if you get any action.

**Action:** You bet $20. He folds.

    He probably had a medium to small pair and just couldn't get involved with the ace and king on board.

# Hand 4-9

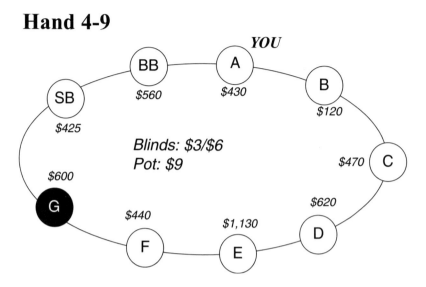

**Situation:** Medium stakes online game. Generally tight table. Player D is very tight, but aggressive. When he plays, he usually has a real hand.

**Your hand:** A♦8♦

**Action to you:** You are first to act.

**Question:** *Do you fold, call, or raise?*

    **Answer:** Ace-eight isn't a very strong hand under the gun, even if the cards are suited. As a means of diversifying one's play, however, it's a useful hand. Here I might raise 15 percent of the time and fold 85 percent. When raising, I would tend to make a mini-raise of twice the big blind rather than a full raise of three times the big blind, just to give myself somewhat better pot odds.

    Why no calls in the mix? I don't like limping with a weak hand in early position. You're advertising that you have a weak hand, and in fact you do. By representing a strong hand, I leave myself in a better position after most flops.

**Action:** You raise to $12. Players B and C fold. Player D, the very tight player, calls $12. Everyone else folds. The pot is now $33.

**Flop:** Q♦T♥2♠

**Question:** *What do you do?*
**Answer:** This would normally be a good situation for a continuation bet. Without knowing anything about my opponent, I would probably bet 60 percent of the time, and check the other 40 percent.

A very tight opponent, however, changes the picture a bit. Normally such a player doesn't call a bet from an early position opponent unless he has a pretty good hand. Against such an opponent I have to reduce my percentage of continuation bets because they just aren't likely to work as much, and I don't want to throw money away. Here I'd adjust my percentages to 30 percent bets, 70 percent checks.

**Action:** You check. He bets $25. The pot is now $58.

**Question:** *What do you do?*
**Answer:** Fold. He had what he thought was a good hand before the flop, and it may have gotten better. You know he bets with value, and you have nothing and no good reason to believe you can take the pot away.

**Action:** You fold.

# Hand 4-10

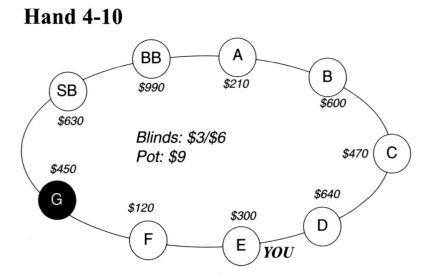

**Situation:** Medium stakes online game. Generally tight table. Both Player A and the big blind have played tight and shown down good hands. You have also played tight.

**Your hand:** A♦J♦

**Action to you:** Player A limps for $6. Players B, C, and D all fold.

**Question:** *Do you fold, call, or raise?*
  **Answer:** You have a pretty good hand for your position — ace-jack suited. A tight player limped under the gun, so he has some kind of hand, and it might be better than yours. Still, my hand is definitely playable and I would mostly be raising. A mixture of 60 percent raises and 40 percent calls looks about right, and when raising, I would raise to four times the big blind with one limper already in the pot.

**Action:** You raise to $24. Players F, G, and the small blind all fold. The big blind calls $18. Player A folds. The pot is now $57.

**Flop:** T♠8♦4♥

**Action:** The big blind checks.

**Question:** *What do you do?*
    **Answer:** Check 100 percent of the time. This isn't a place for a continuation bet. The big blind, a tight player, saw one tight player limp in first position and a second tight player put in a solid raise. The big blind called even though the under the gun player was still active, and the big blind would be first to act after the flop. Calling under those circumstances is practically screaming that he has a pretty good hand. Save your continuation bets for more favorable circumstances.

**Action:** You check behind.

**Turn:** 5♣

**Action:** The big blind bets $36.

**Question:** *What do you do?*
    **Answer:** You have nothing, only one card remains, and the big blind, whom you believe has something, is betting. You fold.
    Tight-aggressive players usually have a hand when they get involved, and loose-aggressive players often don't. However, beginners tend to react to loose and tight players in the opposite way. When they see a loose player pushing the table around, they think "I don't want to get involved with this guy. I'll wait until I have a monster hand, then I'll win all his chips." But when they see a tight player, they think "Oh, he hasn't played many hands. I'm not worried about him. He can't be so dangerous."
    Psychologically, we assume a player will keep doing what we've seen him do before. If a player bets a lot, we're

afraid that he will keep betting at us when we don't have a hand, forcing us out of the pot. But if we haven't seen a player bet much, we imagine that he may not bet at us, letting us see more cards. In fact, of course, loose players are less dangerous when they're in a pot because they're often playing weaker cards. You want to be more willing to bet into loose players, and less willing to bet into tight players.

# Hand 4-11

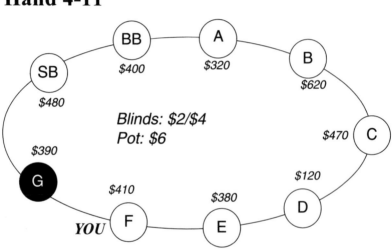

**Situation:** Medium stakes online game. Generally tight table. Several players seem to be playing well. Player D is loose and weak. He's shown down some bad hands and doesn't put much pressure on his opponents when he has a good hand.

**Your hand:** A♠T♣

**Action to you:** Players A through C all fold. Player D limps for $4. Player E folds.

**Question:** *Do you fold, call, or raise?*

**Answer:** I would raise a solid amount, say five times the big blind. Also there's no reason to balance this play with any calls; instead I'd simply raise. It's a specific play for a specific situation. Let's see why.

We've got ace-ten offsuit in the cutoff seat. That's a hand, but not a powerhouse. The hand itself is good enough to raise if everyone had folded to us. It's also good enough to raise a limper if we didn't have three people left to act behind us. But if we put those two factors together, a limper and three people left to act, it's a little below the minimum strength I'd like to have for raising. Ace-jack suited, king-queen suited, or a pair of nines are the sort of hands that meet my requirements.

But there's a third factor to consider. Player D is known to be a loose, weak player, the only one at the table. That's the sort of player you like to play pots against because they'll make a lot of mistakes. So the raise here is really an *isolation play*. I want to raise enough to chase out any marginal hands behind me and leave me one on one with Mr. Fish. Hopefully, he'll be holding something like ace-six or queen-ten where he's dominated, and there'll be no one else in the pot to worry about.

This situation won't happen often enough for me to balance my move with calls. It's a specific play against a specific opponent. If this were a live game against a group of players who played together on a regular basis, then I'd have to think about balancing my strategy in some way. But in an online game, the situation won't arise often enough to be necessary.

**Action:** You raise to $20. The button and blinds fold. Player D calls $16. The pot is now $46.

**Flop: K♣Q♣4♥**

**Action:** Player D checks.

**Question:** *What do you do?*

**Answer:** Given that Player D is a loose, weak player and he checked, this flop probably missed him, and in addition should look pretty scary with the king and queen out there. Make a continuation bet almost 100 percent of the time. Unless Player D caught a piece of the flop, he'll go away.

**Action:** You bet $24. Player D folds.

Let's take another look at the flop action and make the assumption that this time you're up against a tight, tough player who checked when first to act. Under these conditions, checking rather than making a continuation bet becomes reasonable.

To see why, assume your opponent has the better hand right now with something like a pair of sixes, and take a look at the number of outs you have. You have three aces, three tens, and four jacks for a total of ten outs. That's a lot of outs, but if you bet, you give your opponent a chance to raise and take you off the hand. If you think he's tough enough and trappy enough to make that move, the value of your continuation bet goes down. One purpose of a continuation bet is to make him fold a hand, like a low pair, that's currently beating you. But with so many outs, his low pair represents much less of a threat than if you had few or no outs.

The general rule can be stated like this:

> The more outs you have to a big (or winning) hand, the less you want to make a continuation bet.

Suppose, for example, your hand was ace-nine instead of ace-ten. Now I'd be much more eager to make a continuation bet because there are four fewer outs. (I can't make a straight any longer, so my outs are the last three aces and probably the last three nines.) With a hand like ace-three, I'm even more eager to make that continuation bet. In that case, the bet represents by far my best chance to win the pot.

This analysis illustrates why playing cards that are somewhat connected is so much stronger than playing completely disconnected cards. Even with cards that are distantly connected like an ace and a ten, the connection opens up threats that give you options, like checking when you would otherwise be forced to bet.

# Hand 4-12

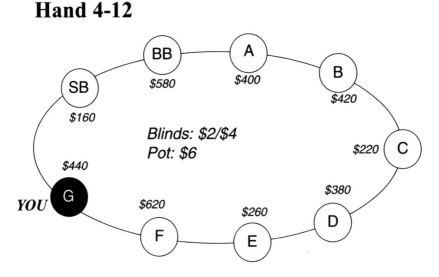

**Situation:** Medium stakes online game. Generally tight table. Player D is loose and likes to bet at pots when the hand has been folded to him. If he is called, he generally bets on the flop. The blinds are average/tight players.

**Your hand: 9♣8♣**

**Action to you:** Players A through C all fold. Player D raises to $12. Players E and F fold.

**Question:** *Do you fold, call, or raise?*
**Answer:** Here you've noticed a pattern. Player D likes to be the first player into a pot and raises far more than his expected frequency when the pot has been folded to him. That's an exploitable situation, and you should call on the button with a lot of hands. Medium suited connectors are good enough for this purpose so long as the blinds are not known to be overly aggressive.

**Action:** You call $12. The blinds fold. The pot is $30.

**Flop: J♥6♠4♣**

**Action:** Player D bets $16.

**Question:** *What do you do?*
**Answer:** The flop has missed you, and you don't have any draws, so the routine play is to fold. There's nothing wrong with that, but under certain circumstances you can try a play called a delayed bluff, which is really just a type of defense against continuation bets.

If a player bets with a high frequency when those in front of him have folded, and follows that with a high percentage of bets on the flop, then most of these bets have to be bets with no hand since players don't get dealt big hands or hit the flop that often. If you only play back when you actually have a hand, you'll end up giving your opponent chips in the long run. To counter such a player, you need to be willing to play back at him on a few occasions when you call and miss your hand.

There are two basic play-back approaches:

1. Raise him on the flop, or

2. Call the flop and bet the turn if he shows weakness.

Both of these plays can work and both involve about the same amount of risk in terms of dollars put into the pot. The second approach, the delayed bluff, is a little safer because you get to see two additional pieces of information before you commit most of your money: the turn card, and his reaction to it.

**Action:** You call $16. The pot is now $62.

**Turn: 2♥**

**Action:** He checks.

**Question:** *What do you do?*
   **Answer:** Good news on both counts. The turn card was innocuous (not an ace or a king), and his reaction was to stop betting. Now you make your move.

**Action:** You bet $30. He folds.

The delayed bluff is a very specific (and somewhat expensive) move, and shouldn't be tried unless the conditions are right. Let's quickly run through the preconditions for the move:

- **Loose opponent who likes to be the first raiser:** How often does the opponent bet when the hand has been folded to him? Imagine that a player was very tight and needed an excellent hand to raise, say a pair or ace-king, ace-queen, ace-jack, ace-ten, or king-queen. Out of 1,324 possible hands, only 158 fit that description. That's 12 percent of the possible hands. So if you see a player who raises 30 or 40 percent of the time when the hand is folded to him, you know he's raising with a lot of weaker hands, some of which are very weak.

- **Cutoff or button position or tight opponents behind you:** You don't need to be surprised by a sudden raise after you call preflop.

- **Heads-up with position when the flop comes:** It's too dangerous to pull this move on two players, and you need to see your opponent act first.

- **Safe flop:** Even a loose opponent will prefer to try to steal pots with high cards in his hand. So skip the flops that have an ace or a king (assuming you don't have one of those cards). You're looking for flops that are headed by a queen or less. Flops with a medium pair are especially good. Your call now looks especially diabolical.

- **You have no hand:** If you have a hand, your bet isn't a bluff. But if it's a medium-strength hand, like middle pair, you're probably better off trying to check the hand down rather than opening up the betting on the turn. If you have a draw, your bet on the turn is a semi-bluff. If he folds, you'll win a hand you might not be able to win on the river. If he raises, you're done with a hand you might have won by getting a free card. On balance, the semi-bluff is probably a better play than checking.

- **Moderately deep stacks at least:** You need to be sure that no one's bets are committing them to the pot.

- **He checks the turn:** If he bets the turn instead, he's probably serious about the hand, and you should just fold.

If all these conditions are met, the delayed bluff has a good chance of working.

One last observation before we let the hand go. There's no leverage with this move. In our example, the amount you were trying to win was $46, the amount of the preflop pot ($30) and Player D's bet on the flop ($16). The amount you risked was also $46, consisting of your call on the flop ($16) and your bet on the turn ($30). That 1-to-1 ratio means you need to win an actual majority of these bluffs to show a profit. If your observations are correct and he is indeed loose and aggressive in these situations, that should be possible to do.

# Hand 4-13

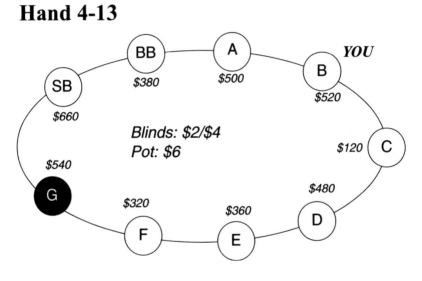

**Situation:** Medium stakes online game. Generally tight table. Player F might be a little loose in his calling requirements.

**Your hand:** A♥K♥

**Action to you:** Player A folds.

**Question:** *Do you call or raise?*
> **Answer:** I mostly like to raise here with calling an occasional option to mix up my play. Raising 80 percent of the time and calling 20 percent of the time seems like a good balance.

**Action:** You raise to $12. Players C, D, and E all fold. Player F calls $12. The button and the blinds fold. The pot is $30.

**Flop: Q♣T♠4♠**

**Question:** *What do you do?*
    **Answer:** I would bet 90 percent of the time and check 10 percent. The bet is a combination of a continuation bet (because you were the preflop aggressor) and a semi-bluff (because aces, kings, and jacks all give you what is likely to be the best hand).
    If you check and Player F bets, you can call or raise. I would mostly call, but I'd mix in a few raises against the loose players.

**Action:** You bet $18. Player F calls $18. The pot is now $66.

**Turn: 6♦**

**Question:** *What do you do?*
    **Answer:** The turn missed you again, and now we get to an interesting question. If you've made a continuation bet, and got called, when, if ever, do you want to fire another barrel on the turn?
    One good guide to firing a second barrel is the exact nature of the flop. Most players call a bet for a reason. If there are no draws on the flop, then that reason is usually either:

1.    They have paired one of their hole cards,

2.    They have a big hand and are slowplaying, or

3.    They have nothing, but are planning on taking the pot away after you check on the turn.

When there are potential draws on the flop, however, a whole new class of hands come into play, namely drawing hands. If the turn card doesn't fill any draws, you now have a lot of situations where your opponent has nothing but a draw with only one card to come. Those hands are very likely to throw in the towel to a significant turn bet.

Of course, other hands may fold to a turn bet as well. The opponent who called the flop with middle or bottom pair may decide to let it go once you bet again, as will the player who was planning to bluff on the turn if you checked. That leaves just the big hands and the top pair/reasonable kicker type hands, which constitute a minority of the possible flop calls, so your turn bet should show a solid profit.

Here the two spades plus the queen-ten coupling creates a lot of possible drawing cards on the flop, and the six of diamonds missed all those hands, so this is a prime situation for firing a second barrel.

**Action:** You bet $45. Player D folds.

This hand illustrates why it's so important to stay completely focused while playing. You need to constantly be asking yourself "Why did my opponent do what he did? What hands fit into his sequence of bets?"

Some players simply decide "I'm going to fire a second barrel" without looking to see just how favorable or unfavorable the situation really is. Imagine that this flop had come Q♣8♦2♠. Now there are no draws, so the calling hands must represent a much stronger group, and hence another bet doesn't make nearly as much sense.

# Hand 4-14

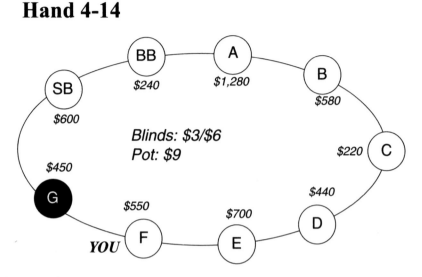

**Situation:** Medium stakes online game. Generally tight table. Player A has been relentless, entering and raising many pots.

**Your hand:** A♥Q♣

**Action to you:** Player A raises to $24. Players B, C, D, and E all fold.

**Question:** *Do you fold, call, or raise?*
> **Answer:** You're certainly not going to fold ace-queen to the table bully. Since you have position and the shorter stack, there's no compelling need to raise yet, especially since his initial raise was a little larger than usual. Keep the pot small and let position work for you.

**Action:** You call $24. Player G and the blinds fold. The pot is $57.

**Flop:** K♥Q♦3♣

**Action:** Player A bets $40.

**Question:** *What do you do?*
**Answer:** We're in a familiar position. You have middle pair, top kicker. He's advertising that he has a king, which might or might not be true. (Probably not.)
If you're behind, you're way behind. If he holds ace-king, he's about a 10-to-1 favorite. With something weaker like king-ten, he's still a 4-to-1 favorite.
If you're ahead, you're way ahead. If he's holding something like ace-nine, you're better than a 40-to-1 favorite. If he has jack-eight, you're more than 20-to-1. Only if he has exactly jack-ten is he somewhat close — A 5-to-2 underdog. So you don't have any real need to chase him away. Very likely whoever is ahead now will win the hand.
What's more, there are no cards that can come on the turn that really scare you since your pair is so high. You'd like to see an ace, and a king doesn't change anything since you'll lose to a pair of kings just as easily as three of them. With your opponent betting, the best plan is just to call the hand down. You don't, after all, have a monster hand — you don't even have top pair. But you have a hand good enough to call down against a very aggressive player.

**Action:** You call $40. The pot is now $137.

**Turn:** 5♠

**Action:** He checks.

**Question:** *What do you do?*
**Answer:** He seems to have run out of steam, but the same logic applies as in the last comment. Just check the hand down.

**Action:** You check.

**River:** 5♥

**Action:** He bets $100.

**Question:** *What do you do?*
**Answer:** He might be telling the truth, or he might be bluffing as the only way to win. Your hand is good enough to find out.

**Action:** You call. He shows A♠T♥. You win.

# Hand 4-15

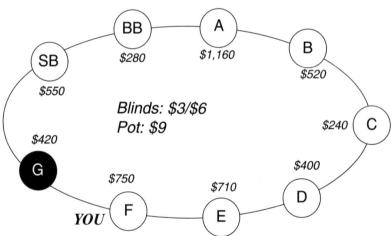

**Situation:** Medium stakes online game. Same table as the previous example. Player A continues to sack and pillage.

**Your hand:** A♠9♠

**Action to you:** Player A raises to $20. Players B, C, D, and E all fold.

**Question:** *Do you fold, call, or raise?*

**Answer:** So far, much like the last hand. Ace-nine suited is a good enough hand to play against someone trying to run over the table.

**Action:** You call $20. The button and the blinds fold. The pot is $49.

**Flop: K♥9♣6♠**

**Action:** Player A bets $30.

**Question:** *What do you do?*

**Answer:** Raise. You should make a good-sized raise, to about $100.

This situation is fundamentally different from the previous example. The two problems together deserve careful study. As before, if you're behind, you're very far behind. If he raised with ace-king, for instance, he's about a 7-to-1 favorite, not very different from before. (Your backdoor spade flush draw helps cut down the odds a little.) If he raised with king-queen, he's a 3-to-1 favorite. So if he has a king, you're in very serious trouble, as in the last example.

The situation where you are ahead, however, isn't as favorable as before. The reason is that there are many cards higher than your pair that can land on the turn and beat you. If he holds queen-ten, you're less than a 2-to-1 favorite. If you just call and a queen, jack, or ten lands on the turn and he bets again, you're in a terrible spot. Your call will indicate that you have a hand, but probably not a king. That makes a pair of nines as your most likely holding. When the overcard comes and he bets, you won't know if he had a king all along, or if he just hit his queen, or if he's just read you properly and understands that a good bluffing opportunity has arisen. If you call the turn, he may put you to a decision for all your chips on the river, and you'll have no idea where you stand. That's an impossible situation.

Instead, you need to raise now. That implies you have a king and puts the pressure back on him. If he calls that bet and bets again on the turn, or if he immediately reraises, you can fold without having lost too much and without the fear that you're walking into a possible major blunder.

**Action:** You raise to $100. He folds.

# Part Five

# Tight-Aggressive Flop
# Play with Multiple Opponents

# Tight-Aggressive Flop Play with Multiple Opponents

# Introduction

When multiple players are seeing the flop, your play will be governed by four key guidelines:

1. If you have a medium strength hand, you need a *stronger* hand than usual to bet.

2. If you have a very strong hand, you *almost never* want to slowplay.

3. If you have a drawing hand, you can accept *smaller* express odds than usual to draw.

4. If you're making a move, circumstances must be *better* than usual to justify your move.

These four rules are all derived from the same idea. With multiple players in the pot, the eventual winning hand will likely be stronger than when fewer players are in the pot. Medium strength hands (like top pair, top kicker) thus drop in value because they tend not to improve over the course of the hand. Very strong hands (overpairs, two pair, sets) need to bet, both to reduce the sheer number of random draws out against them, and because in a large field there is more likely to be someone who can call. Drawing hands go up in value because they both threaten to improve to a hand good enough to win, and they are more likely to be called when they do improve. Moves of any sort are less likely to work because they have to work against multiple opponents, any one of whom might elect to call.

These observations yield a crucial principle for understanding multi-player pots. Since strong hands don't want to slowplay, and since it's more dangerous to bluff, we get *Harrington's Second Law*:

> The likelihood that a player's betting action represents his true strength is directly correlated to the number of players in the pot.

The more players in the pot, the more likely a player's actions represent his actual hand. The fewer players, the more likely that his play is deceptive. This rule, in turn, increases the value of position. The player acting last after the flop has the considerable advantage of seeing the actions of all the other players, actions which telegraph more accurately their actual holdings.

Now let's see how to use some of these ideas in playing various hand types.

# Evaluating Hands in Multi-Way Pots

Strong hands become less strong as more players join the action. This is a crucial point which is nonetheless constantly ignored by many players. To drive the point home, watch what happens to a pair of aces as we match it against multiple opponents:

- **Heads-Up: A♦A♣ versus 4♣4♠.** The aces are favored by 81.3 to 18.7 percent.

- **Three players: A♦A♣ versus 4♣4♠ and J♥T♥.** The aces now win 61.2 percent, the fours win 17.3 percent, and the jack-ten wins 21.5 percent. The aces are still an overall favorite, but they lost one-quarter of their winning chances when the suited connector was added. The fours, on the other hand, were hardly affected at all. This makes sense since the fours have to improve to win, and when they do improve, it's usually to a set which will mostly win.

- **Four players: A♦A♣ versus 4♣4♠, J♥T♥, and 8♦8♥.** The aces drop to 51.6 percent, still a tiny overall favorite. The fours are 15.1 percent, the jack-ten is 17.2 percent, and the eights are 16.1 percent. These three hands are almost even, but the suited connector remains the best of the three.

- **Five players: A♦A♣ versus 4♣4♠, J♥T♥, 8♦8♥, and K♣7♥.** The aces now drop to 45.4 percent. The fours are 15.5 percent, the jack-ten is 16.0 percent, the eights are 15.4 percent, and the random king-seven is a mere 7.8 percent. With five players the aces finally slip below 50 percent. The

342

three coordinated hands are virtually tied, and the random king-seven is a distant fifth with less than 8 percent winning chances.

What lessons can we draw from these statistics? The aces drop off in value once a third player enters the pot, then more slowly as more players pile on (because wins are often sets). Low pairs, relative to other hands, rise in value in these multi-way pots. In a heads-up match between the eights and the fours, the eights would be a 4-to-1 favorite. With two or three other hands mixed in, the fours become equivalent to the eights.

Now look at the situation of the king-seven hand. Note how badly the uncoordinated cards fare when matched against solid hands. Right now they're almost a 12-to-1 underdog to win. Remember that when you're tempted to hop in a big pot with weak cards. You may not be getting the pot odds you *really* need. Suppose, for instance, the king-seven was held by the big blind in a $5-$10 game, the aces opened the pot with a raise to $30, and the fours, eights, and the jack-ten all called $30. The pot would then be $135, and the big blind would have to put in $20 more to play. If he knew his opponent's cards, should he call?

No! He's getting only 6.75-to-1 odds on his money, whereas he needs a minimum of 12-to-1, and since he's out of position, he probably really wants something like 15-to-1 or more. Many players are seduced by the big odds and play all sorts of garbage out of the blinds in these multi-way pots, not realizing just how big an underdog their mediocre hands actually are.

# Playing
# Very Strong Hands

Now let's take a closer look at the problem of playing big hands on the flop. They fall into two categories:

**Group 1: The real monsters.** These are the rare hands that don't fear drawing hands because they're virtually certain to win unimproved. They include quads, full houses, the nut flush, and sometimes top sets.

**Group 2: The merely strong hands.** These are probably best now but which are vulnerable to being beaten by a draw. These include two pair, sets, straights, and non-nut flushes.

Group 1 and Group 2 hands must be played very differently. Group 1 should always be slowplayed. This is a departure from my normal strategy of mixing up my play for various holdings, but there are two good reasons.

The first reason for always slowplaying these hands is that there are plenty of types of hands that you usually want to bet in multi-way pots. Your problem is finding enough good hands to slowplay, and these hands are perfect candidates. By slowall of the Group 1 hands, you get more freedom to bet most of the Group 2 hands.

The second reason for slowplaying these hands is simple: they've sucked all the air out of the deck. Suppose you hold J♥J♣ and the flop comes J♠7♣7♦. You've made a full house, but there's only one jack and two sevens left that can give someone a hand. In order to collect even one bet, you need to give your opponents a chance to catch up. Fortunately, you have multiple opponents, and if you let one or two more cards come, there's a good chance that either someone will try to steal, or someone will catch enough of a hand to call a bet on the end.

Group 2 hands are quite different. Now you need to bet on the flop because your hand is vulnerable to draws and there are likely to be some draws out there with several opponents. Let's look at a not-terribly unusual situation.

You have

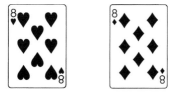

and there are a total of five players seeing the flop. The flop is

You have middle set. Your four opponents have the following hands: A♦J♦, 7♣5♥, 4♠3♠, and K♣9♣. Collectively, they have top pair, a straight draw, and a flush draw. How big a favorite are you right now?

Oddly enough, if the hand is played down to the end, you're not a favorite at all. You're about 49.7 percent to win with no further betting. Is this an extreme case? Only slightly. Most players don't limp with complete junk. They usually have prospects of some sort of draw, and it's not unusual to find a couple of hands with decent draws among four opponents. So your "big hand" often isn't quite as big as it looks, even though it may clearly be the best hand at the moment.

So the rules for Group 2 hands are pretty simple. Bet if you're the first person in the pot, and raise if someone opens ahead of you. At a very aggressive table, or if the preflop raiser is yet to act, consider trapping. Remember that when trapping, you need to have very good reason to believe that someone will open the pot after you. If you're in any doubt, then just open the betting yourself.

# Sample Hand No. 1

Online cash game, nine players at the table, blinds are $5 and $10. The table has been tight with some limping, but not much raising.

This time you have

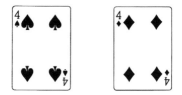

in second position with a stack of $1,100.

Player A, under the gun with $900, calls $10. You call $10 with your pair of fours. Player C, with $1,600, calls $10. Players D, E, and F all fold. Player G, on the button with $600, calls $10. The small blind and big blind, with $1,000 each, call and check respectively. There is $60 in a six-way pot, and you will be fourth to act after the flop.

The flop is

The blinds and Player A all check.

In general, you don't want to slowplay against multiple opponents, and this situation is no exception. True, your set of fours is almost certainly the best hand right now, and it's tempting to want to let the rest of the field improve so you can win a bigger pot. But the more players in the pot, the more likely that someone might catch up a little more than you'd like. Any king, queen, or jack can give someone with two high cards a straight. Any nine through five can give someone with a medium pair a better set. Any deuce, trey, or five can give someone a wheel. None of these possibilities are likely in themselves. But with four opponents drawing, the cumulative effect is substantial.

If you're not convinced by that argument, here's another. What hand (that would currently fold to a bet now) can catch a card that will let them call on the turn, but that you can still beat? Almost no hands fit this category, mostly because someone with an ace in their hand will certainly call you now, and someone with a ten might call as well. So you should bet now and make it a negative expectation play for many of these hands to call. The ace on board is actually a big help since someone who hit a pair of aces will call you now, and might even call another bet later.

With a $60 pot, I would bet $40 to $50 at this point. If everyone folds, then there probably wasn't much money to be won anyway.

# Sample Hand No. 2

Online cash game, nine players at the table, blinds are $5 and $10. The table has been loose, with a lot of limping. You have T♦9♦ on the button, with a stack of $1,500.

Player A, under the gun with a stack of $800, calls $10. Players B and C fold. Players D and E, with $1,100 and $600 respectively, call $10. Player F folds. On the button with suited connectors, you call $10. The small blind folds and the big blind calls. The pot is $50 with five players, and you will be last to act.

The flop comes Q♠J♠8♣. The first four players all check to you.

This might seem an ideal position for slowplaying, but I would still bet here, and it would be a decent-sized bet, say $40. Although you have made a straight, it's a relatively low straight given the board. Any spade either completes a flush draw or puts one out there, and any ace, king, ten, or nine threatens a higher straight.

The only turn card you're really happy to see is a non-spade that's a seven through a deuce. That's a total of 18 good cards, leaving 27 not-so-good ones.

There's another strong reason for betting, besides the defensive one of protecting your hand. You have the nuts right now, and if someone has hit a set or two pair, you'd like to start building the pot. Remember the First Principle of Poker: In general, you want to be betting with a strong hand; slowplaying is the exception, even in heads-up play. If you have a big hand and your opponent has nothing, you don't rate to win anything but the existing pot anyway. But if you have a big hand and he has something he's willing to play, betting early increases the chance that you can trap him into the hand.

Is slowplaying in multi-way pots always wrong? No. An example of a hand where I slightly favor slowplaying would be a flop of queen-nine-eight, two or three suits, where I was holding jack-ten. Now the chances of a higher straight are greatly reduced, and there are almost no possible turn cards that will prevent me from betting. In this case, I wouldn't object to betting half the pot, but my preference is checking.

Really big flops, like the nut flush, a full house, or quads, must be slowplayed on the flop because you almost can't lose, and there's very little chance anyone else can have a bettable hand. With these hands, you have to resign yourself to letting the field catch up, and winning a bet or two on the later streets.

# Sample Hand No. 3

This hand comes from the third season of *High Stakes Poker*. Eight players with blinds are $300 and $600, and $100 antes, so the starting pot is $1,700. The table has been very aggressive. For this hand, the positions and approximate stack sizes are as follows:

| | | |
|---|---|---|
| 1 | Dan Shak | $130,000 |
| 2 | Daniel Negreanu | $300,000 |
| 3 | Dan Harmetz | $140,000 |
| 4 | Ilya Trencher | $90,000 |
| 5 | Phil Laak | $200,000 |
| 6 | Antonio Esfandiari | $200,000 |
| SB | Chris Ferguson | $150,000 |
| BB | Mike Matusow | $90,000 |

**Daniel Negreanu**: Negreanu picks up J♥J♣ and decides to limp, calling $600. This play is in part misdirection, in part consistent with Negreanu's strategy for the third season of this show. In the first two seasons, Negreanu had been very aggressive, attacking the table with raises from every position and with almost any two playable cards. This approach produced big swings and some steep losses when his opponents drew out on him. In the third season, Negreanu seemed to change course, playing more solid cards and frequently mixing limps with raises.

Calling with jacks at an aggressive table isn't bad by any means. Beware the trap of relying too heavily on misdirection. "Normal" plays are normal for a reason. The normal play makes more money, on average, than the alternative. Make sure that with a high pair, you are usually raising and only occasionally calling.

**Antonio Esfandiari**: Calls $600 with 8♥2♥. Esfandiari was one of the surprise stars of *High Stakes Poker*, along with his good buddy Phil Laak. He showed great card sense and an unusual awareness of what the other players at the table were doing, which enabled him to pull off some fine bluffs and make some tough calls. Here he tries a play which is unusual, exciting, and to my mind simply over the top. In cash games, it's essential to mix up your plays and make yourself unpredictable and hard to read. However, you don't need to be playing eight-deuce suited to accomplish your goal. Just playing a mix of suited connectors, unsuited connectors, and hands with a single gap, like ten-eight or eight-six, will provide you with plenty of hands to play. If you find yourself playing combinations like eight-deuce, you've crossed a line that will cost you a lot of money down the road.

**Chris Ferguson**: In the small blind, Ferguson calls $300 with K♣T♣. By now the pot has risen to $2,900, so Ferguson is getting almost 6-to-1 odds on his call, which makes calling with two high suited cards trivially easy.

**Mike Matusow**: In the big blind, Matusow checks with K♦9♥. The pot is now $3,200.

The flop comes K♠T♦8♦.

**Chris Ferguson**: Ferguson has hit top two pair. The board is moderately dangerous, with three somewhat connected cards and two diamonds. He definitely doesn't want to give a free card here, but he has a problem. Up until now he's been the tightest player at the table, so tight that the other players have been joking about him. A leadoff bet from the table's tightest player into three opponents is simply an announcement that he has a very big hand. Since the table is aggressive anyway, and since three of the most aggressive players are in the hand against him, he can wait and let someone else start the betting. Ferguson checks.

**Mike Matusow**: Matusow has top pair with a weak kicker, and a backdoor flush draw. His hand might be best, (*we know it's not*), but with two players still to act, and Ferguson alive in front of him, he prudently checks. I like his play.

**Daniel Negreanu**: Negreanu limped with his jacks preflop, and now he sees an overcard appear. He's in trouble if someone has a king, but his jacks reduce the chance of anyone making a straight from this board. Two checks in front of him might indicate some weakness, so Negreanu reasonably decides it's time to bet and see if his jacks are any good. He bets $2,000, 60 percent of the pot.

**Antonio Esfandiari**: He's made bottom pair, but otherwise this is one of the worst possible flops for his hand. (Not that there were many good ones.) Negreanu says he has something, and that's good enough. Esfandiari folds.

**Chris Ferguson**: Daniel has opened the betting, and now Ferguson has to decide what to do. He probably has the best hand now, but his position is somewhat dangerous. The diamonds and the high cards on board mean that a lot of cards can come which will make Ferguson very uncomfortable, like an ace, queen, jack, nine or any diamond. Given his tight reputation, a check-raise will probably chase the other players away and end the hand, but a call could have the same effect while letting another card come. With the pot now $5,200, Ferguson decides to end matters now and raises to $8,000. I wouldn't have strongly objected to a call, but his play is prudent and reasonable. The pot is now $13,200.

**Mike Matusow**: Matusow now raises to $15,000. This is an unusual play, to say the least. Negreanu's bet into three players indicates he has something, and then the tightest player at the table check-raises! Matusow probably doesn't think that his top pair, weak kicker is best but he may believe that he's pulling off a squeeze play that can bring in the hand. The problem is that the wrong player is getting squeezed. Negreanu, unless he's sitting on a monster, won't call this bet with Ferguson behind him. But he was only the initial bettor, not the check-raiser. It's Ferguson that Matusow needs to be worried about, and he won't be squeezed by the time the action gets around to him. The pot is now $28,200. Matusow should have just folded. You need to pick good spots for making moves, and with all the strength that's already been shown in the hand, this was a particularly bad spot.

**Daniel Negreanu**: Negreanu's opening bet prompted not just one but two check-raises! Most unusual. Negreanu realizes he must be facing at least a king, if not a set somewhere, and prudently folds his jacks. Good play.

**Chris Ferguson**: Ferguson's top two pair isn't a lock, but the only hands that beat him are the sets, and with two kings and two tens accounted for, it's really only a set of eights that he has to worry about. However, he's facing Matusow, who has a reputation for making a lot of unusual plays, so Ferguson has no real choice except to assume he's best and risk his entire stack. Matusow might be on some sort of semi-bluff with a flush or straight draw, and Ferguson can't give him a free draw. He raises to $53,000. The pot rises to $73,200.

**Mike Matusow**: Matusow now knows he's beaten, and Ferguson's bet means he's committed to the pot, so Matusow understands that Ferguson can't be pushed out with any more theatrics. Matusow folds.

When executing a squeeze play, make sure that the player being squeezed is in fact your main threat in the hand. The ideal conditions for a squeeze is when you're facing a bet followed by a call. The initial bet in a hand doesn't indicate overwhelming strength; it may signify just a willingness to see if anyone wants to fight for the pot. The call from the second player shows a willingness to play but an unwillingness to raise, indicating some weakness. A raise at this point squeezes the first player, the one who has indicated the most strength so far.

# Playing Overpair and Top Pair Hands

Overpairs and top pair type hands differ from the strong hands in the extent to which you're willing to get involved in the pot. These are hands where, in general, you're going to bet on the flop. What happens after that is very hand-dependent, but here are a few general guidelines.

1. If everyone folds, you're happy.

2. If you get a caller, it's probably someone with a draw, or top pair as well. The stronger hands would have raised you, and middle pair and weaker hands are reluctant to call a bet on the flop in a multi-way pot. On the turn, you'll need to evaluate the turn card carefully and see if it could fit any available draws. After your flop bet, you'll frequently want to check the hand down rather than get a lot of your stack involved.

3. If you get raised, be careful. You could be against a draw making a semi-bluff, but you could also be up against a really big hand. Depending on the circumstances, it's not impossible to just let the hand go.

I'll call a bet with top pair, especially with position. On the turn, it's time to be very careful.

If someone moves all-in on the flop, then I'm probably letting the hand go unless the bettor is short-stacked or my pot odds are otherwise pretty good.

Now for a couple of examples of play with these hands.

# Sample Hand No. 1

Online cash game, nine players at the table, blinds are $5 and $10. The table has been generally loose and aggressive, with lots of raising, not much limping.

You have

in first position with a stack of $1,200. You raise to $30.

Players B and C fold. Player D, with a stack of $1,000, calls $30. Players E and F fold. Player G, on the button with a stack of $1,100, calls $30. The small blind folds, but the big blind with a stack of $600 calls $20. The pot is $125. Four players will see the flop. You will be second to act.

The flop is

The big blind checks.

At this point you need to bet a healthy amount, between $70 and $100. (I would lean to the higher end of the scale, but I wouldn't quarrel with anyone who wanted to bet just $70.) You have a good hand which is probably still best. You can't check against three opponents with a somewhat connected board. There could be one or several draws against you, and at the very least you need to make them pay to see another card, especially since you're out of position in the hand.

Suppose you bet $80 and get one caller behind you. If a blank hits on the turn (something like the 3♣), I would bet again, this time something like $150, about half the pot. It's important to keep charging the draws while still keeping a grip on the pot and stack sizes.

If I bet $80, get one caller and a danger card hits, say something like the T♣, whether or not to bet depends on what I think of my opponent. If he's a straightforward player who could have called on the flop with a pair, another pop in the $150 range sounds about right. If I've seen him slowplay a big hand before, it's probably best to check and see what happens.

With a hand like a pair of aces and a moderately dangerous board, it's important to be careful that my bets don't commit me to the pot. In this example, my total bets of $260, which is about one-fourth of my stack, leaves me plenty of wiggle room to get away if my opponent socks me with a big raise on the turn and I think he's telling the truth.

If there were two callers on the flop, I'll definitely check on the turn and see what happens. It's a rare situation where I'll call all my chips with just an overpair, so it may be best to be done with the hand at that point.

# Sample Hand No. 2

Online cash game, nine players at the table, blinds are $5 and $10. The table has been loose but not especially aggressive, with lots of players splashing into the pots.

This time you have A♠A♣ on the button with a stack of $1,200.

Player A, with a stack of $1,200, calls $10. Players B and C fold. Player D, with a stack of $500, calls $10. Players E and F fold. You raise to $50 (a good amount). The small blind folds, but the big blind with a stack of $1,500 calls $40. Players A and D also call $40. The pot is $205. Four players will see the flop. You will be last to act.

The flop is Q♥J♥T♣. The big blind bets $100. Player A folds, but Player D calls $100. The pot is now $405.

This is about as bad a situation as a pair of aces are likely to see. Plenty of calls before the flop, indicating some strength even at a loose table, a highly coordinated flop, and now a bet and a call. If out of position, I would fold my aces, but with the advantage of acting last, and getting 4-to-1 pot odds, my money (unhappily) goes in.

By calling, I'm hoping for one of two scenarios. Either a blank comes on the turn and both players check in front of me, in which case my aces are probably still in the lead, or a king comes on the turn and I can at least split the pot. (It's unlikely to get paid off if I'm the only player with an ace, but my hand won't lose the pot either.) Note that I'm not really hoping for a third ace. That gives me trips, but may give a straight to someone with a hand like king-queen or king-jack.

# Playing Middle
# Pair and Low Pair Hands

As we drop down to pairs below top pair, our caution level continues to rise. Still, we don't want to give up on these hands prematurely. To make a play at pots with middle pair, I'm looking for two things:

1. A flop that's not heavy with draws.

2. Some solid indication of weakness at the table.

If I get both of these, then it's time to make a bet and try to claim the pot. In general, if that bet doesn't win the pot, I'm done with the hand.

This strategy might seem excessively conservative to many players, but on a board without a lot of draws, what hands could reasonably call my bet? Top pair might venture a call, or a pair between top pair and middle pair, and against those hands I'm a huge underdog. Other than that, I'm up against middle pair, bottom pair, or a couple of overcards. It's impossible to get a clear idea of where I stand without risking a lot more of my chips than I'm willing to risk. After that first call, checking the hand down and seeing what's happening is a good result for a middle pair hand.

Now let's look at a couple of concrete examples.

## Sample Hand No. 1

Online cash game, nine players at the table, blinds are $1 and $2. The table has been tight. There's a lot of limping, but not very many players making moves. The bets here pretty accurately

357

represent what the players have. The stacks range from $100 to $300.

You're fourth to act. Player A calls $2, Players B and C fold. You have

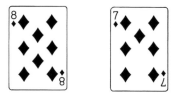

You correctly call $2. Medium suited connectors are an ideal hand for limping into a multi-way pot. Given the tendencies of the table, that's what is likely to occur.

Players E and F call $2. Player G, on the button, folds. The small blind folds and the big blind checks. The pot is now $11, and five players will see the flop.
The flop is

The big blind and Player A check.

You should take the lead and bet. Although you only have middle pair in a five-player hand, your bet represents a better hand than you actually have, and since all draws have been thwarted by the flop, there may well not be anybody inclined to stand up to you. If you don't bet, you'll be giving a free card to four other hands. While there's a good chance your hand is actually best now, that chance goes down quickly as more cards appear.

You bet $7. The other players all fold.

# Sample Hand No. 2

Same table as the previous example, about 20 hands later. You're in the big blind with

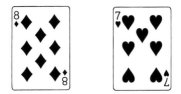

Players A and B fold. Player C limps in for $2. Players D and E fold. Player F limps for $2. The button folds. The small blind calls $1. The pot is $8.

You should check, of course. Eight-seven offsuit is a nice hand for seeing a free flop.

You check. The flop comes

The small blind checks.

This looks superficially similar to the previous example, but it's actually worse in a number of ways. While you still have middle pair, there is an ace on board and two diamonds. Players tend to limp with medium or low aces, but once they make a pair, they'll stick around for awhile. In the same way, someone with a diamond draw isn't going to be chased away except by a massive overbet. Your chances of winning this hand on the flop aren't nearly as good as before, so check and see what the other players do. If everyone checks, you might be able to take the pot on the turn.

You check. Player C bets $4. Player F and the small blind fold.

You should fold. Player C bet with three players still alive, indicating that he has something. He's a huge favorite against you if he has an ace, and even a hand like Q♦T♦ is a small favorite (53-to-47) against your pair of sevens. Let this one go.

You fold.

# Sample Hand No. 3

Medium pairs and pairs below top pair don't do well in multi-way pots that go the distance. Ideally, they'd like to end the hand quickly, on the flop, where their chance of actually being the best hand is highest. Often this isn't possible; when one or two players in the hand start showing real strength, it's too dangerous for the medium pairs to hang around.

But when players at the table don't show strength, a medium-strength pair can make a move at the pot. The next example, from the second season of *High-Stakes Poker*, shows what happens when two players have the same idea.

Eight players at the table. The blinds are $300 and $600, with $100 antes, so the starting pot is $1,700. The table has been very aggressive. All the stacks are at least $100,000.

**Antonio Esfandiari**: Esfandiari picks up the T♣T♠ in early position and raises to $2,000 preflop. The raise is on the smallish size, given that the game uses antes. A raise to $2,500, a little more than four times the big blind, would be equally reasonable and a little more likely to make players lay down playable hands.

**Mike Matusow**: Matusow calls $2,000 in middle position with J♠7♠. It's a much weaker hand than I would use to call a raise with several players left to act, but it's not that unusual a play for a loose-aggressive player.

**Todd Brunson**: Brunson, on the button, calls $2,000 with 9♣8♠. It's a much more reasonable play than Matusow's, partly because his two cards are connected, partly because he's on the button, and partly because he's getting better odds. (The pot now has $5,700 and it costs him just $2,000 to call.)

**Daniel Negreanu**: Negreanu has a pair of fours in the small blind. His pot odds are massive ($7,700 to $1,400), so he calls.

**Jennifer Harman**: Harman has 7♦5♦ in the big blind. She also has an easy call with her huge odds.

The pot now contains $10,800, with five players. The flop is Q♦8♣2♦.

**Daniel Negreanu**: He's missed the flop, but still has a pair, which is conceivably best. Right now, however, he's out of position and knows nothing about what the other players intend to do. In particular, the preflop raiser, Esfandiari, hasn't acted yet, so Negreanu correctly checks.

**Jennifer Harman**: Harman has flopped a low flush draw. She also needs to see what Esfandiari does, and she certainly wouldn't mind getting a free card. She checks.

**Antonio Esfandiari**: This is a pretty good flop for his hand: only one overcard and no straight draws. The flush draw is a little bothersome, but not the end of the world. There's nothing wrong with betting here, and that would be my play. However, he sees that Matusow, a very aggressive player who likes attacking undefended pots, is behind him. Esfandiari checks, sensing that a bigger play may be possible later in the hand. It's a slightly unusual but interesting move.

**Mike Matusow**: Matusow has nothing and isn't inclined to make a play against four other players. He checks.

**Todd Brunson**: Brunson has flopped middle pair and four players have checked to him. He should try to take the pot down right here since his situation will only deteriorate as more cards come. He bets $6,500, about 60 percent of the pot. It's a good bet.

**Daniel Negreanu**: Folds his pair of fours. Brunson may be bluffing, but the other players are yet to act and Negreanu's hand and position are weak. Good play.

**Jennifer Harman**: Calls $6,500. She's getting very good pot odds (almost 3-to-1) for her flush draw. Of course there's a possibility of a higher draw out against her, but that's a problem for later in the hand.

**Antonio Esfandiari**: Esfandiari has now seen four checks, then a bet from the player in last position, followed by a fold and a call. The pot is now $23,800, and Esfandiari still has a pair of tens, with one overcard (a queen) showing.

Although he doesn't even have top pair, Esfandiari now raises to $26,000, a fine move. His check-raise represents, at a minimum, top pair with a good kicker, and perhaps even a set. What sort of hands can call this bet? Anyone with a pair weaker than queens needs to go away, and someone with a hand like queen-jack has to be worried that he's either dominated or facing a set. Anyone with a diamond draw can't get the right price to call. In addition, Matusow and Brunson still have to worry about the actions that may take place behind them, while Harmon with her check and subsequent call, hasn't shown any great strength.

Esfandiari took what appeared on the surface to be a medium-strength hand and used it to execute a squeeze play based on the flop and the action he had seen so far. An excellent maneuver.

**Mike Matusow**: Folds.

**Todd Brunson**: He was hoping to just take down the pot with his bet, but now he's run into a call and a reraise. When you bet with middle pair on the flop in multi-way pots, you're looking to win right there. You're not looking to get a lot of money involved in the hand. He folds.

**Jennifer Harman**: Her pot odds have deteriorated, and there's some possibility she's up against a better diamond draw making a semi-bluff. She folds.

A nice hand in which three players had low to mid-strength pairs after the flop. All three followed the same basic strategy: get some indication of weakness at the table, then try to win the pot with a bet.

# Playing Drawing Hands

Drawing hands are inherently tricky in multi-way pots. If we compare playing a draw in a multi-way pot to playing a draw heads-up, we can see some of the problems.

There are two main negatives to (non-nut) drawing hands:

1. Semi-bluffs are less profitable because the folding equity is smaller.

2. The chance you'll be up against a better draw is somewhat higher.

Balanced against these are a couple of positives:

1. Since players are reluctant to bet into a multi-way pot without a real hand, you often won't be charged to draw.

2. When you hit your hand, you have a better chance of being paid on the end because of the sheer number of opponents.

On balance, the positives outweigh the negatives. I'd rather have a drawing hand in a multi-way pot than against one or two opponents. But mostly I don't play them aggressively until my card comes in. Once I do hit, it's best to size up the action and see if there's a chance to make some real money.

Straight draws are better than flush draws for making money. This is especially true in multi-way pots because players realize that there are probably some draws out there, so the appearance of a third flush card can shut down all the action. Be cautious in assessing your implied odds when drawing to a flush.

In order to semi-bluff with a drawing hand in multi-way pots, I like to see a very favorable flop, one that is likely to have missed players with two high cards, and no action in front of me. Examples would be three low cards, or a low pair and a connected low card that gives me a straight draw. Flops like this produce reasonable fold equity to go with my draw, and now I don't mind taking the lead and trying to win right away.

# Sample Hand

Online cash game, nine players at the table, blinds are $2 and $4. The table has not been aggressive. There's a lot of limping, and several players have been willing to call on the river with relatively weak hands. Stack sizes and relevant hole cards are as follows:

| Position | Amount | Hand |
|---|---|---|
| Small Blind | $285 | Q♠9♦ |
| Big Blind | $400 | Q♥2♣ |
| Player A | $600 | A♥3♥ |
| Player B | $90 | Junk |
| Player C | $990 | Junk |
| Player D | $110 | A♦T♦ |
| Player E | $390 | 7♠7♥ |
| Player F | $450 | Junk |
| Player G (button) | $340 | Junk |

Player A limps for $4 with his A♥3♥. At an aggressive table, with a lot of preflop raising and players who attack limpers, Player A would have to fold. Here, the play is reasonable. A cascade of limpers creates the ideal situation for ace-x suited.

Players B and C fold.

Player D limps for $4 with A♦T♦. He could open for a raise in this position if he were first to act after three folds. The presence of even a single limper, however, requires a stronger hand for raising. (I'd like an ace-king, or a pair down to nines.) I agree with the call.

Player E calls $4 with a pair of sevens. After two limpers, I'd want about the same hand range to raise as I recommended for Player D. Good call.

Players F and G fold.

The small blind has Q♠9♦, but the pot now contains $18 and it costs him just $2 to see the flop. The pot odds of 9-to-1 are easily good enough to justify the call with a two-gap connector.

The big blind has a sad Q♥2♣, but gets to play for free. A good deal. The pot is now $20 with five players.

The flop is

The small blind with his queen-nine has missed the flop entirely. He checks, and he'll fold to a bet.

The big blind with queen-deuce has two long-shot draws, a gutshot straight with a trey and a flush with two running clubs. Since he has the worst possible flush draw, he's really only hoping for a trey to hit. He checks.

At first glance, this looks like a pretty good flop for Player A. He has an open-ended straight draw plus an ace for an overcard, and the low cards on the flop would have missed anyone playing two high cards.

At a second glance, however, the flop isn't really that good. His trey gives him the low end (less charitably known as the "idiot end") of the straight draw. If a seven appears, anyone with an eight has hit a higher straight, and he'll have to be careful not to lose his whole stack. In fact, the only card he's really happy to see is a deuce which isn't a club, and that gives him just three clean outs assuming a higher straight is not yet made. A second problem is that the arrival of either of his straight cards puts a pretty obvious draw on board which means he may not be able to win much even if he has the best hand. Player A prudently checks.

Player D has two overcards plus a backdoor draw to the nut flush. He's happy to see a free card, so he checks.

Player E actually has a hand. His pair of sevens gives him an overpair plus a good open-ended straight draw. He should bet. In multi-player pots, your aggression has to be carefully tailored to your hand strength, position, and actions at the table. His hand strength is actually very good under the circumstances. Although his pair is low, it's still an overpair to the board, and he has no reason to believe from the betting that there's a higher pair somewhere. His straight draw gives him outs to a very big hand. His position has allowed him to see that no one else feels good enough to make a bet yet. And the two clubs on board means he may need to protect his hand against a flush draw.

But the most important factor driving this bet is position. As we discussed in the introduction, betting actions in multi-player pots more closely reflect the actual strength of the hands than in pots with fewer players. Here everyone has checked, showing weakness, so Player E, with a reasonable but not great hand, is perfectly justified in betting. A bet here can't be precisely characterized: it has elements of a value bet, a semi-bluff, and a move to price out some draws. With a $20 pot, I would bet around $14. However, Player E actually checks, and we move to the turn.

The turn card is the T♣, putting a third club on board and pairing Player D's ten.

The small blind and big blind are still out of position with nothing, so they check. Player A's ace-trey still hasn't improved, so he checks.

Player D now has top pair, but his backdoor draw has gone away. He has a very common situation in multi-way pots: a marginally strong hand with little chance of improvement to a big hand. However, he has some valuable information. Everyone checked on the flop, and three of his opponents have checked again on the turn. He has the best possible top pair, and his hand may well be good. He should bet in the neighborhood of $12 to $15. However, he just checks.

Player E's situation has deteriorated. An overcard came, so he no longer has an overpair to the board, and a third club came, so someone could have just made a flush, and some other players must be drawing to flushes. (In reality, only one of the eight outstanding cards against him is a club, and it's the deuce!)

Player E did, however, pick up one more valuable piece of information: everyone checked to him. The likelihood of a made straight or a made flush has decreased with all the checks on the turn. Big made hands only have so many streets to make money, and usually they won't wait until the river to start betting. If no one has a big hand yet, Player E has a perfect chance to represent one, while charging anyone who's waiting with a single club. If someone just made a pair of tens (and in fact someone just did) they may have to fold rather than call a bet now and possibly face a big bet on the river. Player E should make a substantial bet, about $15 to $18. However, Player E just checks.

The river is 3♠ giving Player A a pair, the big blind a six-high straight, and Player E a seven-high straight. The small blind, still with nothing, checks.

The big blind now has the low end of an obvious straight, plus three flush cards on board. He can't feel confident about his hand, but it's possible, given the lack of betting so far, that he's best and he might get a call from a hand like two pair, so he tentatively puts in a small bet: $8. A reasonable play.

Player A made a pair of treys but knows his hand can't be good. He folds.

Player D still has top pair, and only one player remains to act behind him. He's probably beaten, but the pot is offering 28-to-8 odds, or 3.5-to-1. Those odds are worth a call, so he calls $8.

Player E just made what is almost certainly the best straight, but he still has to be worried about the three clubs on board. The big blind might have a flush. Player D's call might represent a medium or low flush, only calling because he's worried about being beaten by a better flush. Player E's call is trivial, but if he raises it's certainly not clear that any weaker hand can call him, while a flush won't be chased away. So he calls $8 and wins the pot with his straight.

**Summary**: This hand actually shows players being too conservative with draws and medium strength hands in a multi-way pot. You can't become so cautious that you only bet the nuts or something close to it. Both Players D and E missed good bets with hands that, while only moderately strong, looked good enough given the quiet action at the table.

# The Problems

## Hand 5-1

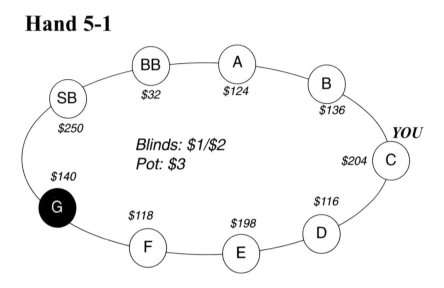

**Situation:** Small stakes online game. You sat down just a few hands ago. The player behind you seems active, willing to limp or call a lot of raises preflop. The small blind hasn't played a hand since you sat down.

**Your hand:** 7♦6♦

**Action to you:** Players A and B fold.

**Question:** *Do you fold, call, or raise?*

    **Answer:** You can't really make a mistake with this hand in this situation. Folding isn't a bad play since you don't need to play every suited connector you're dealt. You've just sat down at the table, so playing tight until you get more of a feel for the situation is perfectly all right. Limping is also reasonable, although you'll probably fold to a raise. And raising is perfectly fine since this is a somewhat misleading hand for your position at the table. If you do elect to raise, I prefer a raise to twice the big blind since you're in relatively early position and your plan is to fold to a reraise.

**Action:** You raise to $6. Player D calls $6. Players E, F, and G all fold. The small blind calls $5, and the big blind calls $4. The pot is now $24, and four players remain. You will be third to act after the flop.

**Flop:** A♦3♦2♣

**Action:** The small blind and big blind check.

**Question:** *What do you do now?*
**Answer:** You put in a solid raise preflop, showing strength, but got three callers. An ace comes on the flop, which is a mixed blessing. The other players have to consider the possibility that you have a pair of aces with a good kicker. You, however, know that with three callers, there's a good possibility that someone called with an ace and now has a pair of aces, perhaps with a medium kicker.

The two diamonds give you a flush draw. That's also a mixed blessing since if one of the other callers also has two diamonds, their flush draw is almost certainly better than yours. (If someone miraculously called you with the 5♦4♦, they just made a straight with a straight-flush draw, but since you hold the 6♦, they can only catch the 2♦ to complete the straight-flush.)

So how do you stand? You're in reasonable shape, but a check is certainly the right play here. Your only asset is a weak flush draw. If you hit the flush, the three diamonds on board will discourage betting, unless someone has a better flush, in which case you will probably lose your stack. You don't have any backup draws, like an inside straight draw, which could give you a concealed monster. The ace on board means you'll have trouble chasing away someone with a pair of aces, at least with one bet.

What would change the situation so I would like to bet here? Fewer opponents or a better flush draw. I would certainly make a continuation bet against one opponent with this board, and would probably make a continuation bet against two opponents. If I had a hand like Q♦J♦, I'd also bet against the players there since now there's a chance of scooping the pot against a weaker flush draw. I'd also like to bet with some sort of combination straight and flush draws, or a flush draw plus a pair, although that would require a different flop.

**Action:** You actually bet $12, half the pot. Player D folds, the small blind calls, and the big blind folds. The pot is now $48. Your remaining stack is $186.

**Turn: 5♦**

**Action:** The small blind checks.

**Question:** *What do you do?*
   **Answer:** You've made your flush and now you have to decide what to do. Your opponent called the bet on the flop indicating that he has something. Given the board and his actions so far, let's look at some of the possible hands he might have, evaluate how likely they are, and see what's likely to happen if you bet or you check.

- **He has a set:** In this case he started with either a pair of aces or a pair of deuces, treys, or fives. None of these holdings are likely given the actions so far. If he had a pair of aces, he should have reraised before the flop after a raise and a call. Aces do best when they narrow the field to one or two opponents, not when they have to face a large field. His check on the flop with top set is possible but risky given the potential draws and the number of opponents. His call after the pot was opened is also possible, but a raise was more likely.

How about a pair of deuces or treys? Not likely either. His call preflop certainly makes sense, but on the flop he's facing a board with an ace and possible straight and flush draws. He should instead lead off with a bet. Once a bet was made and action returned to him, a raise was more likely than just a call.

If he holds a pair of fives, the preflop call is fine, as is the check on the flop with an ace showing and the preflop raiser yet to act. Calling your subsequent bet out of position, with the ace showing, is possible, given that he might have the best hand and he still has an inside straight draw. Most, but certainly not all players, would have folded.

Summation: A set is very unlikely given his plays so far. If he has a set, you're in the lead, but he has ten outs which will win your entire stack if he hits. You need to bet enough to price him out of the draw.

- **He has a straight:** The only likely holding that now has a straight is a pair of fours. He could have called preflop with that hand, and checked on the flop, and called your bet with a gutshot draw. This is an unlikely holding, and he has drawn dead. You should bet because you'll get called or perhaps even raised.

- **He has a medium pair, including a diamond:** With the ace showing, a medium pair is anything from kings down to eights. Kings and queens aren't too likely because they should (and probably would) have reraised preflop. Jacks through eights with a diamond, however, match his play pretty much perfectly. The preflop call makes sense, the check on the flop with an ace showing is fine, the call of your bet with what might be the best hand, plus a backdoor flush draw is sensible, and the check on the turn with an actual flush draw is good.

Against these hands, you need to bet enough to make the call with a flush draw incorrect. You also need to be prepared to fold on the river if another diamond comes and he leads out with a big bet.

- **He has a medium pair, with no diamond:** The analysis above also works here since he didn't need a backdoor flush draw to call on the flop. He's now drawing dead.

   Against this exact hand, your best play is to check the turn and make a modest bet on the river which he can call to pick off a bluff. Betting the turn is too likely to make him fold given the threat of another bet on the river.

- **He has two high cards without an ace, one of which is a diamond:** These are hands like king-queen, king-jack, and queen-jack, possibly with a ten in the mix. The preflop call is okay, although a tight player would have folded. The post-flop call of a bet is very loose however. There's no reason to think you're ahead, and no way to know if you're in the lead once you hit your hand. You don't have many outs and hitting one may just cost you a lot of money. The check on the turn is reasonable with a flush draw.

   This holding isn't likely because of the post-flop call. The right play is now a bet to deny drawing odds.

- **He has two diamonds and a made flush:** The diamonds are probably big, and now all his plays make sense. He calls preflop because his hand is good enough for a three-way or four-way pot, he checks the flop with a diamond draw, he calls your bet with a draw plus some implied odds, and he checks the turn with the nuts or something close to it to trap the player who's been leading with the betting.

You're dead in this variation, and your best play is to check and see what happens. If you check and a fourth diamond appears, you may actually be able to get away from the hand.

- **He has an ace, plus a high diamond:** We're looking here at hands like an ace plus the queen, jack, or ten of diamonds. The preflop call is all right. The post-flop check to the raiser is reasonable, and the call of your bet is also reasonable. (He could check-raise on the flop, but he has to strongly consider the possibility that he's dominated.) The check on the turn with a pair of aces and a flush draw is reasonable given that you've been leading the betting so far.

  You're winning in this variation, but you need to make a solid bet on the turn to make his draw unprofitable.

As we look over the possible hands and their likelihoods given the action so far, it's clear that a solid bet, slightly less than the size of the pot, is the right idea. It's best against the most likely hand which you can beat, which is a medium pair with a diamond. It's also best against a collection of hands each of which is unlikely, but which in total add up to a lot: the sets, two high cards with one diamond, and an ace with one diamond. It's a small mistake against the medium pair with no diamond where you might be able to win a bet on the river, and a big mistake against the made flush where betting now makes it almost certain that you will lose your stack.

**Action:** You bet $40. The small blind raises to $100.

**Question:** *What do you do?*

**Answer:** The pot is now $188. Your stack is $146 and he has you covered. Folding, calling, and reraising are all possible. Let's start by considering calling. If we can eliminate calling as a possibility somehow, our analysis gets simpler.

If we call, the pot goes to $248 and our stack shrinks to $86. If a scary card comes on the river, and the small blind puts us all-in, can we fold? In that case the pot would be $334 and we'd have to put in $86 to call, so we'd be getting almost 4-to-1 odds to call.

The only scary cards that can come are a diamond (putting four diamonds on board) and a card that pairs the board, with an ace being the worst of those. From our analysis of the possible sets, it should be clear that we can't fold if the board pairs since the sets were just too unlikely. Can we fold if a diamond comes?

I don't think we can. Consider the situation from our opponent's point of view assuming he holds something like a pair of tens with no diamonds. He saw us bet preflop, and then continue betting with an ace on the flop, and again on the turn after a check. But in response to his raise we only called. That sequence indicates a player who was happy with a holding like top pair, strong kicker, but was afraid of the three diamonds on board. The appearance of the fourth diamond might signal a stealing opportunity to a player with a medium pair, and he might put us all-in as his only way to win the hand. With 4-to-1 odds, we're getting too good a price to walk away from the occasional bluffer.

So if calling on the end is either clear or marginally correct, we can't call now. We either have to put all our money in or fold. But we can't fold because there are just too many hands we can beat that could be raising now. So we have to push all-in.

**Action:** You raise all-in and he calls. The river is the 7♥, and he shows K♦J♦ for a winning flush.

Although you lost your whole stack, your only clear error this hand was the (relatively innocuous) $6 bet on the flop into three opponents.

I've often heard players justify this bet by saying they wanted to "thin the field." Thinning the field is a valid idea, but in a very different situation. If you have a strong made hand, but there are several players against you who might have draws to beat you, then betting to thin the field is a good idea. You're trying to eliminate all the draws, or reduce them to a single player. If three players are drawing to beat you, all with different draws, then you're most likely an actual underdog in the hand. By thinning the field to one player on a draw, you become a favorite.

However, in reality, when you have a strong hand, you don't bet to thin the field. You bet enough to make it wrong for certain type of hands to call, and now you actually want them to call. So even though it may appear that you want to eliminate the draws, if your bet is of the appropriate size, you want them to stay in.

In this hand, you had no reason to think you were ahead on the flop, so your bet simply reduced the field to the player most likely to beat you, without ever making you a favorite.

# Hand 5-2

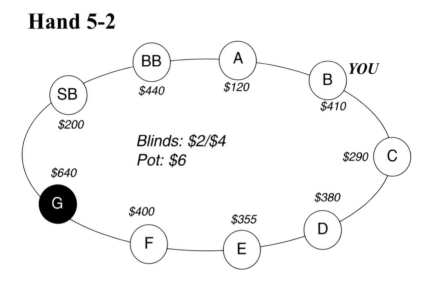

**Situation:** Small stakes online game. You've been playing for a few hands. The table seems tight with not a lot of action so far.

**Your hand:** 7♥7♣

**Action to you:** Player A folds.

**Question:** *Do you fold, call, or raise?*
> **Answer:** You certainly don't want to fold a pair. Raising with a pair of sevens from second position isn't a horrible play. If you're playing a style that always raises when first in the pot, you could raise here to $8 or $10. As we've discussed before, I like to keep open limping as an option, so I would raise to $8 or $10 or limp here in about equal proportions.

**Action:** You call. Players C, D, E, and F all fold. Player G, on the button, calls $4. The small blind calls and the big blind checks. The pot is now $16.

**Flop:** T♠7♠6♣

**Action:** The small blind and big blind check.

You've hit middle set at a four-handed table. You usually don't want to trap with this hand because the board is just a little too dangerous. There are two spades for a possible flush draw, and some coordination for various kinds of straight draws. A lot of cards could come on the turn that could threaten your set: a jack, a nine, an eight, a five, a four, or a trey. In addition, a lot of hands that are losing to you could call right now, and you have three opponents who might have one of those hands, so bet and start building a pot. If they do call and eventually catch a card to win, you want to make sure that they paid their dues along the way.

What sort of board would induce me to trap? A flop like queen-seven-deuce with three suits would do the trick.

**Action:** You actually bet $12. The button calls, and the blinds fold. The pot is now $40.

**Turn:** 4♦

**Question:** *Do you bet or check?*
**Answer:** Again, you need to bet. Your opponent called with something, so he either has a pair he likes somewhat, he has some sort of draw, or much less likely he has nine-eight for the straight. The four looks innocuous, but it could have fit with several different low card holdings to give him low straight possibilities. He might have called with a flush draw, which you still need to charge. He might also have a holding like a pair of eights, which gives him a total of ten outs: eight straight cards (nines and fives) plus the last two eights. In any event, your hand is good but not invulnerable, so you need to keep pressing.

**Action:** You bet $28. The button calls. The pot is now $96.

**River:** 6♠

**Question:** The six put a pair on board. *What now?*
   **Answer:** That's a great card for you. Your best guess was that he was calling with either a straight or flush draw. You made a full house, and if he was calling with a flush draw, he just made his hand. A less likely possibility was that he was calling with bottom pair, in which case he just made trip sixes.
   So should you bet, or should you check with the idea of check-raising? That's a tough problem. Let's quickly run through what will happen in each case with the most likely hands.

- **He has a flush:** If you check, he will bet with any flush. When you raise him, he will call with a high flush, and depending on what kind of player he is, he will call or fold a low flush. Checking certainly gets you one bet and has a good chance of getting two. If you bet, he will probably just call, although he might raise with the nut flush. Summary: both plays get you a bet, but checking has a slightly better chance of picking up the second bet.

- **He has trip sixes:** He'll call if you bet. With the third flush card on board, he probably won't bet if you check. Betting is better.

- **He has top pair:** He'll fold to a bet, and if you check, his hand is good enough to check down and see if he wins. You won't make money in either case.

- **He has a straight (very unlikely):** To have a straight, he either had to have a nine-eight and just called twice, or an eight-five or five-three, and called rather than raised on the turn. This variation is so unlikely that I'd ignore it.

● **He has nothing:** In this case he will fold to a bet, but he may bet to steal if you check. Checking is much better in this variation.

● **He has you beaten:** You don't have the nuts, after all, so you can still be beaten if his hole cards are a pair of sixes for quads, or a pair of tens for a better full house. These are unlikely but not impossible scenarios, and you'll lose your whole stack whether you bet or check. Unlucky.

So of these six scenarios, we can ignore three, which are either unlikely or a wash. Checking is better if he has a flush or nothing, and betting is better if he has trip sixes. Conclusion: You should check.

**Action:** You check and he checks behind you. He shows the T♥8♥ for two pair, and you win the pot.

His hand was good enough to check down on the end, a lucky break for him.

# Hand 5-3

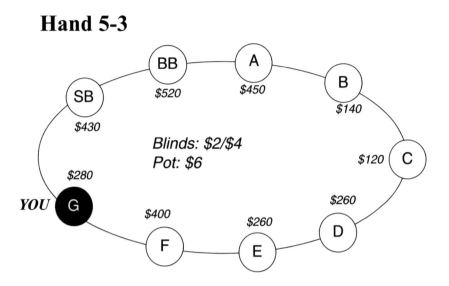

**Situation:** Small stakes online game. You've been playing for an hour. It's a tight, tough game, with mostly tight-aggressive players.

**Your hand:** K♣Q♥

**Action to you:** Players A and B fold. Player C calls for $4. Player D calls for $4. Players E and F fold.

**Question:** *Do you fold, call, or raise?*
> **Answer:** You call. Your hand isn't strong enough to attack two limpers at a tight table, and you'll have position throughout the hand, so you don't need to attack right now.

**Action:** You call $4. The small blind folds and the big blind checks. The pot is $18 and there are four players. You will be last to act after the flop.

**Flop:** Q♣4♠2♣

**Action:** The big blind and Player C check. Player D bets $16. The pot is now $34.

**Question:** *What do you do?*

> **Answer:** That's a very good flop for you. There's a potential flush draw and some possibility of a low straight, but you have top pair and second-best kicker. Given two checks and a bet from a player who could be trying to steal, you have no reason not to make a move for this pot. You should make a substantial raise.

**Action:** You raise to $48. The big blind and Player C fold. Player D calls $32. The pot is now $114.

**Turn:** 9♦

**Action:** Player D checks. Your stack is now $228, Player D has $208.

**Question:** *What do you do?*

> **Answer:** You keep betting even though pot commitment will become an issue after you make a bet that's more than half the pot. In general, you don't really want to get your whole stack involved with top pair. But here you and your opponent both started with relatively small stacks (65 big blinds for him, 70 big blinds for you) and the situation at the table is very favorable. While there are a few hands that beat you, your opponent hasn't given any indication that he has one of them, and there are many hands you can beat that account for his actions so far. He might have queen-jack or queen-ten, or any pair from jacks down to fives. He might be on a club draw. If he's slowplaying a set or he in fact has ace-queen, that's just bad luck. You can't let fear of a concealed set stop you from making good value bets, or from charging players to draw.

**Action:** You bet $72, and Player D folds.

He probably had a pair below nines, and gave up when another overcard came. Or he might have had the flush draw, and realized he wasn't guaranteed to get paid if a third club hit on the river. Or he may have simply called the flop to see if you were on a draw, and saw you instead keep firing on the turn, so he assumed you were playing with a made hand and gave up.

# Hand 5-4

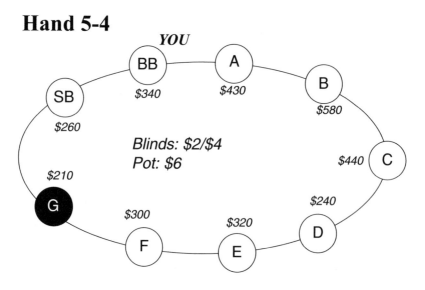

*YOU*

BB — $340
A — $430
B — $580
SB — $260
C — $440
$210
G
D — $240
F — $300
E — $320

Blinds: $2/$4
Pot: $6

**Situation:** Small stakes online game. You've been playing for about two hours. The table is tight and only somewhat aggressive.

**Your hand:** A♠6♣

**Action to you:** Player A folds. Player B calls for $4. Players C, D, E, and F all fold. The button makes a mini-raise to $8. The small blind calls $6. The pot is now $24, and it costs you $4 to call.

**Question:** *Do you fold, call, or raise?*

**Answer:** You call. You're getting 6-to-1 pot odds and you have an ace. True, you're out of position and there's a live player behind who limped from early position, but you still have an easy call.

**Action:** You call $4. Player B calls $4. The pot is $32.

**Flop:** 8♠6♥3♣

**Action:** The small blind checks.

**Question:** *What do you do?*

**Answer:** You have middle pair, top kicker, on a board with relatively few drawing possibilities. You're beating most of the hands that are likely to be out there. Everyone who called with ace-ten or king-queen type hands is now a big underdog to you.

Of course, someone could have an eight, in which case they won't be going away. But right now you stand about as well as you're going to in this hand. Almost any turn card that doesn't hit you will make your situation worse. So bet and see if you win the pot. If you don't, reevaluate on the turn.

**Action:** You actually check. Player B and the button check. The pot remains at $32.

**Turn:** Q♦

**Action:** The small blind checks.

**Question:** *What do you do?*

**Answer:** You now have third pair, and the queen could have hit a lot of hands. No one bet on the flop, which is good news, but with third pair you're better off seeing if you can check the hand down.

**Action:** You check. Player B and the button check again.

**River:** 7♠

**Action:** The small blind checks.

**Question:** *What do you do?*
   **Answer:** Yet another overcard to your pair, and now a few more holdings beat you. Again, you should try to check the hand down.

**Action:** You check, and so do the two players behind you. Your pair of sixes was best, beating a J♣9♥, an A♦3♠, and a K♣9♥.

You had the best hand on the flop, and your bet probably would have won right there. The queen and seven on the turn and river were a lucky break, as any king, jack, or nine would have beaten you.

# Hand 5-5

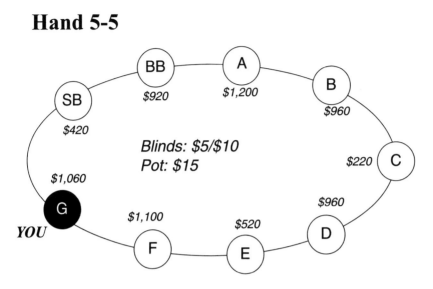

**Situation:** High stakes online game. You just started playing. You have no reads on the table.

**Your hand:** Q♣9♥

**Action to you:** Player A calls $10. Player B folds. Player C calls $10. Players D, E, and F all fold. The pot is $35.

**Question:** *Do you fold, call, or raise?*
> **Answer:** You call. Queen-nine is not a great hand, but you're on the button and one of your main goals in no-limit cash games is to see a lot of cheap flops. This is a good opportunity, so take it. If one of the blinds raises, you may cheerfully throw your mediocre hand away.

**Action:** You call $10. The small blind calls $5 and the big blind checks. The pot is now $50 with five players.

**Flop:** K♦9♠4♦

**Action:** The blinds both check. Player A bets $20. Player C raises to $40. The pot is now $110, and it costs you $40 to call.

**Question:** *What do you do?*

> **Answer:** You fold. This is an easy decision as you should fold if even one player bet. Some players get trapped here with middle pair and pot odds of better than 2.5-to-1, which might look at first like a good pot odds call. But as we've discussed, bets are a more credible indication of a player's strength in these big multi-way pots than in pots with fewer players. Either of the bettors could have a king; one of them might be on a diamond draw. One of the blinds might be on a diamond draw and elect to play along. With middle pair, you don't want to put yourself in a situation where you have to call larger and larger bets with no idea of what you're facing. Instead, you want to get out of the hand early.
>
> If everyone had checked, you could have made a bet with a reasonable chance of success. Here, you're in an untenable situation. Scram.

**Action:** You fold.

# Hand 5-6

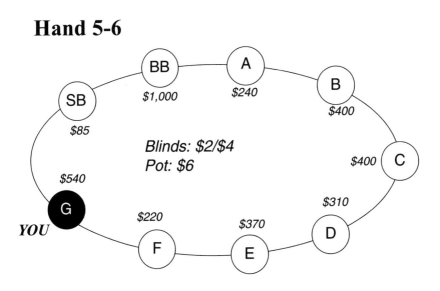

**Situation:** Medium stakes online game. You just started playing. You have no reads on the table.

**Your hand:** 7♦5♥

**Action to you:** Player A calls $4. Players B and C fold. Player D calls $4. Players E and F fold. The pot is now $14.

**Question:** *Do you fold, call, or raise?*
   **Answer:** This is a good enough hand for me to limp on the button. I want to see cheap flops with connected or moderately connected cards, and seven-five offsuit is suitable for that purpose. It's not exactly a mistake to fold, but in no-limit cash games you need to see cheap flops!

**Action:** You call $4. The small blind calls $2, and the big blind checks. The pot is now $20. There are five players and you will be last to act.

**Flop:** K♥8♠6♠

**Action:** The blinds check. Player A checks. Player D bets $16.

**Question:** *What do you do?*

**Answer:** This is a dream flop for your hand, right? Wrong. You need to fold here despite your open-ended straight draw. Three factors are now working against you:

1. **Express odds:** Player D made a big bet, 80 percent of the pot. The pot is now $36, and you need to put in $16 to call, so you're only getting odds of 2.25-to-1, not so good for a straight draw. If you have eight outs, you're a bit less than 5-to-1 to hit on the turn, and 2.2-to-1 to hit if you get to see both the turn and the river.

2. **Outs:** How many outs do you really have? The 9♠ and 4♠ give you a straight but put three spades on board. That's bad for two reasons. Not only might someone have made a flush and beat you out of a big pot, but if the 9♠ or 4♠ arrives and fills your well-concealed straight, you may not get paid because everyone suspects you of having made your flush! Your eight apparent outs should more realistically be counted as six or seven, making your odds to the winning hand even worse.

3. **Position at the table:** No one has folded yet, so three more players remain to act. Any one of them could raise, knocking you out of the pot. If I was truly completing the action, I might call despite the problems with odds and outs, but this last uncertainty is too much.

**Action:** You fold.

# Hand 5-7

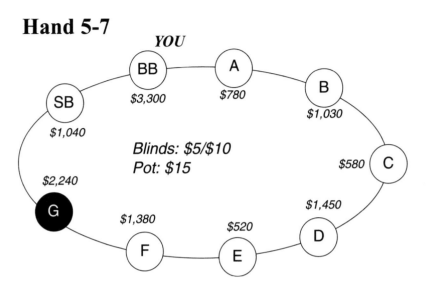

*YOU*

BB
$3,300

A
$780

B
$1,030

SB
$1,040

G
$2,240

C
$580

D
$1,450

F
$1,380

E
$520

Blinds: $5/$10
Pot: $15

**Situation:** High stakes online game. A generally aggressive table. Player A is tight and usually has solid values when he bets or raises. Player G, on the button, is generally solid but has had some big wins today. The small blind will fool around with a lot of middle cards, suited or not. You've been on a roll and generally pushing the table around. You've tripled up so far in the session.

**Your hand:** 8♠6♦

**Action to you:** Player A mini-raises to $20. Players B through F all fold. Player G, on the button, calls $20. The small blind calls $15.

**Question:** *Do you fold, call, or raise?*
    **Answer:** This is an excellent hand for calling in a multi-way pot. Any straight draw should be well-concealed, and if you miss the flop you'll be able to get away from the hand pretty easily. Of course you're also getting great pot odds.

**Action:** You call. The pot has $80 and four players.

**Flop:** 7♥7♦5♦

**Action:** The small blind checks.

**Question:** *What do you do?*
> **Answer:** Although I generally advocate checking draws in these multi-way pots, this is a case where a semi-bluff is reasonable. It's a flop which is likely to have missed the other three players, so there's a good chance that you can win the pot immediately. If you don't win the pot right here, you may have bought yourself a free card on the turn. Checking is perfectly all right as well.

**Action:** You check. Player A bets $60. Player G folds. The small blind calls $60. The pot is now $200.

**Question:** *What do you do?*
> **Answer:** Player A's bet may have been a simple continuation bet. Unless he started with a high pair or two high diamonds, this flop shouldn't have helped his hand. The small blind called out of position, and with you still to act behind him. He may have a draw as well, and if so it's more likely to be a flush draw since you have a couple of the needed straight cards.
>
> The pot is offering you more than 3-to-1 odds, so you should call with your open-ended straight draw.

**Action:** You call. The pot is now $260.

**Turn:** 9♥

**Action:** The small blind bets $120. He has $840 left in his stack.

**Question:** *What do you do?*

**Answer:** You hit your straight, and now the small blind takes the lead in the betting. He's betting into a player who has bet twice (Player A), and another player who has called twice (you). So he's got to realize that there's strength at the table. His bet is small, less than half the pot, so he's not worried about being called. In fact, he probably expects to be called. What can he have?

Let's make the safe assumption that he has something, and see what hands we can put him on:

- His preflop call against multiple opponents indicates that it's not a high pair.

- One possibility is trip sevens. He might have started with ace-seven, or eight-seven, or seven-six, hands which explain the preflop call. He slowplayed the sevens on the flop and now he's betting them on the turn.

- If he started with a diamond draw, he could now be betting it if the nine helped his hand. In that case he has the 9♦ plus a higher diamond, and now he's betting top pair plus a flush draw.

- There's some chance he has a real monster and we're drawing dead. He could have nines, sevens, nine-seven, or even seven-five, all of which are pretty reasonable preflop calls. Except for nines, he might have slowplayed any of these hands on the flop. (I don't advocate slowplaying trips except as a diversification play, but you have to consider the possibility.) He probably would have bet a pair of nines, but he could have just checked and called with it.

If he has either the diamond draw or the trip sevens, you want to raise. Either hand is drawing to beat you, and you need to charge both of them. If he has a pair of nines plus a diamond draw, he has 13 outs. (9 diamonds, 2 nines, and 2 sevens.) In that case he's a 33-to-13 underdog, or 2.5-to-1. If he has trip sevens with something like ace-seven and no diamonds, he has 10 outs. Now he's a 36-to-10 underdog, or about 3.5-to-1.

You can charge him for either draw by giving him less than 2.5-to-1 pot odds on the last card. Raising to something like $620 is enough to deny him his odds since the pot is then $1,000 and he needs to call $500 to see the last card.

Note carefully that this raise will commit you to the pot, at least vis-à-vis the small blind. If he then puts you all-in, the pot will be $1,840 and you'll only need to call the last $340, so you'll be getting better than 5-to-1 odds. You can't fold a straight for those odds when he may be drawing.

What about Player A, who's still alive in the hand? You're not too worried about him. As a tight player who plays solid values, he probably didn't play anything in first position that allowed him to connect with this flop. His flop bet was just a straight continuation bet, and he'll be leaving once he sees the bet and the raise on the turn.

**Action:** You just call $120. Player A folds. The pot is now $500. The small blind has $840 in his stack, and you have him covered.

**River: T♦**

**Action:** The small blind bets $220.

**Question:** *What do you do?*

    **Answer:** That card is very bad news. Of the three groups of hands that we thought he might have, two are now beating you (the monsters and the flush draws) while the third group, the trip sevens, should be scared of the possible flush draw and be checking. The fact that he's betting, and betting an amount that practically invites a call, means that you're probably beaten, but you should call because 3.5-to-1 is a good price and you just might be winning.

**Action:** You actually push all-in. He calls and shows J♦9♦ for a flush.

Oops. That's a quick $620 tossed down the drain unnecessarily. Think of how many blinds you'll need to steal to get that back!

Seriously, this bet is a huge blunder. With three diamonds on the board, a pair on board, possible straight draws, and vigorous betting throughout the hand, what holding would call this bet that you can beat? Three sevens can't call anymore, and every other hand will beat you.

As the pots get large, it becomes hugely important to bear down and focus on the hand. An amazing number of players do just the opposite; as the pots grow, they play faster and faster, as if to convince you that they're totally in control. Get a grip and don't fall into this most dangerous of traps.

# Hand 5-8

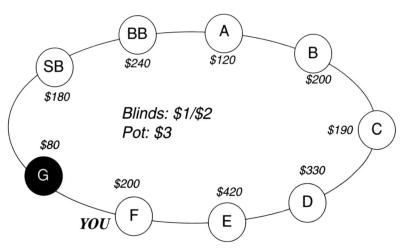

**Situation:** Medium stakes online game. The players have generally been tight. Players bet their hands, and not too much imagination has been shown so far.

**Your hand:** J♦8♦

**Action to you:** Players A and B fold. Player C limps for $2. Player D folds. Player E limps.

**Question:** *Do you fold, call, or raise?*

 **Answer:** I wouldn't routinely play a double-gapped hand, even suited, but it's worth seeing an occasional cheap flop with a hand like this. You have to resist the temptation to play too many of these hands since over time, they'll result in a hand mix that's too skewed towards weaker hands. But no one has shown strength and you may have position here, so it's not a big mistake to play.

**Action:** You also limp for $2. The button and the small blind fold, and the big blind checks. The pot is now $9, and you have position on three other players.

**Flop:** Q♠J♠9♥

**Action:** The big blind checks, as do Players C and E.

**Question:** *What do you do?*

**Answer:** You have hit middle pair and an inside straight draw on a board with a lot of possible threats. Three players have also checked in front of you.

How I play this hand depends strongly on what kind of game I'm in. In a relatively small-stakes game, this hand is bettable. In those games, players tend to limp with a wider variety of mediocre hands and very small pairs. Players also tend to bet their good hands or their drawing hands when they have a chance, rather than sitting back and waiting. So in that environment, my middle pair has a reasonable chance of being best given the three checks I've seen so far.

At a higher-stakes table, I would definitely check. Players are a little fussier about their limping hands, and are more likely to limp with the sort of hands that could connect with this flop. A group of limpers at a high-stakes table is less likely to have the king-four suited or six-three suited hands that you see all the time at lower-stakes tables. In addition, high-stakes players are perfectly capable of taking a hand like A♠7♠, checking the flop, and then check-raising someone in late position who thinks they can steal from the checkers. In short, a bet against a dangerous flop like this requires a much better hand at a high-stakes table.

Since this is a $1-$2 game, the checks probably mean more or less what they appear to mean, so bet at the flop.

**Action:** You bet $6. The other three players fold. You take the pot.

# Hand 5-9

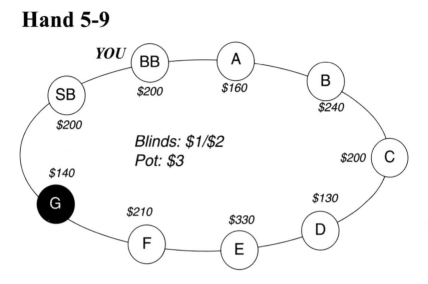

**Situation:** Medium stakes online game. The players have generally been tight. Players bet their hands, and not too much imagination has been shown so far.

**Your hand: J♥7♦**

**Action to you:** Players A, B, and C fold. Player D calls $2. Players E, F and G fold. The small blind calls $2.

**Question:** *Do you check or raise?*
> **Answer:** Check. Your hand isn't strong enough to raise, and seeing a free flop is a better bet than trying to bluff two players who have shown some interest in the pot.

**Action:** You check. The pot is now $7. You have middle position after the flop.

**Flop: Q♠J♣9♠**

**Action:** The small blind checks.

**Question:** *What do you do?*
**Answer:** Check. You have middle pair, weak kicker. That's better than nothing, but it's not very strong. The player who originally limped hasn't acted yet, and you can't be sure what the check from the small blind means. It's still too soon to think you're in good shape, so wait before acting until you get more information.

Many players would bet here. Their reasoning goes as follows:

- I have middle pair, which is something.

- The small blind probably has nothing because he checked, and since most flops miss most hands, Player D may have nothing as well.

- If I bet now, I might win the pot and even bluff out a better hand.

- If I wait, and Player D bets after me, I won't know where I stand or what to do.

- If I wait, Player D checks, the turn doesn't hit me, and the small blind bets, it's impossible to know if he has a hand or is stealing. Plus, the turn card probably won't help me, and it might help somebody else.

- The easiest way for me to win the hand is to bet right now.

All of these statements are true enough. But even collectively, they don't add up to a strong enough case for betting.

When you bet, you want some reasonable assurance that your bet rates to make you some money. You don't have that assurance here. Although your hand did hit the flop, it's not a very strong hand. Except for the small blind's initial check, no one has yet sent a strong signal that they're weak. And worst of all, the flop is not a good bluffing flop. It's actually fairly dangerous. Besides the overcard to your hand, there's the possibility of a flush draw in spades, and if anyone has a ten, they have an open-ended straight draw.

If you bet and someone calls, where will you stand? You won't know if they called you with a queen, with a better jack than yours, with a flush draw, or with a straight draw. That's a lot of unknowns. In fact, if someone calls and you don't think they're just making a move to steal the pot, you'll be very hard-pressed to either bet again or to call a bet on the next round.

On a flop this dangerous, I need more information before second pair and weak kicker becomes a betting hand. Here's a good betting scenario: I check, Player D checks, the turn is an innocuous card like the 3♣, which misses all draws, and the small blind checks again. Now I've picked up three more pieces of favorable information, two checks and a good card. At this point my jack-seven becomes a betting hand.

On a weak flop, I might be willing to bet. For instance, on a flop of K♣J♠3♦ where no draws are present, my jack-seven looks better. Now I'd be willing to bet half the pot or a little more, thinking there was a pretty good chance my bet would pull the pot down.

In the original hand, inexperienced players tend to bet because they think it's their only chance to win. They're afraid of being outplayed as more cards appear and someone else takes the lead. That's a legitimate fear, but the solution is to work on improving your post-flop play rather than betting into the dark.

**Action:** You actually bet $4. Player G and the small blind fold. You take the pot.

# Hand 5-10

**Situation:** Medium stakes online game. Generally tight players so far.

**Your hand:** 8♥7♠

**Action to you:** Players A, B, C, and D fold. Player E calls $4. Player F folds.

**Question:** *Do you fold, call, or raise?*

> **Answer:** Player E could be calling with a light hand. Your hand has a lot of surprise value and you'll be hard to read if you hit. In this spot, on the button behind a late limper, I would always call with this hand.

**Action:** You call $4. The small blind folds. The big blind checks. The pot is $14.

**Flop:** K♠7♣6♦

**Action:** The big blind checks. Player E bets $8.

**Question:** *What do you do?*

    **Answer:** Last hand, we urged caution in opening the betting with second pair. That's because, in part, checking didn't forfeit any of your interest in the pot. Now your choice is between calling and folding, and second pair is certainly worth a call of a half-pot bet that may not be anything but a bluff.

**Action:** You call $8. The big blind folds. The pot is now $30.

**Turn: 5♠**

**Action:** Player E bets $24.

**Question:** *What do you do?*

    **Answer:** Player E fires a second bullet, announcing that he's serious and he really has something. Since he didn't raise preflop, the best guess would be that he has a king with a modest kicker or some sort of draw based on the 7-6-5 that are already on board.

    Meanwhile, you have second pair plus an open-ended straight draw. Fours, sevens, eights, and nines are all working for you. If he's currently ahead, you have somewhere between zero and 13 outs. The pot is offering you a little better than 2-to-1, and you have position.

    Add all the factors together and the call is reasonable. You don't know how many outs you really have, and you don't know what kind of implied odds are actually available, but you have something, you're not getting pot committed, and 2-to-1 plus position isn't bad. Call.

**Action:** You call $24. The pot is now $78.

**River: Q♦**

**Action:** Player E checks.

**Question:** *What do you do?*
    **Answer:** Check. He didn't bet, so the queen didn't help his hand and he doesn't have a straight. Your previous guess is probably on the mark: either a king and a weak kicker or a missed straight. If he missed a straight, you'll win the hand and he won't call a bet, so just check the hand down.

**Action:** You check. He turns over K♣4♣ and takes the pot.

His preflop call with king-four suited was pretty loose, but it didn't cost him. Had a four landed on the river, you might have won a big bet.

# Hand 5-11

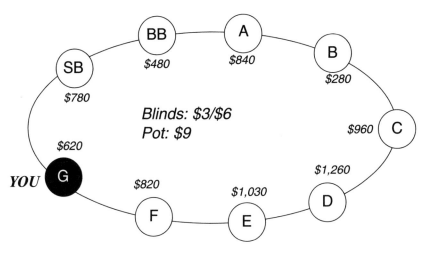

**Situation:** Medium stakes online game. Players A and C seem loose-aggressive. Player D is tight.

**Your hand:** T♠9♠

**Action to you:** Player A raises to $20. Player B folds. Players C and D call $20. Players E and F fold. The pot is now $69.

**Question:** *Do you fold, call, or raise?*
    **Answer:** Medium suited connectors on the button are a nice hand to play in a multi-way pot, even if you have to call a raise. You have position throughout the hand and a better than normal chance of being paid if you can hit your hand. Calling a raise is more expensive than coming in after some limpers, but the extra action indicates that your implied odds in the hand are better than normal.

**Action:** You call $20. The small blind folds, and the big blind calls $14. The pot is now $103, and there are four other players in the pot with you.

**Flop:** Q♠8♠7♣

**Action:** The big blind checks. Player A bets $60. Player C folds. Player D calls $60. The pot is now $223.

**Question:** *What do you do?*
    **Answer:** You have an immense draw, with 15 outs: the last nine spades, plus three more jacks and three more sixes. If you raise, you'll have some reasonable but hard to quantify fold equity, and if you are called you'll be an actual favorite against some hands and only a slight underdog to others. For instance, here's how you would stand in a heads-up confrontation against some possible hands:

- Against A♠A♥, you're a 52-to-48 favorite.

- Against Q♣Q♦, you're a 42-to-58 underdog.

- Against A♠K♠, you're a 38-to-62 underdog.

Two callers would spoil the odds considerably, although you can't assume that would be the case from the betting so far. Against a combination of A♠A♥ and Q♣Q♦, you'd be 38 percent to win, with the other 62 percent divided 54-to-8 in favor of the set of queens.

You should push all-in with a great semi-bluff ensuring that you'll see the last two cards.

**Action:** You push all-in for $600. The big blind folds. Player A calls $540. Player D folds. The turn and river are the J♣ and the 2♥. Player A turns over the A♠A♦, and your straight wins the pot.

# Hand 5-12

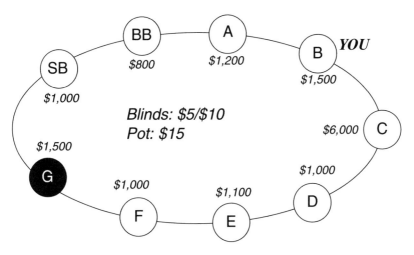

SB $1,000
BB $800
A $1,200
B $1,500 *YOU*
$1,500
G
F $1,000
E $1,100
D $1,000
C $6,000
$1,000

Blinds: $5/$10
Pot: $15

**Situation:** Medium stakes live game. You've played with most of these people several times before. The big blind likes to play a lot of pots, but he'll back off when he doesn't hit. Player D is tight and somewhat unimaginative. He tends to have what his bets represent. Player G is tight-aggressive. He's a good observer of the table and occasionally makes moves.

**Your hand:** T♥T♦

**Action to you:** Player A folds.

**Question:** *Do you fold, call, or raise?*
    **Answer:** You want to raise with this hand. A $30-$40 raise is a reasonable amount.

**Action:** You raise to $35. Player C folds. Player D calls $35. Players E and F fold. Player G calls $35. The small blind folds. The big blind calls $25. The pot is $145, and there are four players. You'll be second to act after the flop.

**Flop:** T♠9♣8♦

**Action:** The big blind checks.

**Question:** *What do you do?*
    **Answer:** You've flopped top set. That's nice, but the board presents a problem. As we've discussed, you don't want to slowplay in general, and this is a super-dangerous flop for slowplaying in particular. You need to make a substantial bet. Anyone with just a pair should go away, but the draws may stick around. I would bet somewhere between $120 and $145.

**Action:** You bet $145, the size of the pot. Player D calls $145. Player G raises to $750. The big blind folds. The pot now contains $1,185. You have $1,320 left in your stack. Player D has $820. Player G has $715.

**Question:** *What do you do?*
    **Answer:** You can fold, call, or raise. To make your decision, you need to estimate what hands Player G might have, and the chances of each hand. You also need to think a little about Player D, and just what he might do. Let's get started.

We know that Player G is a tight-aggressive player. We know that he occasionally, but only occasionally, makes moves. And we know that he's seen a pot-sized bet from the preflop raiser, plus a call from a tight player. From all this we know that he very probably has what he considers to be a premium hand under the circumstances, and the probability of a bluff is very low, but non-zero (because the probability of a bluff is always non-zero).

So what constitutes a hand here that's legitimately good enough for a raise after a big bet and a call? Queen-jack, probably suited, is good enough, as is seven-six, also probably suited. (He had to call with the hand preflop, so the suited connectors are a little more likely than the unsuited connectors.)

He might also be raising with one of the bottom two sets, either nines or eights.

What about hands like jack-ten, jack-nine, or eight-seven? Those aren't really raising hands in this situation. Remember, it's a very dangerous board and he's already seen a bet and a call. There's a distinct possibility that those hands are already facing a made straight. A tight player might call with one of those hands, but he wouldn't raise.

How about a pair of jacks or a pair of sevens? Just barely possible, but again he's much more likely to be calling with those hands rather than raising.

A last legitimate possibility is two pair. That's also more of a calling hand than a raising hand in this situation, but a hand like nine-eight might have elected to raise.

Hands with no draws, like a pair of aces, shouldn't even be calling after these actions on this board. A tight-aggressive, experienced player would know that, so a raise with one of these hands is really just a sort of bluff.

To solve a puzzle like this, I like to figure out what groups of hands are probably in play, estimate the chance I'm facing each group, and then estimate my winning chances against a typical hand in each group. Then I put the information together to get an estimate of my total winning chances in the whole situation. Let's see how this might go.

His bet says he has a top-quality hand, and there are only two candidates: smaller sets, and straights. I'll say that 80 percent of the time he holds one of these hands. There are a lot more possible straight hands than sets. There are 16 ways he can hold queen-jack, and another 16 ways he can hold seven-six, but only three ways he can hold a pair of nines and another three ways he can hold a pair of eights. That's a total of 32 possible straights against just six possible sets. But he would certainly have played a pair if he held one, whereas he might have laid down a connector, depending on how he felt about the situation. My final guess is 60 percent straights, and 20 percent smaller sets.

The last 20 percent I'm going to divide between two types of hands: pure bluffs or hands that are so weak they only count as bluffs, and hands like a pair of jacks, where he has an open-ended straight draw coupled with something extra, like a pair. Under the circumstances, (including the fact that this is a live game), I'll put the probability of a bluff as low as I'm ever willing to make it: 5 percent. If this were an online game, I'd make it higher, perhaps 10 percent, but it's my experience that players are more reluctant to bluff at a live table than they are online. That makes the probability of a drawing hand about 15 percent. Here's our final tally:

- Probability of a made straight: 60 percent
- Probability of a smaller set: 20 percent
- Probability of a drawing hand: 15 percent
- Probability of a bluff: 5 percent

Next we have to figure out how we're doing against each group. This is easy to do at home where we can use tools like *PokerStove*. (And the more problems like this you try to solve at home, the easier it becomes to make good estimates at the table.)

- If we're up against a made straight, our chances are about 35 percent *in a heads-up confrontation with Player G.* It doesn't matter much which straight Player G actually has. Whether he has the high straight or the low straight, we need to improve to a full house or quads to win. But the presence of Player D complicates matters. Player D's call might mean that he holds some of the cards we need. (He might, for instance, have called with two pair, subtracting two of our outs from the pool.) To account for his call, we need to downgrade our winning chances a bit; let's make them 30 percent in this variation.

- If we're up against a smaller set, we're a huge favorite. Any card that gives the smaller set a full house gives us either a better full house or quads. Here we're about 93 percent to win.

- Against a drawing hand like a pair of jacks, we're in pretty good shape: about 68 percent to win.

- If we're against a more or less pure bluff, say a pair of fives or something similar, we're also a huge favorite, in the neighborhood of 97 percent.

Now let's put these two sets of estimates together, round off to the nearest percent, and see what our chances are against Player G.

- He has a straight (our guess is 60 percent) times the chance of winning if he has a straight (30 percent) equals 18 percent winning chances in this variation.

- He has a smaller set (20 percent) times 93 percent equals 19 percent winning chances.

- He has a draw (15 percent) times 68 percent equals 10 percent winning chances.

- He's on a bluff (5 percent) times 97 percent equals 5 percent winning chances.

  Our total winning chances are 52 percent.

  $$52\% = 18\% + 19\% + 10\% + 5\%$$

We're an overall favorite in the hand, so we can't fold. Pushing all-in is certainly a positive equity play. We'd be betting the remainder of our stack ($1,320) to win a total of $1,900: $1500 from Player G, assuming he calls, the $180 we've already put in the pot, $180 from Player D, assuming he folds, and $40 from the blinds. Player G won't call if he's bluffing right now, but we assumed that occurred only 5 percent of the time, not enough to affect the correctness of the move.

Can we do better? Actually the answer is yes, because Player D is still alive in the hand. The reasoning here is pretty simple.

- If Player D has one of the hands that beats us (the two straights) then he'll get all-in anyway, and we'll have to call based on the pot odds.

- If Player D has one of the hands that's losing to us, we want him in the pot, because we're a huge favorite against him.

  Imagine for instance that Player G has the high straight and Player D has the low straight. That's actually a better result for us than just facing Player G's straight alone. If we don't improve we lose our stack in any event, but if we improve our hand and win, we collect Player D's stack in addition to Player G's.

Our best play is to call Player G's bet, hoping that Player D then raises all-in. Then either Player G or us will put the other all-in, and our net profit rises when we actually win the hand.

Does analysis like this seem difficult or tedious? It is, somewhat. But remember, you're making a decision here for all your chips. Those decisions don't arise frequently, and when they do, they're much more important than deciding whether or not to try to steal the blinds. At the table, you're entitled to spend a couple of minutes trying to make a good decision.

What you see all too frequently at the table are players making these big decisions at blitz speed, as though the play were perfectly obvious. In poker, the only "perfectly obvious" decisions occur when you have the mortal nuts, and even there you should take your time so players don't know that's exactly what you have! As long as you're taking home the money, you shouldn't give a hoot whether your opponents think you're slow-witted. In poker, it's an advantage to be dismissed as slow-witted!

**Action:** You actually push all-in. Player D folds. Player G folds. You take the pot.

# Index